Paideia and Performance

ALSO FROM PARNASSOS PRESS

Paideia and Performance

Selected Essays from the Seventh Interdisciplinary
Symposium on the Hellenic Heritage
of Sicily and Southern Italy

edited by

Henry C. Curcio, Mark Ralkowski, and Heather L. Reid

Parnassos Press
2023

First Printing: 2023
ISBN: 978-1-942495-567 (hardcover)
ISBN: 978-1-942495-574 (paperback)
ISBN: 978-1-942495-581 (ebook)

Parnassos Press
Fonte Aretusa Organization
Siracusa, Sicily and Dakota Dunes SD

www.fontearetusa.org

Cover illustration: Terracotta kylix (drinking cup) attributed to the Painter of Bologna, ca. 460–450 BCE. Metropolitan Museum of Art. Accession Number: 06.1021.167 Open access image.

Epigraphs

...as means to a good life *paideia* and virtue would make the most just claim

πρὸς ... ζωὴν ἀγαθὴν ἡ παιδεία καὶ ἡ ἀρετὴ μάλιστα δικαίως ἂν ἀμφισβητοίησαν

-- Aristotle, *Politics* 3.1283a

...for the soul goes to the underworld possessing nothing but its *paideia* and upbringing, which are said to bring the greatest benefit or harm to the dead right at the beginning of the journey yonder.

...οὐδὲν γὰρ ἄλλο ἔχουσα εἰς Ἅιδου ἡ ψυχὴ ἔρχεται πλὴν τῆς παιδείας τε καὶ τροφῆς, ἃ δὴ καὶ μέγιστα λέγεται ὠφελεῖν ἢ βλάπτειν τὸν τελευτήσαντα εὐθὺς ἐν ἀρχῇ τῆς ἐκεῖσε πορείας.

-- Plato, *Phaedo* 107d

Acknowledgments

The editors are grateful to all the participants in the Seventh Interdisciplinary Symposium on the Hellenic Heritage of Sicily and Southern Italy. We also thank the Exedra Mediterranean Center in Siracusa, Sicily for their help and hospitality.

Table of Contents

Henry C. Curcio, Mark Ralkowski, and Heather L. Reid
Introduction

Paideia, a word that combines the concepts of education and culture, is foundational in Ancient Greece — particularly in Sicily and Southern Italy where many Hellenes earned that title through acculturation rather than birth. They had to learn to be Greek in the cultural sense and they learned by participating in a community where the culture was performed through poetry, philosophy, rhetoric, drama, dance, and even gymnastic exercise. Knowing the languge and myriad myths was certainly part of *paideia*, but being Greek was less a matter of knowledge than performance: interacting with others publicly and privately in a way that confirmed shared values and also interrogated them.

In the summer of 2022, an international group of scholars from a variety of disciplines met in Siracusa, Sicily to discuss the relation between *paideia* and performance in Ancient Greece. The Seventh Interdisciplinary Symposium on the Hellenic Heritage of Sicily and Southern Italy revealed the many and important forms that the link between *paideia* and performance takes in ancient culture. Focusing on musical, rhetorical, philosophical, and gymnastic *paideia*, this volume leaves all but a couple of questions about drama to its companion volume on theater. The studies in this volume engage the work of figures as diverse as Sappho, Pindar, Empedocles, Gorgias, Plato, and Aristotle, but they reveal common themes. Performative *paideia* is active, interactive, and often competitive — arguing for its benefits even as it provides them. Choral songs critically engage with mythic paradigms, philosophers use rhetoric to demonstrate their educational superiority over rhetoricians, rhetoricians claim to whip their students into better shape than gymnasia can. The important thing in every case is to strive for *aretē* (virtue, excellence), not just in theory but in performance.

We begin with the "song culture" of Archaic Greece, where Paloma Flavio Betini argues that lyric poetry, repeatedly performed through choral dance, served important educational purposes in the presentation and amplification of a community's values. She uses the examples of Sappho and Pindar to show how lyric poets integrated widely-known mythical narratives called *exempla* with the dancing,

ix

singing, and music of their poetry to provide an education of body and mind. The mythical *exempla* disseminated and reinforced ideas about virtuous behavior, while the performance of the songs in choruses exercised the body and served social cohesion. For both poets, mythical *exempla* made their "arguments"—about married life or aging or filial devotion—easier for an audience to understand and accept, and allowed them to serve as paradigmatic sources of wisdom for communities focused on living a good life.

Next, Michael Goyette shows how Empedocles used rhetorical techniques to establish his authority as a doctor and teacher. In some fragments, he adopts the language of natural philosophy to associate himself with the world of rational medicine. In others, he resembles the character of Dionysus in Euripides's *Bacchae,* claiming to be a "deathless god" and using the language of divination and mysticism to present himself as a healer with privileged access to divine knowledge. We lack conclusive evidence for Empedocles's medical career. But this rhetorical "performance" of medical and pedagogical authority would have given him persuasive powers over multiple audiences in a world where the lines between religion, science, and magic were blurry. They also help to explain why Empedocles was thought to among the founders of the Sicilian school of medicine.

Moving on to avowed rhetoricians, Jurgen R. Gatt and Andrew Debono Gauchi argue that Gorgias's *Encomium to Helen* presents a new educational ideal of "good manliness" (*euandria*), centered on the teachable powers of persuasion instead of the innate virtues of ancestral heroes, nature (*physis*), or birth (*genos*). Gorgias's *Encomium* was not merely a theoretical exposition of the power of logos, a demonstration-piece, or a model defense speech, as other scholars have suggested. It is best understood in its late 5th-century BCE context, as a defense of Gorgias's own pedagogy against the conservative argument, familiar from Aristophanes's *Clouds,* that the "new education" of the "sophistic movement" was emasculating and physically debilitating. While sophists like Protagoras were conciliatory in their counterarguments to this charge, Gorgias was direct and aggressive. He argued that *euandria* is teachable, that the sophists were its best teachers, and that a man with the sophists' acquired wisdom was most fit to compete in life's contest of virtue.

In the next essay, L.M.J. Coulson makes a familiar division of Plato's dialogues into three groups. But instead of ordering them chronologically and arguing for a version of the developmentalism hypothesis, he speculates that Plato's dialogues were written "consecutively and concurrently," and he groups them according to three kinds of *paideia*: "primary," "secondary," and "tertiary," each of which recommends an "evolving philosophy" that is "a quest" for self-knowledge. Primary *paideia* encourages young students to know themselves and introduces them to classic moral questions, emphasizing the importance of caring for the young, distinguishing philosophy from sophistry, and raising hard epistemological and metaphysical questions that are taken up at length in secondary and tertiary *paideia*. Coulson's core claim is that the dialogues are a unified and developing dramatization of Plato's maturing self-knowledge. Philosophy is the hero of the story, and it is presented as a "purifying protagonist" that reaches out to all of time and being while embarking on a quest to liberate the city.

Mateo Duque's essay asks how Plato taught in his Academy. While previous answers to this question have been hypothetical, Duque's historically sensitive arguments avoid engagement in mere speculation. Assuming the dialogues formed the curriculum of the Academy, he suggests that they were likely performed rhapsodically rather than dramatically. Accordingly, their performance, like other rhapsodic performances of the time, would have involved a session of questions and answers post-performance. Suggestively, Duque tells us that such questions and answers may have shaped the final form of the dialogues that we read today.

Discussion of rhapsody naturally leads to questions about poetry—the dominant paradigm of rhapsodic performance and frequent object of Platonic criticism. Veronika Konrádová's essay on the *Ion* highlights Plato's critique of the poets along two axes. First, poetry emphasizes *enthusiazein* rather than critical reflection. We are supposed to be so enchanted by the poet that poetic *paideia* ends in unreflective acceptance of their prose. Second, poetry's emphasis on *mimēsis* allows a corruptive psychological influence: allowing the appetitive part of the *psychē* to remain in the pleasurable state of *enthusiazein*. It is suggested, however, that the division between Plato and the poets may not be as vast as often construed. Michał Bizoń argues just this. Bizoń suggests that Plato's disapproval of the poets is concerned with neither the content nor form of poetry, but rather the authoritative (and rather serious) position poetry occupied in Athenian *paideia*. Noting Plato's frequent suggestion that *paideia* ought to be linked with *paidia* (play), Bizoń argues that until poetry incorporates *paidia*, it fails as a form of *paideia*.

While Plato levels criticism at the poets, he also often criticizes the use of rhetoric. Kristian Sheeley, however, displays the many ways in which Plato uses and endorses a philosophical rhetoric in the *Phaedrus*. Such a rhetorical *technē* not only emerges as a body of knowledge but is also a set of performative skills found in Socrates's use of *psychagōgia* throughout the dialogue. Sheeley suggests that the various tools of Socrates's rhetorical performances include, but are not limited to, speeches, myth, dialogue, and flirtation.

Colin Smith's essay on *Phaedrus* explores the notion of vitality in discourse to understand the connection between performance and education in Platonic philosophy. Beginning from the comparison of *logos* with a living animal, Smith reveals the vitality of discourse to derive from the dialectical connection between living interlocutors. In contrast with other forms of speech-making, dialectic allows *logos* to take root in the soul and reproduce itself through further discussion. As such, it is not only vital but deathless.

For Aristotle, moral education depends on activity and demands moral knowledge. His claim that tragedy is instructive, thus creates a puzzle about how morally ignorant people could learn from what they see on stage. Audrey Anton and Erika Brown solve the puzzle by arguing that these people learn from the reactions of fellow audience members who have the requisite knowledge and react appropriately to the performance. Moral education through activity is also the subject of Georgios Mouratidis and Heather L. Reid's essay on *euexia*, the goal of gymnastic *paideia*. Combining Aristotle's conception of moral virtue as a *hexis* with Plato's description of *gymnastikē* in *Republic,* they argue that the *euexia* cultivated in *gymnasia* should not be understood as beauty, but rather fitness for a task—specifically, the task of citizenship.

Paloma Flávio Betini[1]
Myths as *Exempla* in Archaic Greek Melic Poetry: *Paideia* and Poetic Tradition[2]

In terms of *paideia*, how can we describe Archaic Greece? We could think of dozens of ways to describe it, but perhaps one of the best answers would be that Archaic Greece was a "song culture" — a term coined by John Herington,[3] who explains that "poetry, recited or sung, was for the early Greeks the prime medium for the dissemination of political, moral, and social ideas — history, philosophy, and science."[4] In this dynamic, the songs were well known and repeatedly performed since there was a complex system of poems for each occasion[5]. Moreover, since the poets knew their audience was familiar with myths and other works commonly

---

[1] Paloma F. Betini is a graduate student at the University of São Paulo, Brazil, where she studies the character Paris Alexander in the epic, melic and tragic traditions, supervised by Prof. Dr. Giuliana Ragusa. Her published works include "Stesichorus' four Helens: the heroine's representation in the *Helen*, *Palinode*(s), *Sack of Troy* and *The Returns* fragments," *Codex* 9 (2021): 74-93 (with Giuliana Ragusa); and "Helen and Paris in the voices of the archaic melic Greek poetry: six fragments, four poets," *Phaos* 22 (2022): 1-29.

[2] First I would like to thank the Faculty of Philosophy, Language and Literature, and Human Science of the University of São Paulo for its support, and my advisor Giuliana Ragusa. Secondly, my friends and family who helped with my trip to Sicily and the writing/revision of this text: Angelo, Wanda, Jean, Augusto, Giselle, Thais, Isabella, Raphael, Livia, Lucas dos Passos and Lucas de Freitas. Thirdly, I thank the organizers of the Seventh Interdisciplinary Symposium of the Hellenic Heritage of Sicily and Southern Italy, especially Heather Reid and Susi Kimbell. Finally, but equally important, professors John Stark, Guilherme Motta and my (now) friends Kristian and Filippos who made those days not only intellectually rich, but fun and memorable.

[3] John Herington, *Poetry into Drama. Early Tragedy and the Greek Poetic Tradition* (Los Angeles: University of California Press, 1985), 3-40.

[4] Herington, *Poetry into Drama*, 3.

[5] Leslie Kurke, "The Strangeness of 'song culture': Archaic Greek poetry," in *Literature in the Greek world*, ed. Oliver Taplin (Oxford: Oxford University Press, 2001), 42.

reproduced in the communities, they could make implicit and explicit connections with these narratives, thereby making even the smallest poems part of something bigger, often for educational purposes. In this paper, I shall analyze how the mythical *exemplum* is used for this purpose in three archaic melic songs by two melic poets: Sappho and Pindar. For that end, I intend to expose the general form and use of the *exemplum*, how it relates to the performance of these three melic songs, and how it can reinforce the semantic intention of these poems in the educational context of "song culture."

Firstly, it is important to comprehend the relevance of melic poetry for Greek *paideia* overall. In the archaic period, melic (or lyric) poetry was a genre of songs for performance accompanied by the lyre, divided into subgenres related to the occasion for which it was composed, such as weddings, athletic victory celebrations, symposia, funerals, and other rituals.[6] There were two modalities for melic performances: monodic and choral singing. The latter was also accompanied by a diversity of instruments and dance, executed by a group of chorists that could vary from 7 to 50 members.[7] The choir was trained from an early age to memorize lyrics, melodies, and choreography—a complex activity that had to be perfectly and harmonically executed. Whether performed by adults or teenagers, choral songs were a means of introduction and presentation of the community's values and precepts which, when sung in front of an audience, were reinforced and absorbed by the public. The activity, then, was not only aimed at the formation of good dancers and singers, but also good citizens in general. It was viewed by Greeks not as musical or physical training, but as education, unifying the body and mind.[8]

---

[6] On the definition of "melic," its context, and the preference for this term instead of "lyric," see Felix Budelmann, "Introducing Greek Lyric," in *The Cambridge Companion to Greek Lyric*, ed. Felix Budelmann (Cambridge: Cambridge University Press, 2009), 1-18.

[7] Giuliana Ragusa and Rafael Brunhara, "Paideia na 'Lírica' Grega Arcaica: A Poesia Elegíaca e Mélica," *Filosofia e Educação* [RFE] 9.1 (2017): 45-67.

[8] Wayne B. Ingalls, "Ritual Performance as Training for Daughters in Archaic Greece," *Phoenix* 54 (2000): 1-20; Claude Calame, *Les Choeurs de Jeunes Filles en Grèce Achaïque,* 2 vols. (Rome: Ateneo & Bizarri, 1977).

Educationally speaking, the song's content was also part of the instruction, since it often carried a message that encouraged proper behaviors and passed on the community's history and myths.[9] Usually, these messages were elaborated in or with a mythical narrative which was familiar to the audience and therefore authoritative. They also didactically demonstrated the fragile human condition and its limits through the stories of heroic figures.[10] Finally, in melic songs, the narrative is often related to the occasion of performance, so that the myths serve as a maxim,[11] an argument, or, as I prefer to call it, a lesson relevant to the occasion.

One compositional strategy used by poets to communicate this lesson, argument, maxim, or moral reflection is the *exemplum*, or *paradeigma* (paradigm) in Greek.[12] The lesson can be presented as the poet's opinion or as a general truth, but the goal of the *exemplum* is to illustrate, amplify and confirm propositions as, in the words of Howard Canter, "natural, self-explanatory and true."[13] The general form of the *exemplum* is a quoted narration—historical or mythological—that has a semantic connection with the song's context, which can be implicit or explicit and is dispersed throughout

---

[9] Ingalls, "Ritual and Performance," 3.

[10] Ruth Scodel, "Myth in Sappho," in *The Cambridge Companion to Sappho*, eds. Patrick J. Finglass and Adrian Kelly (Cambridge: Cambridge University Press, 2021), 190-202.

[11] Barbara Graziosi and Johannes Haubold, "Greek Lyric and Early Greek Literary History," in *The Cambridge Companion to Greek lyric,*. ed. Felix Budelmann. (Cambridge: Cambridge University Press, 2009), 107. Graziosi and Haubold also compare lyric songs with epic poems, which they consider to have "broad appeal through anonymity and a notional equidistance from all audiences." Also, "Homeric epic promises an accurate and complete account of past events," as opposed to lyric, that "attempt[s] to preserve their poetry by stressing their individual voice, perspective, context and addressee [...]. Rather than offering a complete and generally accepted account, they focus on examples which are deemed to be relevant to the present."

[12] I use *exemplum* instead of *paradeigma* in keeping with the tradition of using Latin terms to classify features of classical poetry.

[13] Howard V. Canter, "The Mythological Paradigm in Greek and Latin Poetry," *The American Journal of Philology* 54 (1933): 201.

the poem. It varies, of course, with the subject and occasion of the performance and its audience, which are often named and compared with the *exemplum*. Hence, in melic songs, the *exempla* are not only an illustration or a reinforcement of the poet's argument, but they can also be a bridge to the lived moment of performance and a valuable feature of choral education.

The *parthénoi* chorus in Sappho's songs

Sappho's chorality is an increasingly valued aspect of her poetry—leaving aside the image of the poet who sings about herself and her feelings to a restricted group of women, which for a long time dominated our imagination.[14] According to this conception, Sappho played the role of *khorodidáskalos*, that is, the leader of a choir, whose role was to guide the *parthénoi* (unmarried women) in their blossoming discovery of femininity.[15] Thus, the choirs formed by young people can be seen as one of the tribal initiation rituals in which adolescents are introduced to the behaviors and norms of adult sexuality, and since it is still a rite always linked to the sacred, they are also integrated into the religious and cultural life of their community.[16] Specifically regarding the *parthénoi*, the choir has the pedagogical function of preparing them for their transition to *gynē* (adult woman) and to *gámos* (marriage)—the phase in which they will play the role of mother and wife, similar to what happens in the well-known case of Alcman's Parthenians.[17] In this context, the *parthénoi* would perform the song while dancing at civic-cultural events, providing an opportunity to be seen by proud parents and potential husbands alike.[18]

---

[14] Giuliana Ragusa, *Safo de Lesbos: Hino a Afrodite e Outros Poemas* (São Paulo: Hedra, 2021).

[15] Giuliana Ragusa, "Chorality and the World of *parthénoi* in Sappho's Melic poetry," *Aletria* 29.4 (2019): 85-11, 93.

[16] Calame, *Les choeurs*, vol. I, 29-40.

[17] On Alcman's parthenians, see Laura Swift, "Visual Imagery in Parthanaic Song,"in *The Look of Lyric: Greek Song and the Visual. Studies in Archaic and Classical Greek Songs*, vol. 1, eds. Vanessa Cazzato and André Lardinois (Leiden: Brill, 2016), 255-87 and Calame, *Les choeurs*, vol. II.

[18] Ragusa, "Chorality," 92.

In the case of Sappho's poetry, the poet composed songs that elaborated on themes about female beauty and delicacy, and, thinking in the matrimonial context, about sensuality and love—essential elements of the *gámos*. This explains the predominance of the goddess Aphrodite in her poems, since that deity reigns over exactly these domains. However, Sappho does not fail to warn about the dangers that the patron goddess can exert if one gets carried away by her unfettered powers. Such is the case in Fr. 16 or "Ode to Anactoria," a song that uses the myth of Helen as an *exemplum* and tells of her transgression in leaving her husband, daughter, and parents, to sail beside her beloved.[19] Here is the poem:

> Some say a host of cavalry, others of infantry, and others of ships, is the most beautiful thing on the black earth, but I say it is whatsoever a person loves. It is perfectly easy to make understood by everyone: for she who far surpassed mankind in beauty, Helen, left her most noble husband and went sailing off to Troy with no thought at all for her child or dear parents, but (love) led her astray […] lightly […] has reminded me Anactoria who is not here; I would rather see her lovely walk and the bright sparkle of her face than the Lydians' chariots and armed infantry…[20]

---

[19] To the best of my knowledge, the interpretation of this *exemplum* has not been assessed in this way elsewhere, i.e., considering the importance of choral practice for the mythical narrative's sense and intention. On the other hand, Sappho 16 has been widely studied with other interpretative focuses; see Glenn W. Most, "Sappho Fr. 16. 6-7 L-P," *Classical Quarterly* 31 (1981): 11-17; Hardy C. Fredricksmeyer, "A Diachronic Reading of Sappho fr. 16 LP," *Transactions of the American Philological Association* 131 (2001): 75-86; J.H. Barzhuizen and G.H. Els, "On Sappho, Fr. 16 (L.P.)," *Acta Classica* 26 (1983): 23-32; Synnøve B. Thorsen, "The Interpretation of Sappho's fragment 16 L-P," *Symbolae Osloenses* 53.1 (1978): 5-23.

[20] Sappho, fr. 16, 1-20. For the analysis, I am using the Greek text as edited by Eva-Maria Voigt, *Sappho and Alcaeus. Fragmenta* (Amsterdam: Athenaeum, Polak & Van Gennep, 1971); the translation is from David A. Campbell, *Greek Lyric*, vol. 1: *Sappho and Alcaeus* (Cambridge, MA: Harvard University Press, 1982).

It begins with a *priamel*, a generic feature of Greek poetry that consists of a sequence of negatives designed to help the single affirmative gain prominence. In this fragment, the *priamel* aims to answer the indirect question "what is the most beautiful thing on the black earth?" To do this, Sappho uses the oppositional and complementary binomial *éros-mákhē* (love and war), a theme also explored by her in other fragments.[21] To construct this binomial, she oscillates between the precise and the imprecise, the concrete and the subjective, the I and the other. The affirmative, what the persona considers the most beautiful, has a vague and personal nature, described simply as "whatsoever a person loves" (κῆν' ὄττω τις ἔραται, 3-4), in contrast with the concrete and war-like elements as "host of cavalry, infantry, and ships" (*ippéōn stróton... pésdōn... náōn*, 1-2), preferred by "some" and "others" (*oi... phaîs'*, 1-2).

The *exemplum*—Helen's myth—is introduced in this sequence, and here it performs two main roles. The first is to give authority to the argument. At the end of the *priamel*, the construction may appear to be a mere opinion, for "what others say" (*oi... phaîs'*, 1-2) is put in opposition with what "I say" (*égō dè*, 3), as seen above. We do not know who or how many say that horses, infantry, and ships are the most beautiful, but the use of the plural makes us infer that it is a group, leaving the argument developed by the "I" isolated and weakened at first. However, the song gains another dimension by presenting the *exemplum*, because it draws on the listeners' collective memory and knowledge of the mythical tradition. As such, it introduces an element of authority, transforming the poem's "I" into a "we." Of course, this feature is in line with the educational work of archaic poetry because this "I" is always in communion with the audience, occasion, and poetic genre. Moreover, in the case of choral songs, these experiences expressed as individual in the poem take on the character of shared experience by its members.[22]

The second role of the *exemplum* is to illustrate the affirmative that "whatsoever a person loves" is the most beautiful. As previously mentioned, Sappho's affirmative here has a subjective and vague

---

[21] Fragment 1 (Hymn to Aphrodite), for example.
[22] Kurke, "The Strangeness," 44.

nature that needs to be explained and developed through the myth to be understandable. Helen's transgression story is chosen because the heroine is *kalliston*, the most beautiful human being (*kállos [anth]rópōn*, 7), a claim well-attested in the tradition and therefore objective evidence in the ancient mind. Consequently, she is the perfect model when the subject is beauty. The *exemplum* carries with it an expansive web of myths, especially in connection to the beginning of the poem, upon which Sappho puts her personal touch.[23] However, it also exposes Helen's faults in running away with Paris to Troy (*ébas Troïan pléoi[sa*, 9): she leaves her husband, who was the "most noble" (*ar]iston*, 8), and her daughter and parents, who were "dear" (*phílōn*, 10) to her. Those are serious transgressions because they break with the proper fulfillment of female social roles in Ancient Greece: those of wife and mother.[24] The Trojan War, though not directly cited in the legible part of the fragment, was certainly remembered by the audience,[25] showing that Helen's choice of Paris over her legitimate husband had destructive consequences, causing the end of a city and the death of countless warriors.[26]

---

[23] In the Judgment of Paris, for example, the Trojan prince chooses to give the apple of Eris to Aphrodite, goddess of beauty and erotism, rather than Athena and Hera, goddesses better aligned with ideas the poem rejects; it is by choosing beauty that Paris wins Helen. So, contrary to the tradition that made Helen an object of dispute among men, in fragment 16, she is not the object of desire, but rather the one who desires. Therefore, although the structure of the song reminds us of the Judgment myth, it reverses it by making Helen the one who wants Paris. This view is developed by Eric D. Robson, "Helen's 'Judgment of Paris' and Greek Marriage Ritual in Sappho 16," *Arethusa* 43 (2010): 1-20. See also Ruby Blondell, *Helen of Troy: Beauty, Myth, Devastation* (London: Oxford University Press, 2013), 116; and Page Dubois, "Sappho and Helen," in *Reading Sappho: Contemporary Approaches*, ed. Ellen Greene (Los Angeles: University of California Press, 1996), 87.

[24] Elsewhere in melic poetry, this accusation is made by Alcaeus's 283 (Voigt) and Stesichorus's *Helen* 85.

[25] The binomial "love and war" of the *priamel* also helps the public to make this connection.

[26] Betini, "Helen and Paris," 8.

I will not enter into the discussion of whether this casts a positive or negative light on Helen. What is important here is to see what the persona tries to teach through the *exemplum*, namely, how the power of Eros and Aphrodite is invincible and can disturb the senses of even the most noble humans, such as Helen. Sharing this point, Jessica E. Decker explains that the *exemplum* shows how the goddess's force can even "pull [Helen] away from a pleasant marriage and loving family," thereby proving Aphrodite's great power.[27]

In terms of performance, we cannot say with certainty for what occasion fragment 16 was composed; however, there is one piece of information that we must keep in mind—its chorality. The clue that leads us to think that fragment 16 might be part of choral educational practice is the mention of Anactoria at the end. There is an erotic atmosphere that comes along with her image when the speaker wishes to see "her lovely walk and the bright sparkle of her face" (ἔρατόν τε βᾶμα | κἀμάρυχμα λάμπρον ἴδην προσώπω, 17-18) rather than "Lydians' chariots and infantry" (ἢ τὰ Λύδων ἄρματα κἀν ὄπλοισι | πεσδομ]άχεντας, 19-20)—phrases that echo the *priamel* in exemplary ring composition, showing the speaker's choice for love. As is well-documented, homoeroticism is an important feature in the poetry performed by *parthénoi*, especially to highlight their youthful, desirable, and florescent beauty.[28] Secondly, Anactoria represents the memory of a *parthenos* who is not there anymore (*Anaktorí[as... ou pareoísas*, 15-16), who went to another place (maybe Lydia?) for a reason unknown to us, but whose gracefulness and beauty remains in the speaker's mind. Following Ragusa and Lardinois,[29] it is coherent to think of Anactoria as one of Sappho's young choir members, whose leaving may have coincided with her marriage.

---

[27] Jessica E. Decker, "The Most Beautiful Thing on the Black Earth: Sappho's Alliance with Aphrodite," in *Looking at Beauty* to Kalon *in Western Greece*, eds. H. Reid and T. Leyh (Sioux City: Parnassos Press, 2019), 48.

[28] Calame, *Les choeurs*, 420-436.

[29] Ragusa, *Safo de Lesbos*,126; Andre Lardinois, "Subject and Circumstance in Sappho's Poetry," *Transactions of the American Philological Association* 124 (1994): 57-84.

On that account, considering that Sappho's songs were directed to her group of *parthénoi* in the context of choral education, depicting Helen from the song's novel perspective may be a way of demonstrating to these young women the dangers and pleasures of Eros. The desired person is the most beautiful thing, but to possess him may imply reprehensible actions. Neglecting to mention the war while highlighting Helen's family may be a proximity strategy for the instruction of this group since, as Ruth Scodel remarks, "another woman whose desire led her to violate social norms would not start a war, but she, like Helen, would have a family."[30] Thus, the *exemplum* in Sappho's fragment 16 may have served the educational function of preparing *parthénoi* for their future in courtship and marriage—warning them about Aphrodite's power of bringing beauty, but also dishonor if they don't follow her wisely. However, the teachings shared by the poet with the chorus members went beyond the marriage sphere, touching equally on issues about the human condition and the importance of poetry in overcoming our limitations. Such is the case in the song "Old Age Poem" or "Tithonus poem":[31]

> [several words missing] the violet-rich Muses' fine gifts, children, [several words missing] the clear-voiced song-loving lyre: [several words missing] skin once was soft is withered now, [several words missing] hair has turned white which once was black, my heart has been weighed down, my knees, which once were swift to dance like young fawns, fail me. How often I lament these things. But what can you do? No being that is human can escape old age. For

---

[30] Ruth Scodel, "Myth in Sappho," in *The Cambridge Companion to Sappho,* ed. Patrick Finglass and Adrian Kelly (Cambridge: Cambridge University Press, 2021), 201.

[31] Sappho, "Tithonus poem," 1-12. Greek text and translation from *The New Sappho on Old Age: Textual and Philosophical Issues,* eds. Ellen Greene and Marilyn Skinner (Washington DC: Center for Hellenic Studies, 2009). For general views of the fragment, see also Felix Budelmann, "Commentary Sappho 58b" in *Greek Lyric: A Selection,* ed. Felix Budelmann (Cambridge: Cambridge University Press, 2018), 146-52;

people used to think that Dawn with rosy arms [several words uncertain] Tithonus fine and young to the edges of the earth; yet still grey old age in time did seize him, though he has a deathless wife.

The choral aspect is even more evident in this fragment than in the previous one, beginning with the vocative *paîdes* to refer to the female choir, which is instructed to do something related to "the violet-rich Muses' fine gifts [and] the clear-voiced song-loving lyre" (...ἰ]οκ[ό]λπων κάλα δῶρα, παῖδες, ... τὰ]ν φιλάοιδον λιγύραν χελύνναν·,1-2).[32] The speaker uses her own experience to approach the chorists. Like them, she was once nimble in dancing gracefully like young fawns (ποτα λαίψηρ' ἔον ὄρχησθ' ἴσα νεβρίοισι, 6), but today she can no longer do this because she has grown old—an evil that will one day affect these young women as well. The theme of old age is constructed with traditional images of poetry—black hair becomes white (ἐγ]ένοντο τρίχες ἐκ μελαίναν, 4) and the chest, heavy (βάρυς δέ μ' ὀ [θ]ῦμος πεπόηται, 5)—joined by the image, linked to choral dance, of failing knees (γόνα δ' [ο]ὐ φέροισι, 5) that can no longer dance. The persona laments that only her voice is left to sing about this time, signaling the importance of poetry in finding a kind of eternal life and youth.[33]

However, consolation comes with the gnomic phrase "No being that is human can escape old age" (ἀγήραον ἄνθρωπον ἔοντ' οὐ δύνατον γένεσθαι, 8), which changes the individual perspective of

---

[32] Martin L. West restores the first verses with the verb σπουδάσδετε, translated by him as "pursue," but which also has the sense of "pay attention," "to be busy," and even "study." In West's version, therefore, the first two verses would be: "Pursue the violet-laden Muses' handsome gifts, my children, and the loud-voiced lyre so dear to song" (ὔμμες πεδὰ Μοίσαν ἰ]οκ[ό]λπων κάλα δῶρα, παῖδες, | σπουδάσδετε καὶ τὰ]ν φιλάοιδον λιγύραν χελύνναν·), which would further emphasize the paideutic aspect of the song. See Greene and Skinner, eds., *The new Sappho*, 23-24.

[33] Ragusa, "Chorality," 88; Katerina Ladianou, "Female Choruses and Gardens of Nymphs: Visualizing Chorality in Sappho," in *The Look of Lyric: Greek Song and the Visual. Studies in Archaic and Classical Greek Songs*, eds. V. Cazzato and A. Lardinois (Leiden: Brill, 2016), 343-69.

aging to a collective perspective that everyone shares. Contrary to Sappho 16, the argument of this song is not abstract, nor subjective, but clear and objective: the *gnṓmē* is an ethical-moral or philosophical reflection based on human experience and it is represented in the *exemplum*'s narrative. The chosen myth that supports the argument of the sentence is Tithonus's story, a beautiful young Trojan who aroused the desire of the goddess Eos (Dawn). The deity then asks Zeus to make him immortal like her; however, she forgets to also ask him to ward off another human evil besides death: old age. Thus, Tithonus grows old forever, forgotten in a room by the goddess who once desired him so much.[34] In the song, the mythic narrative is brief, and Sappho chooses to mainly remember the beauty of Tithonus (*[k]álon kaì néon*, 11) that is gone, taken by aging (ἀλλ' αὐτον ὔμως ἔμαρψε | χρόνωι πόλιον γῆρας, 11-12), just as it happened to herself, linking the mythic experience with their own lives. The same link happens with the erotic pleasure that the goddess and the mortal enjoy, which was limited to the time that Tithonus retains his beauty and his luster, similar to what occurs with the pleasure of the living choral experience.

Thus, the surviving part of the song leads us to think that Sappho instructs her students to accept this human lot ("But what can you do?" 7), by showing that not even the love of a goddess could make a hero escape aging.[35] Hence, in the beginning, we see the invitation to the young chorists to profit from the Muses' gifts while it is still possible for them.

Antilochus's filial devotion in Pindar's *Pythian* 6:

Another melic species that usually elaborates a mythical *exemplum* to connect with the whole of the song and thus bind a

---

[34] The earliest mention of the myth that we have access to is in the *Homeric Hymn to Aphrodite V*, 218-238. It is relevant to note that, although the lesson intended by the song does not directly address the world of *gámos*, still the chosen story has in its motivation an erotic background. On Homeric hymns, see H.G. Evelyn-White, *Hesiod, the Homeric Hymns and Homerica* (Cambridge, MA: Harvard University Press, 1914).

[35] There are those who maintain that the poem continues in four more verses. See Greene and Skinner, eds., *The New Sappho*, 3.

message or lesson is epinician. Victory odes were composed to celebrate and immortalize the victor in athletic games and they were most frequently performed in palace *symposia* or at the homecoming procession of the victorious athlete (*kōmos*).[36] Thus, the praise of the victor, his lineage, and his achievements are the main characteristic of the epinician genre.[37] This shows the importance of mythical narratives in songs, for they elevate athletic victory beyond something unique and individual, making it collective since the ideals and traditions of the winner are not his alone, but shared with the entire community.[38] This distinctive feature is reinforced by the choral performance, which for epinician odes consists of adult or young male dancers,[39] celebrating the victory of the praised together with the myth in order to unite them all socially, and thus demonstrate that the winner conveys and emphasizes the traditional values and teachings of that community.

We can see this in Pindar's *Pythian* 6, composed for Xenocrates of Akragas, who won the chariot race in the Pythian Games of 490 BCE in Delphi.[40] It is one of the five Pindaric odes related to the

---

[36] For the genre, see Douglas L. Cairns, *Bacchylides. Five Epinician Odes* (Cambridge: Francis Carins, 2010) 1-74; Laura Swift, *The Hidden Chorus: Echoes of Genre in Tragic Lyric* (Oxford: Oxford University Press, 2010), 104-72; and Peter Agócs, Chris Carey and Richard Rawles, eds., *Reading the Victory Ode* (Cambridge: Cambridge University Press, 2012). The *kōmoi* in victory odes are "an element in a larger celebration involving feasting and acclamation of the victor's success, either at the site of his victory or in his home community, and will indicate that at least part of his celebration involved the movement of the festive throng towards a specific location [...]" Cairns, *Bacchylides*, 30.

[37] The songs were commissioned by those who either owned the victorious horses or ruled the victor's city.

[38] Cairns, "General Introduction," 27.

[39] Cairns, "General Introduction," 29. On the performance of the victory ode being monodic or choral beyond Cairns and Swift, see also Christopher Carey, "The Victory Ode in Performance: The Case for the Chorus," *Classical Philology* 86.3 (1991): 192-200.

[40] On Pindar's *Pythian* 6, see also Lucia Athanassaki, "Performance and re-performance: the Siphnian treasury evoked (Pindar's *Pythian* 6 ,

Emmenidai,[41] a family of tyrants who governed various Sicilian cities at the beginning of the 5th century BCE. The honorand of this song is Thrasybulus, the son of Xenocrates and probably the driver of the winning chariot.[42] The *exemplum* here, Antilochus's death for saving his father, has the semantic intention of praising the young Emmenid by comparing him to the hero for teaching the precept of filial devotion. In this regard, the speaker makes Thrasybulus a model of this precept for his generation, since his victory is a way to honor his father and his lineage, in reflection of Antilochus, who was the model for the heroic generation.[43]

The complete ode has 54 lines, divided into six stanzas, which we can summarize in four parts: the praise of Xenocrates and the Emmenidai lineage (1-18); Chiron's precept for filial devotion (19-27); Antilochus's death *exemplum* (28-46); and the last praise of Thrasybulus with a prayer to Poseidon (47-54). Due to the theme, I focus on verses 19-46, where the *gnōmē* and the *exemplum* occur:

> Truly, by keeping him at your right hand
> you uphold the precept,
> whose words of advice they say Philyra's son
> once gave to the mighty son of Peleus in the mountains
> when he was away from his parents: above all gods
> to revere Kronos' son, loud-voiced lord
> of lightning and thunder,
> and never to deprive of like honor
> one's parents during their allotted lifetime.
>
> In the past as well, mighty Antilochos
> bore such thoughts in mind,

Olympian 2, and *Isthmian* 2)," in *Reading the Victory Ode*, eds. P. Agócs, C. Carey, and R. Rawles, (Cambridge: Cambridge University Press, 2012), 134-157.

[41] The other songs are *Olympian* 2 and 3, *Isthmian* 2, and Fragment 124.

[42] It is not unanimous whether it was in fact Thrasybulus who was driving the chariot. See Gregory Nagy, "A Sampling of Comments on Pindar Pythian 6," *Classical Inquiries*, published online at chs.harvard.edu.

[43] Giuliana Ragusa, *Lira Grega: Antologia de Poesia Arcaica*. (São Paulo: Hedra, 2013), 254.

who died to save his father by standing up to
the man-slaughtering general of the Ethiopians,
Memnon. For Nestor's chariot had become entangled
when his horse was struck by Paris' arrows, and he
was brandishing his powerful spear.
In panic the mind of the old man
from Messene shouted to his son,

nor indeed did he hurl forth a word that fell to the ground:
that godlike man took a stand right there
and bought his father's rescue with his own death,
and, for doing that awesome deed, he was deemed
by the young men of that ancient generation
to be foremost in virtuous behavior toward parents.
Those things are past:
but of men now, Thrasyboulos
has come closest to the standard of filial devotion[44]

In Pindar's ode, the *gnṓmē* is in verses 23-27, and precedes the myth, preparing the *exemplum* that justifies its exhortations: to revere Zeus above all gods (μάλιστα μὲν Κρονίδαν | ...θεῶν σέβεσθαι, 23-25) and always honor your parents (μή ποτε τιμᾶς ἀμείρειν γονέων, 26-27). This advice is attributed to Chiron ("Philyra's son," 21), a Centaur and Achilles's tutor, who serves as a didactic authority. Based on a scholium of the poem and other sources, Leslie Kurke argues that these "Precepts of Chiron" (*Philýras uiòn orphanizoménōi*, 23) seem to rely on a lost poem attributed to Hesiod, *Cheironos Hipothēkai*,[45] which circulated widely, especially in Athens, as an educational text for young aristocratic men. Thrasybulus, on this

---

[44] For the analysis, I am using the Greek text and translation by William H. Race, *Pindar: Olympian Odes, Pythian Odes* (Cambridge, MA: Harvard University Press, 1997).

[45] Says Leslie Kurke, "Pindar's Sixth Pythian and the Tradition of Advice Poetry," *Transactions of American Philological Association* 120 (1990): 91, "The genre of *hypothêkai* would be characterized by a proem, an address to a specific addressee, sometimes by mythological material, but mainly by a collection of injunctions and traditional wisdom, loosely strung together with gnomic material."

view, is praised by the speaker for following the traditional precept of filial devotion contained in the lost poem by winning the chariot race, as is marked in lines 19 to 22.

After the *gnốmē*, Pindar introduces Antilochus's exemplum—the son of Nestor who died to save his father—to illustrate the precept of filial devotion. The narrative is introduced with "in the past as well" (*égento kaì proteron*, 28), situating the song no longer in the present moment, but in the mythical past of memory. The myth is elaborated in epic style: Nestor's chariot "became entangled" (*árm' epéda*, 32) after having been "struck by Paris's arrows" (*Pários ek beléōn daïkhtheís*, 33), making it vulnerable to the attack of Memnon, the "man-slaughtering general of the Ethiopians" (*enaríbroton... | strátarkhon Aithiópōn*, 30-31). Hearing his father scream, Antilochus saves him by dying in his place. The scene echoes verses 8.80-87 of the *Iliad* when the same arrows from the Trojan prince hit Nestor's chariot; however, in the Homeric poem, it is Diomedes, not Antilochus, who saves him and it is Hector who advances, not Memnon.[46] This arrangement demonstrates that Pindar composes scenarios that play with the epic-Homeric tradition while designing apparently original situations.[47]

The similarities and relations between performance, *gnốmē*, and *exemplum* are easily seen in the ode. Antilochus is a young and excellent charioteer like Thrasybulus probably was, and both use their abilities to honor their fathers. Also, both were threatened by "foreign forces" and prevailed—in the myth, it is the Ethiopian Memnon, and the Trojan Paris in the context of war. In the ode's world of athletics, Pindar mentions that "neither winter rain, coming from abroad as a relentless army" (τὸν οὔτε χειμέριος ὄμβρος, ἐπακτὸς ἐλθών ἐριβρόμον νεφέλας, 10-11) would collapse the Emmenidai's "treasure house of hymns" (*hýmnōn thēsauròs*, 7-8),

---

[46] Antilochus's killing by the commander of the Ethiopians would only have been told in *Aithiopis*, a lost epic attributed to Arctinus of Miletus (c. 775-741 BCE), though we don't know how it happened in the poem.

[47] On other Pindaric odes related to the Epic Cycle, see Henry Spelman, "Pindar and the Epic Cycle," *The Journal of Hellenic Studies* 138 (2018): 182-201

probably referring to Xenocrates's enemies and/or competitors in the Pythian Games. This "winter rain" anticipates Memnon, "an alien *par excellence*," and they are connected to each other by the similarity of their epithets (*eribrómon*, 11, *enaríbroton*, 31).[48] In this way, Pindar unites the two worlds to corroborate the comparison between the Messenian hero and the young Sicilian prince as they honor their parents by facing foreign forces, following Chiron's precept.

Finally, in Pindar's song, the *exemplum* illustrates the central argument not only to make it more understandable, as was the case of Sappho 16, but also to present its highest model. The heroic model of the *gnómē* is Antilochus, as is stated in verses 40 to 42 where he is considered the "foremost in virtuous behavior toward parents" (ὕπατος ἀμφὶ τοκεῦσιν ἔμμεν ἀρεταν, 42). By winning the chariot race, Thrasybulus follows in the hero's footsteps, being one who is "closest to the standard of filial devotion" (πατρῴαν μάλιστα πρὸς στάθμαν, 45) of his generation. In this way, Pindar instructs the young listeners of the song to be like Thrasybulus and Antilochus by honoring their parents.[49]

---

[48] Seth. L. Schein, "Unity and Meaning in Pindar's Sixth Pythian Ode," *Mètis. Anthropologie des Mondes Grecs Anciens* 2 (1987): 240.

[49] The *exemplum* in the victory ode can also bring heroic models that should not be followed (i.e., with bad behavior), which serve as an illustration of something to be avoided, because they caused misfortune. This is the case of Tantalus in Pindar's *Olympian* 1, where, in the Pindaric reworking, he abuses divine generosity by stealing nectar and ambrosia from the gods and distributing it to his guests. Because of this, Tantalus receives eternal punishment and Pelops, his son, loses the immortality that was granted to him. Thus, the figure of the mythical banquet is linked with that of the symposium banquet, in which Pindar warns his listeners that "...if any man hopes to hide any deed | from a god, he is mistaken." (Lines 64-65, trans. Race), instructing them to be moderate and reverent to the gods. On the ode and myth, see Douglas Gerber, *Pindar's Olympian One: A Commentary* (Toronto: University of Toronto Press, 1982) and Wallace G. Most "Poet and Public: Communicative Strategies in Pindar and Bacchylides," in *Reading the Victory Ode*, eds. Peter Agócs, Chris Carey and Richard Rawles (Cambridge: Cambridge University Press, 2012), 249-276.

Conclusion

In this essay, I have presented some ways that the *exemplum* could be employed in melic poetry, and how this strategy was an efficient way to send an educational message related to its occasion of performance. We have seen that the mythical narrative of the *exemplum* is elaborated harmonically with the rest of the song, and, therefore, the formed lesson is constructed with the full semantic intention of the poem, of which the *exemplum* has the function of being an illustration, an authority, a model, an amplification. This resource becomes important for the education of adults and young people who watch or participate in the song's performance since, in addition to conveying traditional narratives, it also reinforces and teaches the community's values and precepts. Therefore, the content of the song combined with the choral experience of dancing, singing, and music—the *molpé*—forms an educational practice *par excellence* by teaching what virtuous behavior is while at the same time exercising the body and promoting social integration.

This phenomenon was observed in the two songs by Sappho analyzed here. Bearing in mind that Sappho's songs were composed for female choirs whose main purpose was to prepare young women for marriage and adult sexual life, talking about love and its danger is essential, and the poet chooses Helen's myth to illustrate how this feeling can be destructive, despite its beauty. Besides the erotic content, the songs could also deal with the fragile human condition to which everyone is subjected, such as growing old.[50] In the case of "Tithonus's Poem," Sappho seems to teach the young women not to fight this lot because it is humanly impossible. What is left for them is to enjoy the "Muses' gifts" while they are young—demonstrating to them the importance of poetry and of the choral practice in which they are embedded.

On the other hand, Pindar's victory odes are set in the world of the athletic games, with performances likely in palace *symposia*. We

---

[50] I recall fr. 140 which seems to teach the girls (*kórai*) to mourn the death of the young Adonis, Aphrodite's mortal lover, in a dramatized way. This causes the *parthénoi* to experience, through myth, the funeral ritual. See Ragusa, *Safo de Lesbos*, 96.

see in them, therefore, a masculine world of aristocratic values which relate to the actual context of the performance. This is how it plays out in *Pythian* 6. The similarities between Antilochus and the recipient of the song, Thrasybulus, are evident: they are both young charioteers and the pride of their respective families, being perfect models of filial devotion. In this way, the ode reinforces the educational precept of filial devotion that was already circulating within aristocracy and demonstrates to young people what steps they should follow to fulfil it, all while praising and admiring Thrasybulus and the entire Emmenidai lineage.

Michael Goyette[1]

Playing the Doctor: Performances and Pedagogies of Healing in the Fragments of Empedocles and Euripides's *Bacchae*[2]

Although the evidence for Empedocles's medical career is fragmentary and heavily reliant upon later sources (e.g., Diogenes Laertius, *Vitae Philosophorum* 8.52-76; Aulus Cornelius Celsus, *Proem.* 1.7; Pliny the Elder, *Naturalis Historia* 30.9, Galen, *Meth. Med.* I.6), Empedocles's own surviving fragments reflect a distinct interest in matters of healing and the nature of embodiment—all of which contributed to his reputation as one of the founders of the Sicilian school of medicine. This essay demonstrates that these interests are closely connected with performative and didactic elements in Empedocles's Fragments, as reflected in the poetic language and rhetorical strategies[3] he uses to convey authoritativeness concerning questions of healing, illness, and human physiology. In the first part, I consider modern frameworks that utilize the lenses of performance studies to examine power dynamics in doctor-patient interactions. Drawing upon these frameworks, I proceed to argue that Empedocles's work performatively employs a multifaceted approach

---

[1] Michael Goyette is an Instructor of Classics and Ancient Studies at Eckerd College in St. Petersburg, Florida. His research and teaching interests include ancient medicine and the health humanities, ancient science and the history of science, tragedy, gender, reception studies, and pedagogy. He is highly enthusiastic about interdisciplinary inquiry, and in both his research and his teaching he strives to demonstrate how the humanities and the sciences can complement and speak to each other in both antiquity and the modern world.

[2] I am grateful to Fonte Aretusa's editorial staff for their suggestions on this chapter, and to the attendees of the 2022 Symposium for their helpful comments and questions. I would especially like to thank Heather Reid, Susi Kimbell, and their team for their organization and hospitality.

[3] Diogenes Laertius preserves a fragment from the Peripatetic biographer Satyrus attesting to Empedocles's rhetorical skill immediately after Laertius observes that Empedocles was a healer, as if to link the two activities: φησὶ δὲ Σάτυρος ἐν τοῖς Βίοις ὅτι καὶ ἰατρὸς ἦν καὶ ῥήτωρ ἄριστος. ("Satyrus says in his *Lives* that [Empedocles] was both a doctor and the best rhetorician." *Vitae Philosophorum* 8.58–8.59).

to legitimate his claims to medical and didactic authority. I show that, as one part of his strategy, he incorporates religio-magical language to present himself as a healer with privileged access to divine knowledge, in a manner that resembles Dionysus's highly theatrical self-presentation in Euripides's *Bacchae*. I then turn to how Empedocles also lays claim to naturalistic, physiologically-based approaches to healing and to disseminating medical knowledge, which are typically associated with the "rational" physician. I show that this multidimensional approach can be understood as a performative effort to appeal to and to instruct multiple audiences with potentially differing conceptualizations of healing and medicine.[4] Indeed, focusing on the performative aspect of Empedocles's work also prompts one to consider its possible audiences and the medical marketplace in which ideas about healing and the body were developed and communicated to students and to potential patients — and in which healers might acquire power and influence.[5]

Medicine, magic, and performance

In recent years, scholars of the health humanities, bioethics, and medical education have brought greater awareness to the integral role that performative factors can play in doctor-patient interactions. As many may know from personal experience, a doctor's physical presentation, posture, uses of language (including their choices of when or when not to employ specialized medical terminology), vocal intonations, facial expressions, and the amount of time they spend with a patient can all create an impression in the patient's mind as to the doctor's trustworthiness, authoritativeness, ability to empathize,

---

[4] On the theory that Empedocles wrote for multiple audiences who may have held differing perspectives on medicine, magic, etc., see Dirk Obbink, "The Addressees of Empedocles," in *Materiali e discussion per l'analisi dei testi classici* 31 (1993): esp. 89–92.

[5] This aspect of my methodology draws influence from historian John Harley Warner's analysis of the medical landscape in 17th–19th century Britain, which observes how "calculated self-promotion, often played out on a highly visible public stage" can be "a crucial ingredient in the success of learned physician and mountebank alike." John Harley Warner, "Medicine as performance," *Nature* 412 n. 6845 (2001): 377.

and more. While some may take the notion of "performance" in a medical context as something contrived or insincere (possibilities that can certainly occur), these performative elements can, as Roger Kneebone, Will Houstoun, and Natasha Houghton observed in *The Lancet*, "help clinicians build immediate rapport with patients."[6] Their article suggests that medical professionals can learn a lot from professional magicians, especially with regard to winning the trust of their audiences (or patients). This may seem counterintuitive, since magicians typically withhold information in order to dupe—rather than treat or educate—their audiences (and we certainly would not want our doctors duping us in the way a magician might!), but the comparison centers upon the performative techniques and strategies that magicians and doctors both use to gain buy-in from audiences/patients who may be skeptical, anxious, or ambivalent.[7] Kneebone, Houston, and Houghton also consider a magician's ability "to control what is and is not seen" to constitute a skill set that could be "advantageous during a medical consultation;" they find this to be particularly true in the context of online doctor's appointments (which have become increasingly common in the wake of the COVID pandemic), where there is a newfound focus on self-presentation and audio-visual curation.[8] I submit that these abilities to build rapport and "control what is and is not seen" operate in ways that are comparable to Empedocles's careful selection of wording and his deliberate crafting of a persona that would be capable of winning his audiences' trust.

---

[6] Roger Kneebone, Will Houstoun, and Natasha Houghton, "Medicine, magic, and online performance," *The Lancet* 398 n. 10314 (2021): 1868-9.

[7] A similar perspective can be seen in the work of Performing Medicine, an award-winning initiative of the London-based performance company Clod Ensemble which draws on techniques and ideas in the arts "to provide training to medical students and healthcare professionals" (clodensemble.com/learning/performing-medicine). On the work of Performing Medicine and further discussion of the role of performance in medical training and clinical settings, see also Alex Mermikides, *Performance, Medicine and the Human* (London: Bloomsbury, 2020), esp. 21, 67-77, 81-85, 138-141.

[8] Kneebone, Houstoun, and Houghton, "Medicine," 1869.

Daniel J. Sokol, a scholar of medical ethics who is also a practicing magician, has similarly observed in the *Journal of the Royal Society of Medicine* how subtle "verbal manipulations" can have a crucial impact in magic exhibitions and medical interactions alike—imperceptibly leading the audience or patient towards a single option or a specific desired reaction.[9] I would argue that these sorts of verbal cues and powers of suggestion also resemble the subtle ways by which a teacher might steer a student to a certain answer or interpretation. For Sokol, this aspect of performance is a function of the power dynamics typical of interactions in the spheres of both magic and medicine. Expanding upon the nature of power dynamics in medical contexts, Sokol draws upon a framework developed by bioethicist and physician Howard Brody which attributes to medical doctors three specific kinds of power: "Aesculapian power, acquired through an expert knowledge of medicine; social power, arising from the doctor's social status; and charismatic power, derived from personal qualities such as courage, firmness, and kindness" (or "bedside manner").[10] According to Sokol, these forms of power can contribute to positive outcomes for patient and doctor, but they also have the potential to be used deceptively or otherwise abused, such as when a doctor's ambition for social power detracts from their commitment to serving patients and furthering medical knowledge.[11] Indeed, this tension is particularly evident in the world of ancient medicine, where many avowed remedies and treatments would, as we know now, further imperil patients' health.

While Brody's tripartite framework of medical power is not ancient, and we should not expect ancient doctors or healers to adhere to it in the same way as modern doctors, I propose that offers a useful lens for examining constructions and performances of power in both ancient and modern medical contexts.[12] Applying this framework to

---

[9] Daniel K. Sokol, "Medicine as performance: what can magicians teach doctors?" *Journal of the Royal Society of Medicine* 101.9 (2008): 443.

[10] Sokol, "Medicine as performance," 444; cf. Howard Brody, *The Healer's Power* (New Haven: Yale University Press, 2006), esp. 16-18.

[11] Sokol, "Medicine as performance," 445.

[12] Although this framework is modern, manifestations of each of these forms of power can also be seen in ancient medical sources, and perhaps most

analyze the construction of medical authority in the Empedoclean Fragments can illuminate how Empedocles as poet pursues these three aspects of medical power through his performative uses of language and self-presentation. My analysis follows ancient testimonies and modern scholars in taking the first-person "I" speaker in this and other fragments to be representative of the historical figure Empedocles himself,[13] but this identification is not crucial to my arguments since I focus on the text's deployment of language and its performative construction of medical and didactic authority.

Empedocles: performing the divine healer

The performative kinship between magic and medicine detected by these modern medical ethicists is also profoundly evident in Empedocles, an author who has since antiquity been described as a magician, sorcerer, or prophet as well as a doctor or physician. Blurring the lines between such figures, Empedocles was, as Katarzyna Kołakowska puts it, a "master of his own PR" with a deliberately constructed persona that "no PR expert would be ashamed of today."[14] In the context of the highly competitive ancient Greek medical marketplace in which Hippocratic-style physicians vied for influence with sorcerers, herbalists, root-cutters, and healing cults—categories of practitioners whose theories and approaches often overlapped—skills in self-promotion and the ability to associate oneself with multiple forms of healing could have provided a significant advantage.

The intricate nature of Empedocles's self-presentation is on display in Fragment 1, which many commentators (going back as far as Diogenes Laertius)[15] have regarded as the beginning of the

---

vividly in the works of Galen. Cf. Vivan Nutton, *Ancient Medicine* (London: Routledge, 2013), 242–243.

[13] Geoffrey Stephen Kirk, John Earle Raven, and Malcolm Schofield, *The Presocratic Philosophers: A Critical History with a Selection of Texts* (New York: Cambridge University Press, 1983), 282–283.

[14] Katarzyna Kołakowska, "Empedocles of Akragas. Politician and Performer," in *Politics and Performance in Western Greece*, ed. Heather L. Reid (Sioux City, IA: Parnassos Press, 2017), 205.

[15] Diogenes Laertius, *Vitae Philosophorum* 8.54.

Purifications, one of two poems into which Empedocles's Fragments are often divided:

> O friends, who dwell in the great city of the yellow Acragas
> up in the high parts of the city, concerned with good deeds,
> \<respectful harbors for strangers, untried by evil,\>
> hail! I, in your eyes a deathless god, no longer mortal,
> go among all, honored, just as I seem:
> wreathed with ribbons and festive garlands.
> As soon as I arrive in flourishing cities I am revered
> by all, men and women. And they follow at once,
> in their ten thousands, asking where is the path to gain,
> some in need of divinations, others in all sorts of diseases
> sought to hear a healing oracle,
> having been pierced \<about by harsh pains\> for too long a time.[16]

> ὦ φίλοι, οἳ μέγα ἄστυ κάτα ξανθοῦ ᾽Ακράγαντος
> ναίετ᾽ ἂν᾽ ἄκρα πόλεος, ἀγαθῶν μεκεδήμονες ἔργων
> \<ξείνων αἰδοῖοι λιμένες κακότητος ἄπειροι\>
> χαίρετ᾽. ἐγὼ δ᾽ ὑμῖν θεὸς ἄμβροτος οὐκέτι θνητός
> πωλεῦμαι μετὰ πᾶσι τετιμένος, ὥσπερ ἔοικα,
> ταινίαις τε περίστεπτος στέφεσίν τε θαλείοις·
> πᾶσι δ᾽ ἅμ᾽ εὖτ᾽ ἂν ἵκωμαι ἐς ἄστεα τηλεθάοντα
> ἀνδράσιν ἠδὲ γυναιξί, σεβίζομαι· οἱ δ᾽ ἅμ᾽ ἕπονται
> μυρίοι ἐξερέοντες ὅπῃ πρὸς κέρδος ἀταρπός,
> οἱ μὲν μαντοσυνέων κεχρημένοι, οἱ δ᾽ ἐπὶ νούσων
> παντοίων ἐπύθοντο κλύειν εὐηκέα βάξιν,
> δηρὸν δὴ χαλεπῇσι πεπαρμένοι \<ἀμφ᾽ ὀδύνῃσιν\>.

Addressing the denizens of Acragas (the presumptive general audience of his text), Empedocles casts himself as a "deathless god" (*theos ambrotos*) who is lavishly honored (*tetimenos*) and sought after upon his arrival in new cities. He indicates that this influence derives both from his ability to perform divinations (*mantosuneōn*) and from his capacity to provide relief from all sorts of diseases via divinations

---

[16] For all Empedoclean fragments and translations cited, I use the textual edition by Brad Inwood, *The Poem of Empedocles: A Text and Translation with an Introduction* (Toronto: University of Toronto Press, 2001).

and oracles of healing. Boasting of his large, reverent followings and his exceptional powers of healing, Empedocles simultaneously curates (to use Brody's framework) Aesculapian power and social power, while also exuding a larger-than-life, theatrical charisma. Unlike modern doctors who may achieve charismatic power through skills in interpersonal communication and empathy demonstrated during one-on-one interactions with patients,[17] Empedocles's performance of medical charisma hinges upon his own self-professed access to divine knowledge and self-deification.[18] Indeed, according to Diogenes Laertius's testimony the reputation Empedocles had acquired for being both a "doctor" and a "prophet" was directly inspired by the lines of this fragment (*Vitae Philosophorum* 8.62). Furthermore, Diogenes Laertius relates that Empedocles earned this reputation by reviving a woman who had neither breathed nor had a pulse for thirty days (*Vitae Philosophorum* 8.60–61), dramatically surpassing the medical capabilities of ordinary mortals. While this anecdote appears to have been embellished from the medically omnipotent persona Empedocles crafts in his poetry,[19] it reveals his success in developing a reputation for superhuman acts of healing.

Empedocles's conflation of the roles of prophet and doctor is also apparent in Fragment 136:

> And finally they become prophets and singers and doctors
> and leaders among men who dwell on earth;
> thence they sprout up as gods, first in their prerogatives.
>
> εἰς δὲ τέλος μάντεις τε καὶ ὑμνόπολοι καὶ ἰητροί
> καὶ πρόμοι ἀνθρώποισιν ἐπιχθονίοισι πέλονται
> ἔνθεν ἀναβλαστοῦσι θεοὶ τιμῇσι φέριστοι.

Suggesting an affinity between "prophets and singers and doctors," Empedocles relates that all such figures "sprout up as gods" by

---

[17] Sokol, "Medicine as performance," 445.

[18] On Empedocles's self-deification, see also Fragment 27 (vol. 11): "but know these things clearly, having heard the story from a god" ἀλλὰ τορῶς ταῦτ' ἴσθι, θεοῦ πάρα μῦθον ἀκούσας.

[19] Kirk, Raven, and Schofield, *The Presocratic Philosophers*, 282.

assuming these roles or identities.[20] Taken in juxtaposition with Fragment 1, it appears that Empedocles is eager to remind his audiences not only of his own divine nature, but also, as Tom Mackenzie has observed, of "the contrast between [himself as] divine narrator and [his audiences' status] as mortal addressees."[21] This contrast in status is reinforced by Empedocles's choice to write in dactylic hexameter, which is traditionally associated with didactic authority[22] and thus a choice that contributes to his performance of medical expertise.

A stark difference in status between Empedocles and his addressees is also seen in the opening lines of Fragment 15:

> All the potions which there are as a defense against evils and old age, you shall learn, since for you alone will I accomplish all these things.

> φάρμακα δ' ὅσσα γεγᾶσι κακῶν καὶ γήραος ἄλκαρ
> πεύσῃ, ἐπεὶ μούνῳ σοι ἐγὼ κρανέω τάδε πάντα.

Adopting the mantle of the masterly instructor, Empedocles professes his ability to pass on specialized knowledge of *pharmaka* that are capable of averting all manner of "evils," including old age. His use of the word *pharmakon* is fittingly ambiguous: in addition to a potion, this word can refer to a charm, philter, or spell, as well as a medicine or drug.[23] As such, it semantically encompasses the magico-religious claims to therapeutic authority seen in Fragments 1 and 136, as well as the more empirically minded approaches that are discernible in other

---

[20] See Peter Kingsley, *Ancient Philosophy, Mystery, and Magic: Empedocles and Pythagorean Tradition* (Oxford: Clarendon, 1995), 319, on Empedocles's presentation of his teachings as dispensations of divine prophecy.

[21] Tom Mackenzie, *Poetry and Poetics in the Presocratic Philosophers* (Cambridge: Cambridge University Press, 2021), 114.

[22] Kirk, Raven, and Schofield, *The Presocratic Philosophers*, 283; see also Obbink, "The Addressees of Empedocles," 51, 52, 55.

[23] Henry George Liddell and Robert Scott, *A Greek-English Lexicon* (Oxford: Clarendon Press, 1996): s.v. φάρμακον. On the semantic complexities associated with the use of this word in Fragment 15, see Christopher Faraone, "Empedocles the Sorcerer and his Hexametrical *Pharmaka*," *Antichthon* 53 (2019): 14–32.

fragments discussed below. Whichever approach one may find more convincing and/or comforting, one is led to the conclusion that Empedocles offers the most effective protection from illness and old age, in a manner akin to how, in the view of Sokol, modern doctors and magicians subtly lead the patient or audience to one particular option or reaction.

Performative parallels: Dionysus as divine healer

Evidence from other ancient sources indicates that performative assertions of self-deification could serve as a powerful way to lay claim to medical and didactic authority in the ancient medical marketplace. In her analysis of the relationship between medicine and religion in Aelius Aristides's *Sacred Tales*, Georgia Petridou concludes that Aristides's self-attested associations with the god Asclepius help elevate him "to the status of a potent physician" while also providing him "with the essential authority to ground his claims to healing powers analogous to those of the god."[24] Over the course of this text, these highly performative claims effectively amount to a subtle and gradual process of self-deification, or, as Petridou encapsulates it: "by becoming a doctor, Aristides becomes a god."[25] Although the *Sacred Tales* are dated to the Second Sophistic period (2nd century CE), Petridou's analysis offers a compelling methodological model for examining the relationship between performances of healing and deification in significantly earlier sources. I propose that a comparable performative relationship can be seen not only in the Fragments of Empedocles, but also in the representation of the god of theater himself, Dionysus, in Euripides's tragedy *The Bacchae*, which was produced in 405 BCE, as few as 25 years after the death of Empedocles.[26] While scholars such as W.K.C. Guthrie maintain that Euripides was familiar with Presocratic philosophy and that some of

---

[24] Georgia Petridou, "Becoming a Doctor, Becoming a God: Religion and Medicine in Aelius Aristides' *Hieroi Logoi*," in *Religion and Illness*, eds. A. Weissenrieder and G. Etzelmüller (Eugene, OR: Cascade, 2016), 307.

[25] Petridou, "Becoming a Doctor, Becoming a God," 328; on the performative nature of Aristides's claims, see esp. 319 and 323.

[26] Kirk, Raven, and Schofield, *Presocratic Philosophers*, 281; see also Inwood, *Poem of Empedocles*, 6.

his tragedies contain Empedoclean echoes,[27] I do not intend to argue for any direct influence between the two authors; instead, the reverberations that I identify between them are meant to illuminate performative strategies, constructions of medical authority, and elements of characterization in each source and, through these juxtapositions, the highly theatrical nature of Empedocles's self-presentation. These comparisons are also rooted in the observation that both Empedocles and Dionysus present themselves as prophet-healers while blurring the lines between the mortal and the divine and between various approaches to healing.

My discussion of the *Bacchae* will focus on its prologue and first episode, where these aspects of self-presentation and similarities with Empedocles's Fragments are most evident. In the very first lines of the play, Dionysus announces his arrival in Thebes with multiple reminders that he is, though disguised as a mortal, in fact a god:

> I have come to this land of Thebes as the son of Zeus.
> Dionysus is my name. Semele, the daughter of Cadmus,
> gave me birth after being forced into labor by fiery lightning.
> Exchanging my divinity for human form I have arrived
> at Dirce's streams and the waters of Ismenus.
> I see the tomb of my thunder-struck mother here
> near the palace and the fallen ruins of her house
> smouldering with the still living flames of Zeus' blast,
> a memorial of Hera's undying hybris against my mother.
> I praise Cadmus who keeps this ground untrodden,
> a shrine for his daughter. But it was I who covered her sanctuary
> all around with the grape-vine's clustering foliage.
> After leaving the gold-rich fields of the Lydians
> and Phrygians, I moved on to Persia's sun-parched plateaux
> and Bactra's walls and the bleak land
> of the Medes and opulent Arabia
> and all of Asia Minor whose parts hug the salty sea
> with beautifully-towered cities

---

[27] W.K.C. Guthrie, *A History of Greek Philosophy*, Vol. II (Cambridge: Cambridge University Press 1969), 262.

full of Greeks and barbarians mixed together.
I first came to this Greek city
only after I had roused to dancing all those Asian lands
and established my rites there so that I might be seen by
mortals as a god.

᾽Ήκω Διὸς παῖς τήνδε Θηβαίων χθόνα
Διόνυσος, ὃν τίκτει ποθ' ἡ Κάδμου κόρη
Σεμέλη λοχευθεῖσ' ἀστραπηφόρῳ πυρί·
μορφὴν δ᾽ ἀμείψας ἐκ θεοῦ βροτησίαν
πάρειμι Δίρκης νάματ' Ἰσμηνοῦ θ᾽ ὕδωρ.
ὁρῶ δὲ μητρὸς μνῆμα τῆς κεραυνίας
τόδ' ἐγγὺς οἴκων καὶ δόμων ἐρείπια
τυφόμενα Δίου πυρὸς ἔτι ζῶσαν φλόγα,
ἀθάνατον Ἥρας μητέρ' εἰς ἐμὴν ὕβριν.
αἰνῶ δὲ Κάδμον, ἄβατον ὃς πέδον τόδε
τίθησι, θυγατρὸς σηκόν· ἀμπέλου δέ νιν
πέριξ ἐγὼ 'κάλυψα βοτρυώδει χλόῃ.
λιπὼν δὲ Λυδῶν τοὺς πολυχρύσους γύας
Φρυγῶν τε, Περσῶν θ' ἡλιοβλήτους πλάκας
Βάκτριά τε τείχη τήν τε δύσχιμον χθόνα
Μήδων ἐπελθὼν Ἀραβίαν τ' εὐδαίμονα
Ἀσίαν τε πᾶσαν, ἣ παρ' ἁλμυρὰν ἅλα
κεῖται μιγάσιν Ἕλλησι βαρβάροις θ᾽ ὁμοῦ
πλήρεις ἔχουσα καλλιπυργώτους πόλεις,
ἐς τήνδε πρῶτον ἦλθον Ἑλλήνων πόλιν,
τἀκεῖ χορεύσας καὶ καταστήσας ἐμὰς
τελετάς, ἵν' εἴην ἐμφανὴς δαίμων βροτοῖς.[28]

With the very first words of the play Dionysus unambiguously
declares that he is the son of Zeus, and then repeatedly reasserts his
godly nature in subsequent lines (vv. 4, 22). These declarations of his
own divinity, along with the way in which he touts his ability to attract
a jubilant and reverential following in diverse geographical locations

---

[28] For the *Bacchae*, I follow the text of E.R. Dodds, *Euripides: Bacchae* (Oxford:
Clarendon, 1960), and the translation of Stephen Esposito, *Euripides:
Medea, Hippolytus, Heracles, Bacchae* (Newburyport, MA: Focus, 2004).

(vv. 20-22), recall Empedocles's self-presentation in Fragment 1, which, as noted above, may have also comprised the beginnings of one of his own works of poetry, the *Purifications*.

While Dionysus's assertions of divinity are substantiated later in the play, they are also highly performative.[29] Indeed, Dionysus's claims to divinity appear to conflict with his mortal appearance at this juncture in the play, and Dionysus himself admits to having a mother who was mortal (vv. 2–3). These seeming contradictions contribute to the skepticism with which some Thebans—most notably Pentheus—regard Dionysus's claims to divinity, and, by extension, his ability to enact healing. With these preemptive pronouncements, Dionysus attempts to forestall such skepticism and to show that he knows how to play the part of the divine healer—not unlike a medical doctor competing for the approval of potential clients and for broader social legitimacy. Applying Brody's framework to this scene, it becomes apparent that Dionysus seeks to cultivate social power and charismatic power by referencing his throngs of followers, in a manner reminiscent of what we have seen in Empedocles. Moreover, Dionysus expresses Aesculapian power through his claims to rouse people to dancing, since in Greek culture ritual dance is often associated with restoration, rejuvenation, and healing.[30] These assertions of powers associated with doctors and healers provide affirmation for Dionysus's claims to divinity.

The facets of Aesculapian power exhibited by Dionysus in the opening lines of the play are also on display in the first episode, in which Tiresias and Cadmus assume the mantle of bacchants and endeavor to climb up Mt. Cithaeron. Despite their advanced age, Tiresias and Cadmus enthusiastically take up the task:

---

[29] On the highly performative role that Dionysus assumes in the *Bacchae*, see Thomas Rosenmeyer, "'Metatheater': An Essay on Overload," *Arion* 10.2 (Fall 2002): 100-101.

[30] Ian Rutherford, "Paeanic Ambiguity: A Study of the Representation of the παιάν in Greek Literature," *Quaderni urbinati di cultura classica* 44.2 (1993): esp. 78; Anna Lazou, "The Concept of Therapy in Ancient Greek Texts & Dance Practices," *Annals of Bioethics and Clinical Applications* 4.3 (2021): 1–10.

Though I'm an old man and he still older, we will twine together thyrsi and wear fawnskin cloaks and crown our heads with shoots of ivy.

...πρέσβυς ὢν γεραιτέρῳ,
θύρσους ἀνάπτειν καὶ νεβρῶν δορὰς ἔχειν
στεφανοῦν τε κρᾶτα κισσίνοις βλαστήμασιν.

According to E.R. Dodds, these lines "exhibit a Dionysiac miracle of rejuvenation,"[31] showcasing the god's knowledge of healing and his capacity for transformative restoration. This ability to invigorate old men, to the extent that they feel capable of climbing a mountain, calls to mind Empedocles's self-professed abilities to heal people who have "been pierced about by harsh pains for too long a time" (cf. Frag. 1.12). As male devotees of the god, Cadmus and Tiresias complement the female followers whom Dionysus mentions in the play's opening passage; this combination exhibits a broad, potentially universal, charisma that parallels Empedocles's statement that he is "revered by all, men and women" (Frag. 1.8). Moreover, the fact that these lines are delivered by Tiresias—a prophetic figure himself—augments the charismatic powers of healing associated with Dionysus in this play.

Later in this episode Tiresias underscores Dionysus's ability to relieve pain and distress through his role as the god of wine:

Dionysus introduced [wine]
to mortals to stop their sorrow and pain.
Whenever men are filled with the stream of the grape-vine
they can sleep and forget the evils of the day.
No other medicine alleviates human suffering.
Dionysus, being a god, is poured out as a libation to the gods
so that it is through him that men receive blessings.

...ηὗρε κεἰσηνέγκατο
θνητοῖς, ὃ παύει τοὺς ταλαιπώρους βροτοὺς
λύπης, ὅταν πλησθῶσιν ἀμπέλου ῥοῆς,
ὕπνον τε λήθην τῶν καθ' ἡμέραν κακῶν
δίδωσιν, οὐδ' ἔστ' ἄλλο φάρμακον πόνων.

---

[31] Dodds, *Euripides: Bacchae*, 90.

Michael Goyette

οὗτος θεοῖσι σπένδεται θεὸς γεγώς,
ὥστε διὰ τοῦτον τἀγάθ' ἀνθρώπους ἔχειν.

As Tiresias recounts, Dionysus's divine power traces not only to his knowledge of wine, but also to his eagerness for imparting that knowledge to mortals in order to relieve their suffering more effectively than any other medicine. Tiresias's messaging concurs with Dionysus's own self-presentation at the beginning of the play, where he mentions his cultivation of the grape vine (vv. 11–12) immediately prior to cataloguing the various regions he invigorated to dance (vv. 13–22). Through these references to Dionysus's expertise with wine and its revitalizing effects, Tiresias reinforces the Aesculapian power to which Dionysus lays claim. It is also telling that Tiresias refers to Dionysus's gift of wine as a *pharmakon*, particularly in light of Empedocles's use of this word in Fragment 15. As observed above with Empedocles, the semantic range of this word highlights the breadth of Dionysus's appeal, leaving open the possibility that his healing powers stem from magic or divine intervention as much as the medicinal properties of wine. Thus, Euripides portrays Tiresias— much like Dionysus himself—as a figure capable of appealing to traditional religious thought as well as newer mindsets interested in "seeking a rational basis for the old stories about the gods."[32]

It is also noteworthy that Tiresias, in a later part of this episode, uses language of disease (*nosos*, vv. 311; 327) in reference to Pentheus, a character who forcefully opposes Dionysus and all he represents. These uses of language establish a contrast in which Dionysus embodies medicine and healing, while Pentheus personifies disease and suffering[33]—elements of characterization evident in his name, with its etymological connection to *penthos* (grief).[34] Pentheus explicitly doubts Dionysus's divinity and therapeutic capabilities at

[32] Paul Roth, "Teiresias as Mantis and Intellectual in Euripides' *Bacchae*," *Transactions of the American Philological Association* 114 (1984): 67.

[33] On the play's use of language and imagery of disease, see Robin Mitchell-Boyask, *Plague and the Athenian imagination: Drama, History, and the Cult of Asclepius* (Cambridge: Cambridge University Press, 2007), 35, 135, 189.

[34] Liddell and Scott, *A Greek-English Lexicon*, sv. πένθος. Cf. *Bacchae* v. 367; Esposito, *Euripides*, 219.

numerous points in the first three episodes of the play, and at one point even describes Dionysus as a "new disease" (*noson / kainēn*, v. 353–354). The events of the play, however, eventually reveal that Pentheus is in fact the one whose mind is "diseased", in contrast with those who revere Dionysus and the god's healing potential.

In such ways Dionysus's healing powers serve to validate his divinity, and his claims to divinity likewise affirm his therapeutic capabilities. Dionysus is not typically regarded as "a medical deity" in the same way as an Asclepius or an Apollo, but Euripides's play highlights how the god's theatrical and performative nature is pertinent to the sphere of healing and medicine. Moreover, these aspects of Dionysus's characterization convey cultural perceptions of a close link between performances of medical authority and demonstrations of divine power, even at a time when some of the works in the Hippocratic Corpus had begun to emerge.[35] Some of the Hippocratic medical treatises confront this perception head-on, perhaps most famously *On the Sacred Disease* (circa 400 BCE), which criticizes unnamed individuals who invoked divine elements in the treatment of disease. *On the Sacred Disease* characterizes such practitioners as "magicians, faith-healers, quacks, and charlatans" (μάγοι τε καὶ καθάρται καὶ ἀγύρται καὶ ἀλαζόνες, 4.1); here these terms (especially *alazones*) connote the performance and teaching of knowledge or abilities one does not actually possess.[36] The existence and forcefulness of such critiques expose the prominence that such approaches to cultivating and performing medical authority retained even in the late 5th century BCE,[37] along with a contemporary increase in tensions concerning the legitimacy of such approaches.[38]

---

[35] On affinities between magico-religious and so-called rational approaches to healing (and the challenges associated with distinguishing between such approaches) in ancient Greek medicine, see Philip van der Eijk, "Introduction" in *Magic and Rationality in Ancient Near Eastern and Graeco-Roman Medicine*, eds. Manfred Horstmanshoff and Marten Stol (Leiden and Boston: Brill, 2004), 1–9.

[36] Liddell and Scott, *A Greek-English Lexicon*: sv ἀλαζών.

[37] Nutton, *Ancient Medicine*, 114; Kingsley, *Ancient Philosophy*, 220.

[38] Julie Laskaris, *The Art is Long: On the Sacred Disease and the Scientific Tradition* (Leiden: Brill, 2002), 33–43, 97–108.

Empedocles: performing the rational physician

In a cultural milieu that was not universally receptive toward medical and didactic authority rooted in claims to divine knowledge and self-deification, Empedocles found other, less divinely oriented ways to procure an impression of Aesculapian power. While some fragments celebrate Empedocles's powers of divine intervention, others attempt to explain aspects of the physical universe in materialist and naturalistic terms,[39] including the workings of the human body; it is in these fragments that Empedocles displays an interest in educating his audiences rather than simply holding them in awe of his healing powers. This feature is highly apparent in Fragment 106, which provides a detailed description of various biological activities involved in the process of respiration:

> And all [animals] inhale and exhale thus: all have channels
> empty of blood in the flesh, deep inside the body,
> and at their mouths the extreme surface of the nostrils is
>   pierced right through
> with close-packed furrows, so that
> they cover over the blood but a clear passage is cut in
>   channels for aither.
> Next, when the smooth blood rushes back from there,
> seething air rushes down in a raging billow;
> and when it [blood] leaps up, it exhales again –
> as when a little girl plays with a clepsydra of gleaming
>   bronze:
> when she puts her fair hand over the passage of the pipe
> and dips it into the smooth frame of shining water,
> no water [lit. rain] enters the vessel, but it is checked by
> the bulk of air from within, which falls against the close-
>   packed holes,
> until she uncovers the dense flow. But then,
> when the breeze leaves it, water enters in turn.

---

[39] Inwood, *Poem of Empedocles*, esp. 37–39, 50–51; Anthony A. Long. "Thinking and Sense-Perception in Empedocles: Mysticism or Materialism?" *The Classical Quarterly* 16.2 (1966): esp. 270–276.

In the same way when she holds water in the depths of the
   bronze,
plugging the passage and pore with her mortal hand,
and aither is outside longing to enter, and checks the water
   [lit. rain]
around the gates of the harsh-sounding strainer by
   controlling the extremities,
until she releases her hand; then again, conversely to before,
when the breeze enters it water in turn runs out.
In the same way, when smooth blood surging through the
   limbs
rushes back into the interior [of the body],
straightaway a stream of air comes down / back, seething in
   a billow,
but when [blood] leaps up, it exhales an equal amount in
   return.

ὧδε δ' ἀναπνεῖ πάντα καὶ ἐκπνεῖ· πᾶσι λίφαιμοι
σαρκῶν σύριγγες πύματον κατὰ σῶμα τέτανται,
καί σφιν ἐπὶ στομίοις πυκναῖς τέτρηνται ἄλοξιν
ῥινῶν ἔσχατα τέρθρα διαμπερές, ὥστε φόνον μέν
κεύθειν, αἰθέρι δ' εὐπορίην διόδοισι τετμῆσθαι.
ἔνθεν ἔπειθ' ὁπόταν μὲν ἀπαΐξῃ τέρεν αἷμα,
αἰθὴρ παφλάζων καταΐσσεται οἴδματι μάργῳ,
εὖτε δ' ἀναθρώσκῃ πάλιν ἐκπνέει, ὥσπερ ὅταν παῖς
κλεψύδρῃ παίζουσα διειπετέος χαλκοῖο·
εὖτε μὲν αὐλοῦ πορθμὸν ἐπ' εὐειδεῖ χερὶ θεῖσα
εἰς ὕδατος βάπτῃσι τέρεν δέμας ἀργυφέοιο,
οὐδεὶς ἄγγοσδ' ὄμβρος ἐσέρχεται, ἀλλά μιν εἴργει
ἀέρος ὄγκος ἔσωθε πεσὼν ἐπὶ τρήματα πυκνά,
εἰσόκ' ἀποστεγάσῃ πυκινὸν ῥόον· αὐτὰρ ἔπειτα
πνεύματος ἐλλείποντος ἐσέρχεται αἴσιμον ὕδωρ.
ὡς δ' αὔτως ὅθ' ὕδωρ μὲν ἔχει κατὰ βένθεα χαλκοῦ,
πορθμοῦ χωσθέντος βροτέῳ χροΐ ἠδὲ πόροιο,
αἰθὴρ δ' ἐκτός, ἔσω λελιημένος, ὄμβρον ἐρύκει ἀμφὶ πύλας
ἠθμοῖο δυσηχέος, ἄκρα κρατύνων,
εἰσόκε χειρὶ μεθῇ. τότε δ' αὖ πάλιν, ἔμπαλιν ἢ πρίν,
πνεύματος ἐμπίπτοντος ὑπεκθέει αἴσιμον ὕδωρ.

ὡς δ' αὕτως τέρεν αἷμα κλαδασσόμενον διὰ γυίων
ὁππότε μὲν παλίνορσον ἐπαΐξειε μυχόνδε,
αἰθέρος εὐθὺς ῥεῦμα κατέρχεται οἴδματι θῦον,
εὖτε δ' ἀναθρῷσκῃ, πάλιν ἐκπνέει ἴσον ὀπίσσω.

While not directly concerned with matters of healing, this fragment nonetheless contributes to Empedocles's cultivation of Aesculapian power in several ways. First, in stating that his theory of respiration applies to all living things (v. 1), Empedocles proposes an explanatory model purported to have a universal application, as though he is unlocking a unifying principle of nature for his audiences. Next, he sets out to demonstrate detailed, empirical knowledge of both external and internal anatomical features and physiological processes, (vv. 1–8), including his ideas about how blood and air flow in and out of vessels in the body in a complex interplay which constitutes the act of breathing. Then, in the poem's remaining lines (vv. 8–25), Empedocles offers an extended simile intended to make these obscure respiratory processes more vivid to his audiences through analogy with the workings of a clepsydra, or a container with perforations capable of regulating the outflow of liquid; this type of device was sometimes used as a time-keeping device, but it could also serve other purposes, such as lifting and perhaps measuring liquids.[40]

Sometimes referred to as "the clepsydra experiment," this passage is perhaps better described as a persuasive didactic analogy,[41] both because the simile contains a number of details that are quite challenging to connect with the respiratory processes described earlier in the fragment, and because it "lacks certain essential features of the experimental method."[42] Moreover, from both the initial description (vv. 1–8) and from the clepsydra simile it is apparent that Empedocles's understanding of respiration falls far short of modern scientific understanding.[43] Despite the vexed nature of the passage, in

---

[40] David J. Furley, "Empedocles and the Clepsydra," *The Journal of Hellenic Studies* 77.1 (1957): 31.

[41] F.A. Wilford, "Embryological Analogies in Empedocles' Cosmogony," *Phronesis* 13.2 (1968): 114; cf. Furley, "Clepsydra," 34.

[42] Furley, "Clepsydra," 34, see also 32–33.

[43] Furley, "Clepsydra," 34.

terms of tone and argumentation it is strikingly confident and assertive in performing its purported knowledge of vital physiological processes. Rather than simply passing his explanations off as divine wisdom, here Empedocles descends from his exalted mount to explain the process of respiration in detail and in highly mechanical terms that do not entail divine causes, thereby educating his audiences about the workings of their own bodies. This performance of Aesculapian power can be seen as an attempt to build trust by providing his audiences with a deeper understanding of their own bodily processes, not unlike a modern physician helping a patient comprehend the physiological details of a medical condition. Furthermore, he strives to make this knowledge more familiar and more comprehensible to his audiences through the use of an extensively developed analogy which they could presumably try to test out for themselves or at least visually imagine. Similar uses of mechanical analogies commonly occur in Hippocratic medical treatises, where they often serve both didactic and persuasive purposes.[44] As in modern medicine, even if the analogy itself is flawed or inexact, the practice of drawing a comparison with a more familiar or vivid process may still be didactically or rhetorically effective and help gain trust from a patient or other intended audience.[45]

Another instance in which Empedocles presents his audiences with a purely physiological explanation for an essential biological process is seen in Fragment 96:

> [the heart] nourished in seas of blood which leaps back and forth,
> and there especially it is called understanding by men;
> for men's understanding is blood around the heart.
>
> αἵματος ἐν πελάγεσσι τεθραμμένη ἀντιθορόντος

---

[44] G.E.R. Lloyd, "The Transformations of Ancient Medicine," *Bulletin of the History of Medicine* 66.1 (1992): 121.

[45] Cf. Gwinyai Masukume and Alimuddin Zumla, "Analogies and Metaphors in Clinical Medicine," *Clinical Medicine* 12.1 (2012): 55. Masukume and Alimuddin also briefly discuss potential pitfalls of certain medical analogies, including analogies that may be "inappropriate" or "unfamiliar" to speakers of certain languages (55–56); I would add that using misleading or deceptive analogies could pose dangers for a patient and constitute medical malpractice.

τῇ τε νόημα μάλιστα κικλήσκεται ἀνθρώποισιν·
αἷμα γὰρ ἀνθρώποις περικάρδιόν ἐστι νόημα.

Here, Empedocles relates that *noēma* (understanding or cognition) is induced by the oscillation of blood in the region of the heart. As with Fragment 106, he emphatically lays out a concrete, corporeal explanation for an important but otherwise unobservable biological phenomenon. Moreover, he espouses a theory of cognition, namely cardiocentrism, that was rather widespread in ancient Greek thought.[46] In this way Empedocles displays his familiarity with contemporary medical conversations and conceptualizations of the human body, and again showcases his Aesculapian power and didactic authority.

Conclusions

Rationalistic and naturalistic explanations of bodies, then, reside in Empedocles's fragments alongside assertions of divine and prophetic ways of healing. From a modern perspective, these juxtapositions may seem contradictory and even counterproductive, but in archaic and classical Greece the boundaries between religion, science, medicine, and magic could be extremely blurry;[47] this rings particularly true of Empedocles.[48] In appropriating the medical knowledge of the divine healer as well as the earthly physician, the Empedoclean *oeuvre* not only reflects the contemporary ambiguities surrounding these epistemic categories, it also represents a performative strategy that would have made Empedocles well-positioned to appeal to and to instruct multiple audiences with differing perspectives and approaches to medicine and healing.

As in the modern world, it is plausible that some people in antiquity would have been more moved by Aesculapian power demonstrated through expert knowledge of the body and medicine, along with the ability to educatively disseminate that knowledge to one's patients. By the same token, it seems likely that others would

---

[46] François P. Retief and Louise Cilliers, "The nervous system in antiquity," *South African Medical Journal* 98.10 (2008): 768–772.

[47] Mackenzie, *Poetry and Poetics*, 105; van der Eijk, "Introduction," 1–9.

[48] Kingsley and Parry, "Empedocles," Nutton, *Ancient Medicine*, 46, 113–114; Obbink, *The Addressees of Empedocles*, 90.

have gravitated more to doctors or healers known for their powers of charisma, and that yet others would have been particularly affected by a doctor's reputation or status (their social power). While these categories of power belong to a modern framework rather than an ancient one, each type of power is recognizable in Empedocles's fragments (even though he develops them in ways that differ greatly from what one would expect of a modern physician), and each type figures into the poetic language with which he crafts a multi-faceted medical persona. As with the portrayal of Dionysus in Euripides's *Bacchae*, Empedocles theatrically fashions a therapeutic identity that transcends simple dichotomies and that pursues legitimacy and influence among diverse potential audiences, evincing various forms of medical power while he modulates between the natural and the magical, and between the mortal and the divine. Revealing more than just a similar personality archetype, these comparisons between Empedocles and Dionysus underscore the performative element that was often crucial for establishing the impression of medical legitimacy and didactic authority during Greek antiquity, and which continues to play a significant role in the medical sphere today. This ability to perform an authoritative posture arguably contributed to the reputation Empedocles acquired as the founder of the Sicilian school of medicine as much as any of the specific medical remedies or medical ideologies that he put forth.

Jurgen R. Gatt & Andrew Debono Cauchi[1]
"Contests of Virtue" in Gorgias's *Encomium to Helen*

The aim of this paper is to re-examine Gorgias's *Encomium to Helen*—a speech written in the heyday of the "sophistic movement"[2] —and to integrate it more closely with the Sophists' most characteristic role, namely as exponents of a new form of *paideia*. Focusing on the *Encomium*'s proem (*Helen* 1-5) and its reference to *euandria* (*Helen* 1), as well as Gorgias's fourth argument dealing with the powers of Eros/*opsis* (*Helen* 15-19), we argue that this speech presents and recommends to its audience a new educational ideal of "good manliness," one centered on the powers of persuasion. In so doing, the speech defends Gorgias's own pedagogy against the conservative backlash, brilliantly represented by Aristophanes's *Clouds*, which attacked the "new education" as "emasculating." The essay is divided into two sections. The first discusses the "sophistic movement" in its most pressing pedagogical context, namely the late 5th century BCE clash between the "new" and "old" education. Concentrating on Aristophanes's criticism of the physical effects of Sophistry, we outline two strategies which the Sophists adopted as a "counter-response" to the conservatives, one direct and aggressive, the other indirect and conciliatory. In the second section, we situate the *Encomium* in the context of these "counter-responses," focusing on just one aspect of Gorgias's multifarious program of *paideia*: his re-interpretation of *euandria*.

Greek *paideia* and the "Sophistic Movement"

The 5th century BCE proved to be a decisive turning point in the history of Greek education. The long-lived monopoly of aristocratic *paideia* based on physical and musical training slowly gave way to a different sort of instruction, one offered to new classes of people, and

---

[1] Jurgen R. Gatt is a Visiting Lecturer in the Department of Classics and Archaeology at the University of Malta. Andrew Debono Cauchi is a recent graduate of the Department of Classics and Archaeology at the University of Malta and is currently a postgraduate student in Classics at Leiden University, in the Netherlands.

[2] On the possible dates of the *Encomium* see Edward Schiappa, "Gorgias's Helen revisited," *Quarterly Journal of Speech* 81 (1995): 311.

delivered in novel ways.[3] In the first half of that century, the teaching of letters (*grammata*) became more or less a fixed part of the "curriculum" across the Greek world, and the education of boys took an increasingly institutionalized shape.[4] In the second half, even more momentous changes took place. Prose emerged as a rival to poetry and became the dominant medium for instruction,[5] and in tandem with this shift, the written word emerged as an essential component of education.[6] More generally, the concept of *paideia* was expanded, not only to include non-aristocrats,[7] but also beyond its original reference merely to the education of children.[8] In all of these late 5th-century changes, the Sophists were deeply involved. The new cultural dominance of prose was intimately bound to the early development of

---

[3] Important literature on this topic includes Werner Jaeger, *Paideia: The Ideals of Greek Culture*, vol. 1, trans. G. Highet (Oxford: Blackwell, 1946); Henri-Irénée Marrou, *A History of Education in Antiquity*, trans. G. Lamb (New York: Mentor, 1964); Rudolph Pfeiffer, *History of Classical Scholarship from the beginning to the end of the Hellenistic Age* (Oxford: Oxford University Press, 1968); Jacqueline de Romilly, *The Great Sophists in Periclean Athens*, trans. J. Lloyd (Oxford: Clarendon, 1992), esp. 30-36; Neil O'Sullivan, "Written and Spoken in the First Sophistic," in *Voice into Text: Orality and Literacy in Ancient Greece*, ed. Ian Worthington (Leiden: Brill, 1995), 113-27; T.J. Morgan, "Literate Education in Classical Athens," *The Classical Quarterly* 49.1 (1999): 46-61; Andrew Ford, "Sophists Without Rhetoric: The Arts of Speech in Fifth-Century Athens," in *Education in Greek and Roman Antiquity*, ed. Yun T. Loo (Leiden: Brill, 2001), 85-109; Mark Joyal, Ian McDougall, J.C. Yardley (eds), *Greek and Roman Education: A Source Book* (London: Routledge, 2009).

[4] Herodotus, *Histories*, 6.27.1-2., which reports the collapse of a school in 496 BCE killing all but one of the students as they were learning letters, neatly illustrates both points. For more on these changes, and their relation to the sophistic movement see Joyal et al., *Greek and Roman Education*, 31-32; Ford, "Sophists without Rhetoric," 85.

[5] Pfeiffer, *Classical Scholarship*, 65-46.

[6] Pfeiffer, *Classical Scholarship*, 25-31; Edward Schiappa, *The Beginnings of Rhetorical Theory in Classical Greece* (New Haven: Yale University Press, 1999), 30-33.

[7] Jaeger, *Paideia*, 286-87.

[8] Jaeger, *Paideia*, 286.

rhetoric, and its increasing importance in the *polis*.[9] (The Sophists were, of course, central figures in these developments even if the concept of rhetoric post-dates their activities.)[10] Moreover, many of the Sophists are said to have *written* pamphlets on "rhetoric"—the so-called *technai*[11]—as well as distributed written examples of their speeches. Writing, in other words, was an intrinsic part of the sophistic movement.[12] Moreover, the Sophists' pamphlets on rhetoric, written with an eye to their (re-)useability, may have provided an important incentive for the acquisition of written works, while greatly increasing access to "rhetorical" education.[13] As to the latter point, many have remarked that the sophistic movement thrived best in "middle-class" democracies such as Athens,[14] and their promise to teach anyone— including (rich) non-aristocrats—was inclusive and fundamentally democratic in spirit.[15] Further, the "core subjects" of Sophistry, rhetorical skill and "good judgment,"[16] seem well suited to the

---

[9] See Jaeger, *Paideia*, 290-91; W.K.C. Guthrie, *The Sophists* (Cambridge: Cambridge University Press, 1971), 38-39; H.D. Rankin, *Sophists, Socratics and Cynics* (London: Croom Helm, 1983), 20; de Romilly, *Great Sophists*, 57, among others.

[10] Schiappa, *Beginnings*, 33-34. See also Michael Gagarin, "Did the Sophists aim to persuade?" *Rhetorica* 19.3 (2001): 276; Ford, "Sophists without Rhetoric," 89.

[11] On the nature of the *technai* and their role in education see esp. Thomas Cole, *The Origins of Rhetoric in Ancient Greece* (Baltimore: John Hopkins University Press, 1991), 81-92.

[12] Pfeiffer, *Classical Scholarship*, 25-31 argues that Sophists play a key role in this transformation. See also the more modest positions of O'Sullivan, "Written and Spoken," 121-22; Cole, *Origins of Rhetoric*, 76, and Rankin, *Sophists, Socratics*, 15, who emphasizes the Sophists' orality.

[13] Cole, *Origins of Rhetoric*, 78-79.

[14] See especially George B. Kerferd, *The Sophistic Movement* (Cambridge: Cambridge University Press, 1981), 15-22.

[15] See Kerferd, *Sophistic Movement*, 1-2; de Romilly, *Great Sophists*, 45.

[16] Plato, *Protagoras*, 318e. Whether the Sophists had any "core curriculum" is controversial. See esp. Theodor Gomperz, *The Greek Thinkers: A History of Ancient Philosophy*, tr. G.G. Berry (London: John Murray, 1964), 415; Marrou, *History of Education*, 79; Guthrie, *The Sophists*, 44-48; Kerferd,

political opportunities offered by a democracy. The Sophists, in short, can be seen as the embodiment of the "new education" that revolutionized *paideia* in the late 5th-century BCE,[17] and which promised the youth of Athens unrivalled expertise in civic *aretē*.[18] As such, the Sophists threatened the traditional aristocratic monopoly on "innate" virtue, their methods of instruction, as well as the educational ideal of *kalokagathia*.[19]

These innovations in the educational milieu of Greece were sure to produce a reaction. Indeed, the earliest reaction to the very idea of instilling *aretē* by education appears well before the Sophists, in the poetry of Theognis and Pindar. For the former, the *aretē* of the aristocrats, which distinguished them from the *kakoi* (the "bad"), however wealthy, could only emerge out of *"physis,"* (birthright) and *genos* (lineage).[20] Pindar goes further, contrasting those who have wisdom by nature with those who have *learnt* just a chattering *"panglossia"* (garrulity).[21] Thus even wisdom, according to Pindar, cannot be learnt but is inborn. These two poets, then, can be said to oppose education "holistically," as a fruitless endeavor; a fool's errand

---

> *Sophistic Movement*, 218-20, among others. Though the authors believe that the Sophists possessed closely overlapping methods and interests, the following argument does not depend on this

[17] E.g., Teresa Morgan, *Literate Education in the Hellenistic and Roman Worlds* (Cambridge: Cambridge University Press, 1998), 52.

[18] Gorgias famously disavowed teaching *aretē* to his students and, accordingly, is often seen as a "specialist" in rhetoric; see e.g., Marrou, *History of Education*, 85; Pfeiffer, *Classical Scholarship*, 45-46; Martin Ostwald, *From Popular Sovereignty to the Sovereignty of Law* (Berkeley: University of California Press, 1986), 242-43. It must be noted, however, that Sophists often claimed to have "unique" teaching methods and subjects even when there is evidence of considerable overlap (e.g., Plato, *Protagoras*, 318d7-319a2; see Kerferd, *Sophistic Movement*, 41). We might start to agree with Guthrie's assessment that Gorgias's disavowal to teach *aretē* was a "little disingenuous" (Guthrie, *The Sophists*, 45).

[19] On traditional 6th c. BCE education, see Marrou, *History of Education*, 64.

[20] Jaeger, *Paideia*, 287; Kerferd, *Sophistic Movement*, 37; Joyal et al., *Greek and Roman Education*, 6-7.

[21] Pindar, *Olympian Odes*, 2.86-88. Pindar contrasts the wise who know "by nature" [εἰδὼς φυᾷ] and "those who learn" [μαθόντες].

in the face of mighty *physis*. This "conservative backlash" against the "new" education in favor of the "old" only intensified as the 5th-century unfolded, acquiring a more focused target in the Sophists and a vociferous exponent in Aristophanes.[22] The poet's response to the Sophists was multifaceted, and none of their predilections were above scrutiny or ridicule. In his *Tagenistas* (fr. 490 K), for example, we read that "either a book or Prodicus has ruined this man."[23] One of Aristophanes's more sustained attacks, however, focused on the alleged *physical* ill-effects of exposure to "new education." Indeed, in the *Clouds*, the contrast between the "old education" of the *Marathonomachoi* (soldiers who fought at Marathon) and the "new education" offered by "Socrates" takes on a palpably "physical" shape: "an opposition between the wrangling of intellectuals and the traditional physical training."[24] The poet favors the physical hardiness instilled by the "old" education (965), which led to soundness of body (1012ff.)—in stark contrast to the neglect of physical training in the "new" education (1054), which led in turn to a weakening of the body (987ff. and 1017ff.). Perhaps the apogee of this strategy comes at the end of the Just Speech's defense of "old education," in which she compares the effects of the traditional pedagogy to that offered to the "youths of today":

> If you do those which I am describing and turn your mind to them, you will always have a stout chest, clear skin, mighty shoulders but a tongue that's weak, a large posterior but a small 'anterior.' But if you pursue the pursuits of today's youths, you will have, in the first place, a dark look about you, small shoulders, a narrow chest but a broad tongue, small buttocks and a large 'ham'… (1009-1018)[25]

---

[22] See K.J. Dover, ed., *Aristophanes: Clouds* (Oxford: Clarendon, 1968), lviii-lxiv; *Aristophanic Comedy* (London: B.T. Batsford, 1972), 109-20.

[23] Pfeiffer, *Classical Scholarship*, 30.

[24] Dover ed., *Aristophanes: Clouds*, lix. For the rest of the paper, this criticism against the physically debilitating effects of the "new education" shall be called the "Aristophanic Critique" for shorthand. See also Marrou, *History of Education*, 72-73; de Romilly, *Great Sophists*, 38.

[25] Unless otherwise stated, the translations are the authors' own.

The effects of sophistry are here presented as the inverse of physical education: producing physical atrophy where there should be hypertrophy, and excess where there should be deficiency. Sophistry, in other words, is presented as an anti-athleticism; corrupting the body of the student it professes to teach, as well as their "manhood." And thus, Just Speech argues, the educational endpoints of the Sophist's education are precisely the inverse to the superior "old education" which they are threatening to replace.

It cannot be imagined, surely, that the Sophists took these charges lying down. Indeed, there is strong contemporary evidence that a "counter-reaction" was in full swing by the end of the 5th-century BCE. And just as in the case of the conservative backlash to the "new education," this counter-reaction also had an early 5th-century precedent: Xenophanes.[26] As Jaeger and Marrou point out,[27] the Colophonian poet not only impugns the ethical teaching of Homer and Hesiod as worthless, but also attacks the ideal of the aristocratic athlete, setting up his own wisdom in its place as the pre-eminent civic *aretē*. The Sophists, as Jaeger also argued, inherited Xenophanes's reactionary position.[28] So did the Hippocratic physicians.[29] Yet this defense of "intellectual education" against the traditional ideals of the aristocratic elites, and especially competitive displays of physical prowess—such as *eudandriae* (see below)—was not mounted only in "intellectual circles." It also seeped into public addresses and popular forms of entertainment. In Pericles's funeral speech,[30] which sets up a

---

[26] Zinon Papakonstantinou, "The Athletic Body in Classical Athens: Literary and Historical Perspectives," *The International Journal of the History of Sport* 29.12 (2012): 1161 notes that Tyrtaeus also questions the value of gymnastics for military virtue. This contrast, not so much between sport and intelligence, but between sporting and military activity continued into the 5th century BCE. As Marrou, *History of Education*, 93 points out, Xenophon's *Cynegitus*—which also mentions the conflict of the old and new education—is partly a response to this line of critique.

[27] Jaeger, *Paideia*, 289; Marrou, *History of Education*, 77.

[28] Jaeger, *Paideia*, 296-97.

[29] Papakonstantinou, "Athletic Body," 1162-63.

[30] On this important piece of evidence, see Jaeger, *Paideia*, 319 and de Romilly, *Great Sophists*, 41, who both interpret the statement similarly.

contrast between two ideals of "manliness," the Spartan and the Athenian, the speaker claims that the Athenians pursue "philosophy without effeminacy" as if to assuage any anxieties about the enervating qualities of "philosophy." In Euripides's fragments, on the other hand, we get wind of a far more direct response: open ridicule of athletes as useless to the city-state as well as for their *amathia*.[31]

When we turn to the Sophists' own counter-reaction to the old education generally, and to the "Aristophanic critique" in particular, we find coping strategies roughly analogous to those found in popular culture, some direct and aggressive, others more conciliatory. As an example of the former type, commentators have often noted that their claim to be able to teach *aretē* at all functions as a response to the traditional vision of "virtue" being dependent entirely on *physis* and lineage.[32] At the same time, even this "radical" theory shows signs of an appeasing strategy.[33] Protagoras, then, insisted that *aretē* needed both *physis* and practice,[34] and Prodicus also emphasized the value of *ponos* (effort),[35] which Pindar too had praised. A similar "push and pull" tactic with respect to the traditional ideals and methods of education can be detected elsewhere, especially in the Sophist's relationship to the poets. Thus, at the same time as they entered into direct rivalry with their poetic forebears,[36] the Sophists went to great lengths to emphasize "continuity." Even their promise to teach *logos* as the instrument of political success has a venerable poetic antecedent in Hesiod's description of Muse-inspired Kings.[37] More dramatically, Gorgias and Hippias are said to have delivered public orations

---

[31] de Romilly, *Great Sophists*, 39-40.

[32] de Romilly, *Great Sophists*, 46-47.

[33] Jaeger, *Paideia*, 306; de Romilly, *Great Sophists*, 50.

[34] Ford, "Sophists without Rhetoric," 97.

[35] Ford, "Sophists without Rhetoric," 97.

[36] Protagoras, for example, openly critiqued the diction and sense of epic and lyric poems, thereby demonstrating his own superiority (Pfeiffer, *Classical Scholarship*, 34). Gorgias's definition of poetry as "*logos* having metre," as well as his style, has also been read as an attempt to rival the poet's authority. See Jacqueline de Romilly, *Magic and Rhetoric in Ancient Greece* (Cambridge, MA: Harvard University Press, 1975), 8.

[37] Jaeger, *Paideia*, 290.

wearing rhapsodic clothes,[38] and Protagoras claimed that Homer and Hesiod were "Sophists" in disguise.[39] Rankin is surely correct in saying that Protagoras intended to give his profession a long and respectable history.[40] More generally, we may characterize such conciliatory tactics in terms of "anchoring," as described by Sluiter.[41] The Sophists, conscious of the radical nature of their teachings, sought to describe the new in terms of the old and familiar.

As we have seen, the Sophists "anchored" their own educational program in various ways: they acknowledged the importance of *physis* and *ponos* in their educational theories and emphasized their similarity with the poets in their role as educators, their subject matter, even in their attire. It was not, however, the only "anchor" which the Sophists sought, and with good reason since the traditional education comprised not merely *mousikē*, but also *gymnastikē*. Furthermore, as Aristophanes's criticism and the broader contrast between "wrangling intellectuals" and "athletes" clearly testify,[42] the purported physical effects of the new education made for a common line of attack. It was, therefore, within the Sophist's self-interest to link his own teaching up to the old tradition of physical education, and to the values such an education was thought to promote. We find, accordingly, that among the "Sophists" whom Protagoras names as predecessors are not only poets, but also gymnastics and athletics instructors.[43] Just as this ancient "sophistry" produced "real men," so can Protagoras's own more recent brand of *paideia*. Furthermore, Protagoras sought to assuage the conservatives in even more dramatic ways, applying a gymnastic metaphor to his own educational program: the shaping of the soul.[44] Prodicus's own concern for *ponos* may also reflect the

---

[38] Kerferd, *Sophistic Movement*, 28-29.

[39] Plato, *Protagoras*, 316d-e.

[40] Rankin, *Sophists, Socratics*, 14. See also Ostwald, *From Popular Sovereignty*, 239; de Romilly, *Great Sophists*, 33-34; O'Sullivan, "Written and Spoken," 116; Joval et al., *Greek and Roman Education*, 48.

[41] Ineke Sluiter, "Anchoring Innovation: A Classical Research Agenda," *European Review*, 25.1 (2017): 20-38.

[42] Emphasized by de Romilly, *Great Sophists*, 39-41.

[43] Plato, *Protagoras* 316d-e. See de Romilly, *Great Sophists*, 33-34.

[44] Jaeger, *Paideia*, 314.

importance of this concept in gymnastic circles.[45] We can tentatively conclude from this admittedly meager evidence that Protagoras's response to the "Aristophanic critique" was largely a conciliatory one, not unlike that of his associate, Pericles. Sophistry, Protagoras seems to have argued, is continuous with, indeed analogous to, the old gymnastic education.

In what follows, we take up the invitation offered by the prominently placed word *euandria*, and argue that the *Encomium to Helen* showcases another response to the "Aristophanic Critique" and the makings of a different counter-reaction to traditional education based on *physis, mousikē,* and *gymnastikē.*

The *Encomium to Helen* and the rhetoric of *euandria*

Gorgias's *Encomium to Helen* is typically read under three main guises:[46] as a theoretical exposition of the power of *logos,*[47] as a demonstration-piece,[48] and as a model defense speech.[49] Though these functions seem to pull the short speech in three different directions— respectively, toward philosophy, *epideictic,* and forensic oratory—the evidence for each reading appears strong. As many commentators have observed, the longest part of the speech discusses *logos,* focusing on the psychological mechanism of its actions and the epistemological underpinnings of this power.[50] Indeed, in view of the singularity of

---

[45] Heather L. Reid, "Athletic Beauty in Classical Greece: A Philosophical View," *Journal of the Philosophy of Sport* 39.2 (2012): 286.

[46] See esp. Schiappa, *Beginnings,* 115-19.

[47] E.g., Charles P. Segal, "Gorgias and the Psychology of Logos," *Harvard Studies in Classical Philology* 66.1 (1962): 102 argues that *Helen* 8-14 is a "formal procession of the aims and methods of Gorgias's art."

[48] E.g., Marrou, *History of Education,* 67; Scott Consigny, "Gorgias's Use of the Epideictic," *Philosophy and Rhetoric* 25.3 (1992): 281. Yet, Consigny, "Use of Epideictic," 288 argues that Gorgias adapts his style to suit the situation and this constitutes his chief rhetorical lesson.

[49] E.g., Gagarin, "Did the Sophists," 276. See also Jonas Grethlein, *The Ancient Aesthetics of Deception: The Ethics of Enchantment from Gorgias to Heliodorus* (Cambridge: Cambridge University Press, 2021), 12.

[50] Commentators have focused especially on "tragic deception," e.g., Willem J. Verdenius, "Gorgias's Doctrine of Deception," in *The Sophists and their*

this discussion—it is the only extant theoretical treatment of *logos* by a Sophist[51]—and the obvious importance of the subject to Gorgias,[52] some have argued that this "expository" function was Gorgias's primary aim. The *Encomium to Helen*, under this reading, is "really" an exposition of the subject of the Sophist's art and his teachings.[53] As to its functions of *epideixis*, implicit in the title of the speech, Wardy points to the prominence of "praise" (*epainos*) and "blame" (*mōmos*), the defining theme of epideictic oratory, as well as Gorgias's use of the verb *epideixai* in the proem.[54] Once again, the choice of Helen is generally understood to be a pretext: the real objects of valorization are rhetoric generally and, most of all, Gorgias's own skills.[55] Finally, the apologetic function of the *Encomium*, already noted by Isocrates,[56] is also alluded to in the proem,[57] and obviously animates the argumentative part of the speech. Under this "apologetic" reading, the

---

Legacy, ed. George B. Kerferd (Wiesbaden: Franz Steiner, 1981), esp. 125; Gorgias's analogy of *logos* to medical processes, e.g., Segal, "Psychology of Logos," 105-06; and Gorgias's reference to magic, e.g, de Romilly, *Magic and Rhetoric*, 15-17.

[51] Gagarin, "Did the Sophists," 277 points out that the results of this analysis are also extrapolated to all Sophists because of the unavailability of other discussions on the topic.

[52] de Romilly *Great Sophists*, 67, for example, comments that the section on *logos* "strikes a more personal note."

[53] Wardy and de Romilly argue that the subject matter, Helen, is merely a pretext that soon disappears from the speech. See Robert Wardy, *The Birth of Rhetoric: Gorgias, Plato and their successors* (London: Routledge, 1989), 25, and de Romilly, *Great Sophists*, 67. Untersteiner and Versenyi go further, integrating *Helen* with the third argument of *On Not Being* which, together, spell out an elaborate theory on the communicative limitations of *logos*. See Mario Untersteiner, *I Sofisti* (Milan: Bruno Mondadori, 2008), 173-75 and Laszlo Versenyi, *Socratic Humanism* (New Haven: Yale University Press, 1964), esp. 46-48.

[54] Wardy, *Birth of Rhetoric*, 25-29.

[55] E.g., Consigny, "Use of Epideictic," 291.

[56] Isocrates, *Helen*, 21-22.

[57] Especially in reference to the obligation of refuting those who blame Helen (ἐλέγξαι τοὺς μεμφομένους Ἑλένην, *Helen* 2) and to the speaker's aim to "put a stop to the accusation" (παῦσαι τῆς αἰτίας, *Helen* 2).

Encomium to Helen comes rather close to Antiphon's *Tetralogies* as a treatment of a *cause celebre*, as well as a piece of rhetorical instruction to be used by future litigants. Indeed, many have observed that the speech showcases "commonplaces,"[58] explores interesting and new forms of argument,[59] and elucidates with great clarity how a forensic speech is to be divided.[60]

The "choice" of the *Encomium*'s genre—if a choice is to be made at all—influences the sort of "pedagogy" that the speech offers. This is especially true of the latter, "apologetic" reading of the speech, which would delimit the *Helen*'s instruction to purely "rhetorical" matters, as proposed by Thomas Cole.[61] If such a reading were correct, the *Encomium to Helen* could hardly mount any response to the backlash against the Sophists or, indeed, make any overarching point whatsoever. There are reasons, however, to question Cole's atomistic reading of the speech, for it risks obscuring even some of the most important rhetorical lessons which Gorgias's *epideixeis* have to offer, namely the intricate architecture of Gorgias's arguments,[62] the use of *ethos*, and the structure of his speech.[63] More generally, any reading which sees in the *Helen* only a "rhetorical" or "intellectual" exercise,

---

58 For example, George A. Kennedy, *The Art of Persuasion* (Princeton: Princeton University Press, 1963), 53; Kerferd, *Sophistic Movement*, 31; Cole, *Origins of Rhetoric*, 88-89.

59 See especially Demos G. Spatharas, "Patterns of Argumentation in Gorgias," *Mnemosyne* 54.4 (2001): 393-408.

60 Douglas M. MacDowell, *Gorgias: Encomium of Helen* (Bristol: Bristol University Press, 1982), 17.

61 Cole, *Origins of Rhetoric*, 75 argues that its epideictic functions are not allowed to interfere with its pedagogical aims.

62 On architecture, see Spatharas, "Patterns of Argumentation," 406-408.

63 Typically, the 5th-century orators are believed not to have much use for *ethos* (e.g., Cole, *Origins of Rhetoric*, 73). Yet Gorgias, *Palamedes*, 28-36 is one such argument. See also Colin Higgins, "Gorgias," in *The Sophists: An Introduction*, ed. Patricia O'Grady (London: Bloomsbury, 2008), 51. On Gorgias's disposition, see esp. George H. Goebel, "Early Greek Rhetorical Theory and Practice: Proof and arrangement in the speeches of Antiphon and Euripides" (PhD dissertation, University of Wisconsin-Madison, 1983), 175-83.

risks obscuring the larger pedagogical context of the speech, its relevance to the instruction of *aretē*.

Part of this larger pedagogical context has already been amply discussed by commentators, namely Gorgias's positioning with respect to the traditional educators, the poets, a positioning which can best be described as ambivalent. On the one hand, Gorgias's promise to defend Helen's innocence even if she went to Troy threatens to outstrip all his poetic rivals.[64] More explicitly, the proem attacks the poets who have censured Helen as having perpetrated a mistake (*hamartia*) and a feat of ignorance (*amathia*).[65] In contrast to the poets, Gorgias promises to add *logismos* to his *logos*, a word closely associated with prose, thus promising once again to do something the poets simply could not.[66] And yet, some of the most important functions Gorgias will attribute to his own speech—praising Helen and bringing joy (*terpsis*) to audiences—appear to draw it closer to the traditional functions of poetry. The same ambivalent positioning can be detected in Gorgias's definition of poetry as "*logos* having meter."[67] On the one hand, this definition dethrones poetry in favor of a more all-embracing *logos*.[68] The definition, then, would place the poetic and prosaic accounts more starkly against one another, as two equivalent and combating "*logoi*," such as those of the meteorologists and philosophers which Gorgias describes.[69] On the other hand, Gorgias also chooses poetry as a paradigm of powerfully persuasive *logoi* and the key to understanding the doctrine of deception.[70] In relation to his poetic rivals and predecessors, then, Gorgias appears to employ a mixture of tactics within the same speech, a push-and-pull, sometimes

---

[64] Wardy, *Birth of Rhetoric*, 25-26.

[65] As de Romilly, *Great Sophists*, 39 notes, the word *amathia* was also dragged into the conflict between the old and new education (e.g. Thucydides, *The Peloponnesian War*, 1.84.3).

[66] See esp. Wardy, *Birth of Rhetoric*, 30-31.

[67] Gorgias, *Helen*, 9.

[68] Pfeiffer, *Classical Scholarship*, 46; de Romilly, *Great Sophists*, 66.

[69] Gorgias, *Helen*, 13.

[70] In fragment 23 (DK), Gorgias speaks of the just deception of tragedy. On Gorgias's views of deception, see Versenyi, *Socratic Humanism*, 49-51; Grethlein, *Aesthetics of Deception*, 12-13.

emphasizing rivalry, sometimes continuity. In what follows, we make the case that a similar "push-and-pull" strategy can be detected with respect to precepts of the "old education" more broadly and, in particular, to the substance of the "Aristophanic Critique."

This broader pedagogical picture, which moves the *Helen* well beyond formal, rhetorical instruction, appears early in the speech, indeed in the very first clause:

> Good order, for a city, is the courage of its men [κόσμος πόλει μὲν εὐανδρία]; for a body, beauty; for a soul, wisdom; for an action, virtue; for a speech, truth; while the opposite of these is disorder. And in the case of a man and woman, word and deed, city and act, one must honor them with praise if they are worthy; and ascribe blame, if they are unworthy. For it is equally erroneous and ignorant to blame the praiseworthy and to praise the blameworthy. It is the same man's task to correctly say what should be said and to refute those who blame Helen, a woman about whom the belief of those who have listened to poets, as well as the sound of her name—which recalls disaster—have become univocal and unanimous. Yet, by adding a certain reasoning to my speech, I want to save the slandered woman from the accusation, to show that those who blame her are lying, to reveal the truth, and to put a stop to ignorance. (*Helen*, 1-2)

Considering its rarity in literature, the word *euandria*—literally "good manliness"—makes for a remarkable opening in any speech, but especially a speech which is purportedly about a woman.[71] Its use, then, especially in such a prominent place, as the first contributor of *kosmos* to the *polis*, deserves some explanation.[72] The *Suda* glosses this

---

[71] Wardy, *Birth of Rhetoric*, 29 argues, convincingly, that the "purpose of the opening sentence is evidently to enumerate across a wide range of cases that might properly be the subject of an encomium." Commentators also say that Gorgias's emphasis is on the connection between truth and *logos*, e.g., Gagarin, "Did the Sophists," 279.

[72] On the meaning of *kosmos*, see Dimos Spatharas, "Gorgias: an edition of the extant texts and fragments with commentary and introduction" (PhD dissertation, University of Glasgow, 2001), 127-28.

word as "an athletic competition which took place in Athens,"[73] and this technical use is confirmed both by inscriptions, the earliest of which coming from the 380s BCE,[74] and by Aristotle,[75] who adds that the prize for this competition was a shield. Though, as we show below, this term was also used in another, less technical sense—one more directly relevant to Gorgias's *Helen*—it is clear that the nature of these *Euandriae* is material to any "broader" meaning of the word. It is unfortunate, therefore, that great controversy exists on this very issue. Scholars differ both on the question of whether the competition involved a choral or an individual contest,[76] and, more crucially, on the question of what the contest entailed. Some have argued that it was a straightforward beauty contest,[77] others that the competition involved some element of performance.[78] Some also propose that the competition involved not only physical, but also intellectual and psychological dimensions.[79] The diversity of opinion, however, need not obscure the chief characteristics of the *Euandria*: namely that it was a competition, one which was associated with athletics and open only to Athenian citizens, in which competitors were judged against some normative standard related to "masculinity." It is also clear, from Ps. Andocides, that a great deal of civic pride was involved in setting up the competition, competing and, of course, winning.[80]

---

[73] Suda, s.v. εὐανδρία.

[74] The evidence is discussed by Nigel B. Crowther, "Male 'Beauty' Contests in Greece: the *euandria* and *euexia*," *L'Antiquité Classique* 54.1 (1985): 285-91; Alan L. Boegehold, "Group and Single Competitions at the Panathenaia" in *Worshipping Athena: Panathenaia and Parthenon*, ed. J. Neils (Madison: University of Wisconsin Press, 1996), 97-99; Thomas F. Scanlon, *Eros and Greek Athletics* (Oxford: Oxford University Press, 2002), 205-10.

[75] Aristotle, *Constitution of the Athenians*, 60.3.

[76] For a brief summary of the controversy, see Scanlon, *Eros*, 404.

[77] Nancy B. Reed, "The Panathenaic Euandria Reconsidered," *Ancient World* 15.1 (1987): 59–64.

[78] E.g., Crowther, "Male Beauty Contests," 287-88.

[79] E.g., D.G. Kyle, "The Panathenaic Games: Sacred and Civic Athletics," in *Goddess and the Polis: The Panathenaic Festival in Ancient Athens*, ed. Jennifer Neils (Princeton: Princeton University Press, 1992), 95–96.

[80] [Andocides], 4.42.

Even such a partial description of the Athenian *Euandriae* is enough to inform our reading of Gorgias's proem. Thus, its partnership with bodily beauty (*kallos*), referred to next in the list of desirables, is quite straightforward, as is its association with the *polis*. Indeed, Socrates's reference to inter-state competitions, where no other city can rival Athenians in *euandria*, also helps explain how *euandria* brings *kosmos* (good order and ornament) to one's city, namely by winning.[81] Some commentators have noted the aptness of these references, suggesting that Gorgias is referring to this very competition, perhaps even ironically.[82] Though this is possible, concentrating exclusively on this formal meaning risks obscuring the larger moral and educational picture of "good manliness." For surely, even the Athenian competition itself was intrinsically bound to such value-laden terms as *kalos* and *kalokagathos*.[83] These terms, as Adkins argued,[84] remained intrinsically linked to the aristocratically-minded evaluative framework of Homer and the epinician poets and, therefore, to the values of the old education of *mousikē* and *gymnastikē*. *Kalos* and *agathos*, in the other words, did not refer only to physical beauty,[85] for it was also a moral and pedagogical concept.[86] So was *euandria*.[87] Indeed, these terms were pedagogical endpoints,[88] markers of the physical and cultural education of aristocrats.[89] As such, these

---

[81] Xenophon, *Memorabilia*, 3.3.12.

[82] Boegehold, "Group and Single Competitions," 99,

[83] I. Karamanou ed., *Euripides: Alexandros.* (Berlin: De Guyter, 2017), 221-22. On athletics being a space for displaying manly *aretē*, see esp. Heather Reid, *Athletics and Philosophy in the Ancient World: Contests of Virtue* (London: Routledge, 2011), 58-90. Papakonstantinou, "The Athletic Body," 1160 also discusses the relation of the normative body of the athlete and the "construction of gender and *civic identities*."

[84] Arthur W.H. Adkins, *Merit and Responsibility: A Study in Greek Values* (Oxford: Clarendon Press, 1975), 156-64.

[85] Reid, "Athletic Beauty," 283 also refers to the importance of *kalokagathia* in Greek aesthetics, especially statuary.

[86] Jaeger, *Paideia*, 3-4; Marrou, *History of Education*, 73.

[87] Karamanou ed., *Euripides: Alexandros*, 222.

[88] An "educational ideal" according to Reid, "Athletic Beauty," 293.

[89] Jaeger, *Paideia*, 3-4.

concepts could not help but be drawn into the debate between the "new" and "old" education and their respective merits in generating "virtuous men."

This pedagogical backdrop of *euandria,* understood in a non-technical sense,[90] is amply confirmed by the tragedies of Euripides, and most powerfully of all in the *Supplices*:

> For to be brought up not basely brings a sense of honour. Every man who has practised what is good is ashamed to become base. Courage [*euandria*] is something that can be taught, since even a young child is taught to speak and to be told things which he does not understand. And whatever things someone understands, he usually preserves them till old age. (Euripides, *Supplices* 911-17; *trans.* Morwood).

The preoccupation of this play with education has long been noted by Collard and others.[91] This concern is most evident in Adrastus's "Funeral Speech" and, especially, in the generalizing epilogue quoted above, which explicitly associates *euandria* with *paideia,* seemingly as its ultimate object.[92] The association between *euandria* and education, therefore, is clear enough. What is unclear from the speech, however, is the sort of education being recommended. Some aspects of the speech point in a decidedly traditional direction. Thus, the speech as a whole is delivered in response to Theseus's request that Adrastus relate "however did these men come to be pre-eminent among mortals

---

[90] It is useful to note that the negative *anandria* is occasionally also associated with pedagogy (e.g., Isocrates's *Ad Archidamum* 15).

[91] Christopher Collard, ed., *Euripides: Supplices* (Groningen: Bouma's Boekhuis b.v. Publishers, 1975), esp. 334-37; James Morwood ed., *Euripides: Suppliant Women* (Oxford: Aris and Philips, 2007), 3-4; Ian C. Storey, *Euripides: Suppliant Women* (London: Duckworth, 2009).

[92] Even its location at the end of a Funeral Speech, where didactic *gnomai* are often placed, is appropriate for such a "lesson" (Collard ed., *Supplices,* 337). Moreover, the repeated references to educating "these youths" has a meta-theatrical touch to it, as commentators often note (e.g., Collard, *Supplices,* 320; Storey, *Suppliant Women,* 64) and imports into the theater considerations of how Athenian youths are to be educated.

in courage (*eupsychia*)?"[93] The epilogue quoted is a direct response to this question and, as such, associates *euandria* to the *eupsychia* of aristocratic warriors who have died in combat. A further "Homeric" ring to *euandria* may be detected in the shame that such a man would feel at the prospect of becoming *kakos*.[94] Furthermore, Theseus's initial request, as well as Adrastus's speech, stress the importance of *physis* in education—even that of lineage—as well as that of toil and of the dangers of being *agymastos* (untrained). All of these features would associate the *euandria* promoted with the "old education." Yet, there are ample suggestions to the opposite, starting with the fact that Adrastus is delivering an *epitaphios*, a genre of rhetoric of interest to the Sophists. Moreover, we find in the epilogue an explicit declaration that *euandria* can be taught. Such an idea seems singularly "Sophistic," especially when it is defended by way of a striking analogy to language acquisition.[95] Even the reference to *askēsis* a few lines prior may refer to one part of the Sophistic "trinity" of education found in Plutarch's *On the Education of Children*.[96] In Adrastus's speech, then, *euandria* features prominently in a discussion about education and is referred to as its object. Moreover, the bold declaration and defense of the idea that *euandria* can be imparted by *paideia*, also suggests a specific context for its deployment, namely the highly charged conflict between the "old" and "new education" and their respective ability to produce "good manliness." This impression is further strengthened by a reference to *euandria* in another Euripidean drama:

> Wealth and too much luxury are, after all, a bad instruction [*paideuma*] in manly virtue [*euandria*]. Poverty is miserable,

---

[93] Trans. Morwood, 106-07.

[94] In a fragment from the late *Archelaos* (Euripides, fragment 237), *euandria* is associated with fame. See Annette Harder ed., *Euripides's Kresphontes and Archelaos* (Leiden: Brill, 1985), 220-21.

[95] On the Sophists and language acquisition, see Deborah L. Gera, "Two Thought Experiments in the *Dissoi Logoi*," *The American Journal of Philology* 121.1 (2000): 21-45. Jaeger, *Paideia*, 296 makes the important observation that Theognis and Pindar, unlike the Sophists, "presented their positions [about education] without argument." It is possible that we get wind of one such Sophistic argument here.

[96] Jaeger, *Paideia*, 311, traces this "educational trilogy" to the Sophists.

but, for all that, it breeds children who are better at toiling and effective. (Euripides. Fr. 541 *trans.* Karamanou)

This fragment is firmly attributed the non-extant play *Alexander* which, besides concerning Helen's accomplice—referred to by way of a *recusatio* in Gorgias's speech—is generally dated to 415 BCE,[97] close to the purported date of the *Encomium*. As such, its use here may be especially relevant to Gorgias's exordium. Unfortunately, the fragmentary state of the text makes any reconstruction speculative. It is likely, however, that these lines come from the concluding part of a messenger speech which announces Paris's victories in some athletic competition.[98] As Harder also notes, the contrast between wealth and poverty, given Paris's origins, must be framed in an "Orientalist" context.[99] Yet the explicit association of *euandria* with education, as well as the reference to the educational importance of *ponoi* for engendering this trait—an idea also evident in other fragments[100]—allows for another interpretation, one supported by the use of *euandria* in Euripides's *Electra*.[101] Here, Orestes, dismayed by his sister's poor husband but surprised by his virtuousness, comments on the difficulty of ascertaining the *euandria* of another. The central point of both speakers, surely, is the fact that the poor are sometimes able, indeed better able, to acquire *euandria*, and this because, at least in the fragment above, their poverty "educates" them by hardships. Compared to the poor man, the rich aristocrat, the traditional exponent of *euandria* in athletic competitions and in general, is at a disadvantage. Once again, then, we find the importance of "education"—here understood in terms of *ponoi*—to produce *euandria*, and in the most unexpected of places, which evokes the contentious world of 5th-century *paideia*.

We hope to have shown by this long excursus on *euandria*, that the idea of "good manliness" was deeply intertwined with the idea of

---

[97] Ioanna Karamanou ed. and trans., *Euripides, Alexandros*. (Berlin: De Guyter, 2017), 31-37.
[98] Karamanou, *Alexandros*, 220.
[99] Karamanou, *Alexandros*, 220.
[100] E.g., Euripides, fragment 237: "ἀλλ' οἱ πόνοι τίκτουσι τὴν εὐανδρίαν."
[101] Euripides, *Electra*, 367.

education. This is evident in Euripides, but also in Xenophon's *Memorabilia*, where the word, though probably referring to a competition, is used in an argument about the education of youths for political life.[102] Moreover, this term—at least in Euripides—became involved in the ideological war between the old and new education. One side espoused a position implied by the "Aristophanic critique," professing *euandria* to be the preserve of elites and the product of *physis*. Meanwhile, the references to *euandria* in Euripides collectively suggest a counter-response: *euandria* depends more on *ponos*, and thus on education, than on *physis,* and is thus available to all. This Euripidean backdrop of *euandria*—present most suggestively in his *Alexander*—as well as this debate, gives vital context to Gorgias's use of the word at the very start of the *Helen*. In using this term, we suggest that Gorgias indicates to its audience that he has entered into the fray. More straightforwardly, it also highlights, from the very first words, the speech's pedagogical theme, which is taken up in the second part of the proem:

> That the subject of the speech is a woman who, by nature and birth, is preeminent among men and women, is not unclear even to a few. For her mother was clearly Leda, and though her real father was a god, Zeus, it was said to be a man, Tyndareus. The one was suspected to be by being so, the other was proven to be by say-so. And the one was the best of men, the other the overlord of all things. Born of such parents, she acquired a beauty equal to the gods, which she seized upon and did not hide, stirring in several men several desires for love. With one body, she drew together many bodies of men who were thinking of great deeds and their great rewards. Of these, some possessed an abundance of wealth, others a fame of ancient lineage, others a good-form of innate strength, and others the power of acquired wisdom. All of them came, moved by love, by a desire for victory, and an unconquerable desire for honour. (*Helen*, 3-4)

---

[102] Xenophon, *Memorabilia*, 3.3.12.

The first half of this passage, which concerns Helen's nature (*physis*) and birth (*genos*), explains how it is that Helen acquired such beauty (*kallos*), the very same "desirable" mentioned in the first sentence. Helen's beauty, in other words, is entirely explicable under the paradigm of the old education, in terms of innate *physis* and lineage. Next comes the only description of Helen which ascribes to her some form of agency: she seizes upon her "god-like beauty" and draws the bodies of men to her, as if drawing like to like. The reference to her beauty being "god-like" may, in alluding to Sappho's *Fr. 31*, also suggest a mechanism of this "attraction": overwhelming emotion.[103] The men whom she attracts are also described, as Spatharas has noted,[104] in terms of their "education." The reference to "acquired wisdom" appears particularly apt for a Sophist given their theory of education. Moreover, the fact that their "wisdom" is *acquired* emphasizes the innate qualities of the other figures with whom the "wise man" is competing, especially those armed with good repute (*eudoxia*) of good-lineage (*eugeneia*) and the good-form (*euexia*) of innate strength.[105] These suitors are, like Helen, products of the old education. Aside from the solitary reference to "acquired wisdom," then, what emerges from the proem is a largely traditional picture of *paideia*. It suggests, in other words, that like Helen's *kallos*, and like the suitors' *eudoxia, euexia,* and *eugeneia, euandria* more generally is the preserve of the aristocrats and semi-divine figures, and explicable in terms of *physis*.

These three interconnected themes—of bodily beauty, its motivating power, and the formative importance of *physis*—reappear in the fourth argument of the *Helen*, Gorgias's own "theoretical" treatment of bodily beauty and of the medium through which it affects the soul, namely *opsis* (appearance). Indeed, the association between (Paris's) *physis* and his beauty is alluded to early in the first part of this

---

[103] Like Sappho, Gorgias describes the *physical* effects of emotions (*Helen* 8).
[104] Spatharas, "Gorgias," 141-42.
[105] The reference to *euexia* is particularly suggestive since it too is the name for an athletic competition. See Nigel B. Crowther, "*Euexia, Eutaxia, Philoponia:* Three Contests in the Greek Gymnasium," *Zeitschrift für Papyrologie und Epigraphik* 85.1 (1991): 301-304.

argument. Gorgias calls to our attention the fact that the objects which we see do not have the *physis* we want, but that which they happen to have (ἔχει φύσιν οὐχ ἣν ἡμεῖς θέλομεν, ἀλλ᾽ ἣν ἕκαστον ἔτυχε).[106] This trite observation, in fact, is an essential part of Gorgias's apologetic argument. Since Helen did not *want* to see Paris, the consequences of this encounter—dependent on Paris's *physis* and beauty—cannot be used to blame her. This is all the more so in view of Gorgias's analysis of vision which, like *logos*, acts materially and directly on the soul.[107] Her body was, just like the body of Helen's suitors in the proem, moved by *force majeure* of Paris's own beauty. Gorgias reiterates the nub of this argument, referring both to *erōs* and *tychē*, in his memorable conclusion of this section: the vision-induced psychic disturbance happens "because of the bonds of Chance, not the counsels of the mind, and with the necessities of love, not the preparations of craft (*technē*)."[108] The last argument also spells out what was implicit in the allusion to Sappho: like *logos*, it is through the passions that beauty, and *opsis* more generally, affects the human soul. There is, however, a notable inversion when one passes from the *epideictic* proem to the *apologetic* argument: Helen's own beauty, her most infamous trait, and her propensity to act, remain unmentioned, and this for obvious argumentative reasons. The attention, rather, has shifted to Paris's beauty and, through him, to the effects that the *masculine* form has on the soul. The topic of conversation, in other words, has returned to *euandria* and masculine *kallos* understood in its fullest sense. Thus, the first concrete example of the effects of *opsis* on the soul—presumably his strongest—comes straight from the gendered world of warfare:

> For example, whenever it gazes upon hostile bodies, a hostile and good order [*kosmos*] of bronze and iron decked out with hostile intent, the bronze for defense, the iron for offence, then sight [*opsis*] is immediately troubled and troubles the mind. In such a way, people often flee, driven beside themselves by dangers which are yet to come as though they

---

[106] Gorgias, *Testimonia*, Part 2: Doctrine (D), 15.
[107] See esp. Segal, "Psychology of Logos," 106-08.
[108] Gorgias, *Helen*, 19.

were present. For a pressing truth is established for the mind on account of fear [*phobos*] which comes through sight. And it, advancing, makes one careless of what is fine [*kalos*], as judged in accordance with law, and of the good which is brought about by justice. (*Helen*, 16)

It is noteworthy, first of all, that Gorgias returns to the word *kosmos* in the context of warriors fighting, presumably for their *polis*. This, surely, is more evidence that the notion of *euandria* is not far from Gorgias's mind. More generally, we also find the same "conciliatory" attitude to the precepts of old education. Thus, the description of the ordered soldiers evokes lyric war poetry and, in particular, Tyrataeus's own descriptions of the *kosmoi* Spartan soldiers, fighting—and dying—in his ranks.[109] The image of the *kosmos* of soldiers, therefore, evokes not only military virtue but its celebration in song. The power of the military *kosmos* in this case, however, lies not so much in their fighting ability. In fact, we are left with the impression that the opposing army fled when the *kosmos* was still advancing from afar. Rather, the power of "fighters" lies primarily in their visual form, their perceived appearance. Furthermore, its effects on the enemy are described in psychological, indeed moral terms. Confronted by the *kosmos* of the marching soldiers, the enemy's own internal sense of what is beautiful and worth pursuing—the *kalos*—becomes disturbed.[110] The battlefield, therefore, becomes not a place where arms are tested, but a competition of *euandria*. The overlap with the old education, and with the world of poetry in particular, is also evident in the mechanism by which this *kosmos* operates: fear (*phobos*). The effects of the soldier's appearance, therefore, comes close to the effects of poetry on its audience (*Helen* 8): provoking "shuddering fear" (*phrikē periphobos*) for troubles that are not one's own. This close overlap between Gorgias's treatment of *opsis* and poetry continues in the rest of the argument:

---

[109] Tyrtaeus, fragment 6.

[110] We owe this observation to Heather Reid's insightful comments on the original article.

Next, painters delight [*terpousi*] the sight whenever they create one complete body and shape out of many colours and bodies. The creation of portraits and the making of statues also provide a delightful illness [*noson*] to the eyes. It is natural, then, that some things distress [*lupein*] the eyes and others stir yearning [*pothein*]. (*Helen*, 18)

Once again, the effects of vision—joy (*terpsis*), distress (*lupein*) and yearning (*pothos*)—are precisely the same as those of poetry. Like poetry, and like Gorgias's own discourse (*Helen* 5) which he has usurped from the poets, painters are able to provoke pleasure (*Helen* 5) in their "audiences." Moreover, the effects of statues—distress and yearning—are analogous to those of poetry: "grief-stricken yearning" and "tear-drenched pity."[111] Even the subject matter of most statues in the late 5th-century BCE would overlap considerably with the subject matter of poetry. Such a close connection between the effects of the visual form, particularly the visual form of soldiers, and those of poetry is extremely suggestive. It points not only to the archaic connection of poetry, soldiery, and masculinity which animated much of the "old education," but also speaks to Gorgias's rhetorical strategy with respect to *euandria*. In affirming the connection between poetry and the male form—whether that of Paris's beauty or of the fear-inducing soldiers—as he previously affirms between *physis* and beauty more generally, Gorgias adopts a conciliatory attitude toward the "old education." The male form—like *euandria*—depends on *physis* and has an effect analogous to poetry. Moreover, in emphasizing the power of Paris's conquering *euandria* even to the point of eulogy, and equally the *kosmos* of soldiers, Gorgias's *epideixis* moves ever closer to the genre of praise-poetry.

And yet, Gorgias's own ambivalent positioning to poetry in the *Helen*, as well as various features of the argument, should make us question the extent of his conciliatory attitude. First of all, the formative nature of *physis*, despite the early (and oblique) allusion, seems to have slipped out of the discourse. Instead, various *technai* (sorcery, medicine, painting) have become the main objects of focus.[112]

---

[111] Gorgias, *Helen*, 9.
[112] Gorgias, *Helen*, 10-11.

Moreover, the close overlap between *opsis* and poetry must be placed side by side with the more general overlap of *opsis* and *logos*, as noted long ago by Segal.[113] *Opsis*, like all *logoi*, shares the same fundamental psychology: it operates directly on the passions of the soul. Even the mechanisms of their actions are explained in analogous ways. The medical analogy that was used to explicate *logos* recurs in the discussion of eyesight. Furthermore, eyesight, like all *logoi*, also works by a form of "deception." In the case of the soldiers, then, the "truth" which is established by the soldier's fearful form is based on a counterfactual, their enemies behave "as if they were present." Even the painter's creation of one body out of many colors smacks of deceit. Moreover, *opsis* shares the same fundamental characteristic of *logos*: it also operates by a form of persuasion which is tantamount to necessity.[114] There is, in other words, a close overlap between *opsis* and *logos* which transcends the observed closeness of *opsis* and poetry.

This close nexus of ideas, we argue, is fundamental to Gorgias's reinterpretation of the goal of education, *euandria*. It suggests, moreover, an overall strategy and an overall response to the tenets of the old education. Just as poetry has been subordinated to the Sophists' primary province, *logos*, one which grounds them on equal if not better footing, so too are *opsis* and *euandria* subordinated to a common domain, that of persuasion. All domains, not only poetry, sorcery, and philosophy, but also painting, military prowess, and even physical beauty, must compete on the same basis: asserting power over the emotions of another's soul. It is this ability, more than any other, which characterizes the citizen possessed with *euandria*. Just as a soldier confronts his enemy in the psychological and moral domain, all speech, whether poetry or oratory, operates on this level. All human endeavor, in other words, has been reduced to one "basic" type: a contest of virtue. In one fell swoop, all educators—whether poets, gymnasts, or Sophists—were turned into "orators" understood in a narrow sense: the promulgators of a "*technē*" for persuasion. And on those grounds, Gorgias knew he could compete.

---

[113] Segal, "Psychology of Logos," 106-10. Cf. Wardy, *Birth of Rhetoric*, 46-48.
[114] Segal, "Psychology of Logos," 106.

Conclusion

Gorgias's *Encomium to Helen* begins as a defense of a mythological subject. As the speech progresses, however, Helen recedes further and further into the background, and the speech is transformed into a Sophistic "educational toy" through which Gorgias can convey and explore other ideas. We have argued that one such idea relates to the Aristophanic critique of the new education as emasculating and physically debilitating. In responding to this critique, the *Helen*, like Adrastus's speech in Euripides's *Suppliants*, finds itself in a grey zone. At the outset, the prominent reference to *euandria*, the description of Helen, and of her suitors fit more neatly into a traditional scheme of *aretē* as the preserve of elites reared in the "old education." Helen herself is the greatest embodiment of this paradigm, her beauty being determined by *physis* in the strictest sense, her illustrious parentage. But as the speech drifts away from its "god-like" subject, numerous *technai* are discussed, which, due to their teachability, contrast sharply with these notions of the *physis*. Moreover, the fourth argument in the *Encomium to Helen* contains an implicit counter-response to Aristophanes's criticism. In short, Gorgias subordinates *opsis* and *euandria* to persuasion, thus rendering them analogous to *logos*, the domain of the Sophists par excellence. Just as the man with "acquired wisdom" can compete for the greatest rewards against ancestral heroes and mighty warriors, so too can the Sophist compete at the game of *euandria*—as long as it is reframed in this way. Moreover, in equating Paris's *euandria* to the workings of *logos*, which the Sophist professed to teach, Gorgias also implies that *euandria*, like "rhetoric," can be taught. In this, Gorgias not only echoes the thoughts of Euripides's Adrastus, but he also finds himself drawn closer to that famed professor of *aretē*, Protagoras.

L.M.J. Coulson[1]
Performing Platonic *Paideia*: Philosopher, Know Thyself

Why did Plato the educator write dialogues to cultivate virtue and wisdom? Perhaps he believed that narrative has neither the explanatory nor the persuasive force of discourse. The literary constructs that scaffold Platonic *paideia* intend to attract, charm, agitate and alter. Their appeal and sway rests on the spectators' cognitive immersion in the actors' performance. In short, to achieve his pedagogic aim the words spoken by Plato's characters must apprehend his audiences' attention.

Plato's players mimic the values and foibles of the infamous and esteemed in order to characterize human virtue and ignorance. The *mise-en-scène* of these philosophical dramas disclose their instructive context and purpose. At the agora, festivals, lawcourts, and gymnasia, in the intimacy of symposia and private conversations, Plato invites an elite, historically informed audience to listen, engage, partake, and preferably activate the inner dialogue that quickens self-discovery.

Platonic enactments are written to educate. Thus, they present the author's pedagogic intent, which implies that Plato the teacher frequently speaks directly to the audience in *propria persona*, albeit masked by a *dramatis persona*. It is perverse to assert that none of Plato's actors tell his teachings. Aristotle was Plato's student for about 20 years and probably knew his work better than most. He wrote that Plato's characters often voice his views.[2] Diogenes Laertius was also adamant that Socrates, Timaeus, the Athenian, and the Eleatic Stranger speak for Plato.[3]

I do not here address debates about the dialogues' compositional chronology or the related unitarian/developmental theories, save to ask if they are necessarily mutually exclusive. This essay is concerned

---

[1] L.M.J. Coulson is an Honorary Associate of the Department of Classics and Ancient History, University of Sydney, Australia, and Publisher at Academic Printing and Publishing.

[2] For Aristotle's view on Plato's voice in the *Republic* and *Laws* see *Politics* II i-vi, especially 1266b5, 1271b1, 1274b9.

[3] Diogenes Laertius, *Lives of Eminent Philosophers,* tr. R.D. Hicks, vol. I (Cambridge, MA: Harvard University Press, 1925), 3.52.

with why Plato wrote his school's texts and proposes the idea that they can be categorized as primary, secondary, and tertiary *paideia*.[4] I attempt to show that this division reveals three intentional terms of cumulative schooling that employ often revised dialogues written consecutively and/or concurrently. Moreover, I argue that Plato's characters frequently mask the practice of an evolving and amended philosophy that is a quest for him and would-be philosophers to heed the Delphic entreaty, "know-thyself."

Primary *paideia*

The *Apology, Crito, Ion, Hippias Minor, Protagoras, Gorgias, Laches, Charmides, Euthyphro,* and *Lysis* are classified here as primary *paideia* texts. These shorter works attract and entertain students using familiar language to discuss and encourage self-refection about moral conduct, reasoning, beliefs, and discernment. Plato disrupts typical attitudes about being *pepaideumenos* (an educated person) and begins to articulate the relationship between introspection and the acquisition of true knowledge.

The *Apology* is arguably Plato's first or second dialogue. It was purportedly written prior to 387 BCE when he made the first of three visits to Sicily that initiated his lasting friendships with Dion of Syracuse and the Pythagorean, Archytas of Tarentum.[5] Plato began his teaching career at this time, establishing the Academy and writing its so-called Socratic texts. Personal experience aside, he was doubtless aware of commentaries on Socrates's life and ethics. Some known to us include those of Xenophon, Antisthenes, Aeschines, Phaedo, Eucleides, and anecdotally Aristippus, a renowned Socratic disciple and chronicler who Plato probably knew.[6] It is unlikely that Plato's

---

[4] I crave readers indulgence for the necessarily scant adumbration of multifaceted Platonic dialogues.

[5] Our knowledge of Plato's visits to Sicily is based primarily on his *Seventh Letter,* the authenticity of which is disputed. On Plato's relationship with Sicily, see Heather L. Reid and Mark Ralkowski (eds.), *Plato at Syracuse: Essays on Plato in Western Greece,* (Sioux City, IA: Parnassos Press, 2019).

[6] Klaus Dôring, "The Students of Socrates" in *The Cambridge Companion to Socrates,* ed. Donald R. Morrison (Cambridge: Cambridge University Press, 2010).

depictions contradicted the commonly known aspects of Socrates's elenctic method, ethics, trial, and death. Even where Plato casts him to present un-Socratic philosophy, the character of this revered teacher unites and spiritually grounds the fruition of Platonic *paideia*.

The theatre of the *Apology* defends elenchus, critiques Athenian politics, and pointedly acknowledges the cautioning voice of Socrates's *daimōn*'s daimonion.[7] Plato refutes Aristophanes's depiction of Socrates in the *Clouds* as head of the "Thinkery" absorbed in measuring flea jumps. The *Apology*'s Socrates, attested to be wise by the Delphic oracle, is a good Athenian martyred by the ignorance of his fellow citizens who "neither care nor take thought for wisdom and truth and the perfection of [their] soul" (29e).[8] Hence, the performance of Platonic *paideia* opens with the principal actor delivering a primary lesson: perfecting your incarnate soul requires the courage to care for and cultivate wisdom and truth.

This dialogue emphasizes Socrates's moral integrity, establishing a remarkable literary protagonist: the philosopher warrior. He is distinctive truth-seeking hero who bravely performs the ethics of a well examined life while exposing ignorance, albeit often indifferent to consequence, like "a gadfly to a horse [spur]" (30e). Socrates's heroics transcend the visceral metaphors of Homeric bloodletting. Yet, Plato also harkens traditions of physical valor, citing Socrates's exploits at Potidaea, Amphipolis, and Delium (28e), referencing them again in the *Laches*, *Charmides*, and notably at *Symposium* 221a where Alcibiades extols Socrates's character.

---

[7] I argue for the differentiation of the Platonic *daimōn* and *daimonion*. That evoking the *eide* and *eikons* of *euetheia* (*Rep.* 400de), can enable a *daimōn's daimonion* to function as a personally known tutelary genius (cf. *Phd* 107d, *Rep.* 402e): perhaps akin to so-called human conscience, or synteresis. I submit that for Plato where an embodied soul is cultivated by devotion to learning and true thoughts a *daimonion* amplifies the essential *daimōn*. Therefore, a *daimonion* (as described by Socrates), is a perceptible ethical guide for those fit to activate a reality of the *daimōn's* divine guidance.

[8] All translations of Plato's dialogues are from Plato, *Plato in Twelve Volumes* (Cambridge, MA: Harvard University Press; 1921/25, 1966/67/68).

In the *Crito*, Socrates is a condemned citizen who dutifully accepts the verdict of his beloved Athens, declining the option of flight as unjust. What might the audience do in similar circumstances? This drama might stimulate students' empathy and activate their inner dialogue, primary merits of a would-be philosopher.

The *Ion* teaches a recurring lesson: avoid the rhapsode's error of thinking you know what you do not. Socrates tells Ion that he cannot correctly speak about Homer without both the appropriate *technē* (craft/skill) and *epistēmē* (knowledge/understanding), (532c). Here Plato's voice begins to diverge from Socrates's limited notion of *technē*. Platonic *technē* is more complex and extensive, as it can apply to philosophical method and practice, even metaphysics. For Plato, a reasoned discussion requires the related *epistēmē* to underpin a *technē* (533a, 534c). Clever words can mask ignorance, learn that praise *per se* does not necessarily infer that someone has sufficient knowledge to be admirable. Self-knowledge initiates epistemic understanding worthy of emulation.[9] Given his critique here of the pedagogic harm caused by some, poetry might Plato nevertheless suggest that appropriate knowledge can elevate dramatists' *technē* to a "light and winged and holy thing" (534b)?

The succinct *Hippias Minor* promotes awareness of dialectic's benefits as opposed to its abuse in the linguistic contests known as eristic. Socrates ironically says to the sophist Hippias: "Certainly you are the wisest of men in the greatest number of arts, as I once heard you boast, recounting your great and enviable wisdom in the market-place at the tables of the moneychangers" (368b). Plato concludes the dialogue by iterating the warning to not mistake astute *technē* as false evidence of goodness and moral excellence (*aretē*).[10]

The challenging *Protagoras* dramatizes the need for and purpose of moral education, casting Socrates in the dynamic Periclean age to confront celebrated sophists who claim to teach virtue. Socrates refutes that, and Protagoras responds with his "great speech" (320c-328d). Plato encourages students to reflect on the relationship of

---

[9] Raphael Woolf, "The Self in Plato's *Ion*," *Apeiron* 30.3 (1997): 189-210.

[10] Plato's long held view that all wrongdoing is involuntary (*Hippias Minor* 376ab) is not elaborated here.

knowledge and virtue. And understand that while Protagoras might love the virtue of "wisdom, temperance, courage, justice, and holiness" (349b), he does not truly know what it is.

In the *Gorgias*, named for the famous Sicilian sophist, a defiant Socrates decries sophistic's civil and moral influence, alerting students to the power and peril of such instruction. The potency of teachers and education underpin the dialogue (cf. 453d-457c, 470e, 485b-486b). Plato's articulation of good rhetoric's merit amplifies his political and ethical voice.

The *Laches* opens with two fathers, Lysimachus and Melesias, seeking advice on how to ensure their sons can be educated to succeed in Athenian society. They engage two brave generals, Nicias and Laches, in a debate about armor and battle arts. Socrates is then asked to arbitrate their attempts to definite the virtue of courage, and uses astute elenctic to demonstrate that the brave generals have in truth no knowledge of courage. The dialogue thus recurs the leitmotif of questioning interlocutors' beliefs and assumptions to teach and test students fitting introspection. What do they consider good moral instruction, how and where does their courage manifest? The onus to value an ethical education is underscored by this retrospective assessment of Athenian politics, arguably inferring that self-knowledge helps nurture honorable Athenians' *aretē* (goodness/ virtue). As Nicias remarks, "I knew pretty well all the time that our argument would not be about the boys if Socrates were present, but about ourselves" (188b). In this important exploration of virtuous courage students are "drawn round and round" (187e) by dialectic volleys of cognition aimed at their barricades of doxastic certainty. Plato's primary educational *technē* encourages students' fearless reflection and assessment of beliefs and opinion; to muster the valor crucial for learning and teaching themselves.

The *Charmides* echoes the *Laches* in numerous ways. Both cite Socrates's military service: the *Charmides's* historical context places Socrates as a recently returned veteran from the siege of Potidaea. Each dialogue illustrates his renown as a teacher of noble youth, and the aporetic struggle to define virtue contrasts good and evil. Notably, unlike the *Laches's* admirable interlocutors, the *Charmides's* characters, Charmides (Plato's uncle) and Critias (Plato's mother's cousin), are notorious as among the Thirty Tyrants; notwithstanding that they are historically located before that eight month attempt to Spartanize Athens.[11] Is Plato juxtaposing the excellence of learning temperance as a youth with adult folly of not doing so?

Socrates's celebrated disposition makes him an ideal narrator and exemplar for this text about the virtue of temperance. His glimpse behind beautiful Charmides's robes explicitly demonstrates knowledge of the *technē* that moderates self-control (*enkrateia*), thus he embodies the relationships between knowledge, *technē*, and virtue. For "temperance is good, if its presence makes men good" (161a). Critias alludes to the Delphic Oracle when he remarks that "temperance/ sound mindedness (*sōphrosunē*) is to know oneself" (164d). Arguably, one of the most illuminating instructions in Platonic primary *paideia* occurs in the *Charmides* (166cd):

> If my main effort is to refute you, that I do it with any other motive than that which would impel me to investigate the meaning of my own words—from a fear of carelessly supposing, at any moment, that I knew something while I knew it not? And so it is now: that is what I am doing, I tell you. I am examining the argument mainly for my own sake, but also, perhaps, for that of my other intimates. Or do you not think it is for the common good, almost, of all men, that the truth about everything there is should be discovered?"

Socrates then explains that temperance aids such knowing: "Only the temperate person will know himself and be able to discern what he really knows and does not know and have the power of judging what other people likewise know and think they know (167a).

The *Euthyphro* imparts the need to know the basis of reasoned argument. It attempts to identify and define the virtue of piety/ holiness (*to hosion*): "Just consider this question: —Is that which is holy loved by the gods because it is holy, or is it holy because it is loved by the gods?" (10a). Plato grapples with the difficult issue of godliness and justice, which Socrates's fellow citizen apparently sufficiently

---

[11] Rex Stem, "The Thirty at Athens in the Summer of 404," *Phoenix* 57.1/2 (2003): 18-34.

knew to warrant executing him, and Euthyphro thinks he knows enough to justify prosecuting his father.

The *Laches, Charmides,* and *Euthyphro* try to respectively define the virtues of courage, temperance, and piety, all ending in aporia. Yet they serve the aim of Platonic *paideia* to motivate self-education by directing students to scrutinize values and opinions. Simplicius reports that Plato routinely taught more advanced students by "giving a problem,"[12] which is a core tenet of Platonic philosophy.

The *Lysis* retains the wrestling school staging of the *Laches* and *Charmides*. It is notable that as this dialogue about *philoi* (friends) and *philia* (friendship), begins Socrates is walking between gymnasia. From one that becomes the location of Plato's Academy to a another which is the future site of Aristotle's Lyceum. Plato's efforts to raise *eros* beyond physicality are more incisive in a play of friendship and temperance that recounts Hippothales's erotic infatuation with the younger Lysis. The latter and Menexenus are easily deceived and incapable of rebutting Socrates arguments, so he does it for them to retell the folly of uncritically agreeing with supposed experts.

Platonic primary texts endeavor to identify and differentiate the widely admired and mimicked sophistic *technē* from Plato's educational quest for true knowledge. He disrupts complacency and awakens curiosity to abet students' understanding of themselves and their world. Each aspect of this elementary education instructs Socratic integrity while signaling the more abstract metaphysics and epistemology to follow. The dialogues increasingly emphasize the need to care for the young (*epimeleia*) by nurturing the pursuit of wisdom through good education, a theme elucidated in the *Protagoras, Meno, Republic* and other texts.

The *Ion, Hippias Minor, Laches,* and *Euthyphro* feature men of prestige and authority who prove incapable of defending their sophisticated beliefs as they mistake skillful *technē* for true knowledge. Plato's Socratic dialogues thus challenge the complacency of justifying beliefs based on presumed authority and status. Hence, irrespective of each primary dialogue's topic, Plato persistently urges identification

---

[12] Shigeru Yonezawa, "Aristotle's Testimony Regarding Plato's Philosophical Development," *Rheinisches Museum für Philologie* (2017): 276-298.

of binary beliefs and false certainty, so that students may discern and compare what they deem politically and ethically important, and authentically *aretē*.[13] That inaugurates his primary *paideia's* substrate: have the courage to change by learning from corrective self-reflection that cultivates soul and society: teach yourself how to know yourself.

Secondary *paideia*

Ready acolytes might advance to the decidedly more Platonic curriculum here classified as secondary *paideia*. The *Euthydemus*, *Cratylus*, *Meno*, *Menexenus*, *Phaedo*, and *Symposium* advance self-surveillance of habitual narratives' sway and attempts to elevate that to a higher perspective of observing one's observations. Socrates's masterful presence personifies truth as he continues to deliver the more probing analytical *paideia* intended to sort seed from chaff.

In the public setting of the Lyceum gymnasium, the *Euthydemus* explores the technical relationship between persuasive language and politics. Plato reiterates the lessons of *Hippias Minor* and *Gorgias*, again contrasting the social effects of genuine dialectic and caustic eristic. The *Euthydemus* concludes with earnest advice: "Let those who practice philosophy have their way [...] and when you have tested the matter itself, well and truly [...] if you find it to be such as I think it is, pursue and ply it without fear" (307bc). Plato beckons those willing to "pursue and ply [philosophy] without fear" —a daunting challenge that obliges one to assimilate the puzzling aporias and stalking inconclusion of the primary dialogues. The *Cratylus* provides an extensive etymological review to express its namesake's, and probably Plato's, belief that word names can disguise reality. Hence, would-be *dialektikoi* must look beyond linguistic conventions to find truth.

The *Meno* also explores the unity and teachability of virtues, reviving the argument that Protagoras addresses in his "great speech" (*Protagoras* 320c-328d). The *Meno* ratifies intuitive knowledge and encourages students to desire virtue (*aretē*) as a beneficial good of the soul, which "you understand [as] temperance, justice, courage,

---

[13] The comic poet Epikrates, Plato's contemporary, had a character say that at the Academy Plato "very mildly encouraged" puzzled younger students "to define again the pumpkin from the start" (fr. 10(11), 33-34 K.-A; cited in Shigeru. "Aristotle's testimony," 296).

intelligence, memory, magnanimity, and so forth" (88a). Plato mentions of certain priests, priestesses (81a), and Pindar (fr. 133), as among "many another poet of heavenly gifts [...] if you judge them to be true. They say that the soul of man is immortal, and at one time comes to an end, which is called dying, and at another is born again, but never perishes" (81b). Arguably, Plato acknowledges that the Orphic Mysteries' notion of reincarnation is the source of his self, acquired by recollection theory. [14] He makes the relationship between teaching, knowledge, wisdom, and the soul more evident (87c, 88e).

The *Menexenus* is named for Socrates's close friend who was present at his death.[15] Its account of Pericles's Funeral Oration (as reported by Thucydides) is feasibly Plato's commentary on the folly of Athenian imperialism (238cd). He reasserts the *Gorgias'*s warning that useful rhetoric avoids the harms of gratuitous flattery, and that fame and acclaim do not necessarily infer veracity.

In the *Phaedo,* the ontological influences of Plato's travels heighten his engagement with complex metaphysics that supplant Socratic ethics. His four intricate arguments for the immortality of an incarnate soul,[16] and supposition about Forms/absolutes (65d) elaborate on the primary works' brief metaphysical forays. This instructive, intimate text restates Plato's recollection (*anamnēsis*) theory (71e-72e), enriched by the audience's familiarity with the Homeric hymns, Eleusinian Mysteries, myths of Persephone and Demeter, and Orpheus and the Pythagorean underworld.[17] On this retelling of his execution day Socrates voices Plato's valuation of philosophical education as a necessary and sufficient preparation for the soul's continuance:

> Those who care for their own souls [...] believe that
> philosophy, with its deliverance and purification, must not

---

[14] Max Latona, "The Tale is Not My Own (οὐκ ἐμὸς ὁ μῦθος): Myth and Recollection in Plato," *Apeiron* 37.3 (2004): 181-210,

[15] Cf. *Phaedo;* Menexenus is also the name of Socrates's son.

[16] David Bostock,"The soul and immortality in Plato's Phaedo," in *Essays on Plato's Psychology,* ed. E. Wagner (Lanham: Lexington, 2001), 241-62.

[17] Francesc Casadesús Bordoy, "On the origin of the Orphic-Pythagorean notion of the immortality of the soul," in *On Pythagoreanism,* G. Cornelli, R. McKirahan and C. Macris, eds. (Berlin: De Gruyter, 2013), 153-176.

be resisted, and so they turn and follow it whithersoever it leads. [For] the lovers of knowledge [...] perceive that when philosophy first takes possession of their soul it is entirely fastened and welded to the body and is compelled to regard realities through the body as through prison bars, not with its own unhindered vision. (82de)

The *Phaedo* concludes with Plato's emphatic homage to his teacher: "who was, as we may say, of all those of his time whom we have known, the best and wisest and most righteous man" (118a).

The *Symposium* confirms Socrates's eminence in elite Athenian society. Notoriously, Alcibiades venerates him "for the sake of truth" (215a-216d): yet another Platonic repudiation of Socrates's indictment for corrupting Athenian youth. Diotima expresses Plato's concept of soul nurture. To live and die well one must know that only philosophical ascent can transmute physical desire into a longing for the good of true beauty (205d). The simile of giving birth to such knowledge is a persistent theme: "for there are persons [...] who in their souls still more than in their bodies conceive those things which are proper for soul to conceive and bring forth" (209a). This much is suggestive of would-be philosophers' transition from the conception of secondary *paideia* to tertiary *paideia*'s potential "birthing," which also extends the Socratic midwife metaphor.[18] Plato also notes here that dramatists write tragedy and comedy, as indeed he does.

Secondary Platonic *paideia* stretches epistemic parameters, advances would-be philosophers' knowledge of analytical *technē* and, crucially, teaches that the wise love self-knowledge, which is the purpose and practice of Athenian *aretē*. Philosophy is the hero in these dialogues, a purifying protagonist that champions unconstrained reality in a quest to liberate souls. Socrates's circle tightens in the latter secondary texts where he discloses confidences with intimates more receptive to the *Phaedo's* religiosity and the *Symposium's* dialectic. Those who progress to Plato's tertiary *paideia* are a more select cohort.

---

[18] See David Sedley, *The Midwife of Platonism: text and subtext in Plato's Theaetetus* (Oxford: Clarendon Press, 2004).

Tertiary *paideia*

The *Republic, Phaedrus, Parmenides, Theaetetus, Sophist, Statesman, Philebus, Timaeus, Critias* and *Laws* are here understood as tertiary texts. If Plato's primary *paideia* is deemed Socratic, then we may surely designate his tertiary works Platonic. Like other teachers Plato might have held that in-person tuition and discussion (unwritten doctrine), better facilitates higher learning than the written word.[19] Nonetheless, he did write dialogues intended to express and teach advanced philosophy. The tertiary dialogues feature a more diplomatic Socrates who mitigates candor to persuade more tactfully. Metaphysics pervades this advanced *paideia*'s provocative synthesis of rationalism and mysticism. Mortals are in and of a cosmic union: our best and vital purpose in that cosmos is to harmonize and liberate our tripartite soul, achieved in the *Republic* by education, and in the *Philebus* by beauty-inspired love.

The remarkable *Republic* alludes to the *Meno, Gorgias, Euthydemus,* and *Cratylus,* among other texts. It is classified as tertiary despite the possibility that its first books were drafted during Plato's early teaching career.[20] This drama pedagogically affiliates and melds primary and secondary *paideia* to convey and anticipate the ascending arc of Platonic tertiary schooling. The quest to define justice aside, the *Republic* unambiguously teaches that dialectical method is obligatory for the wise cultivation of just guardians' statecraft. Socrates, gadfly sting abated, adroitly motivates a multi-rung ascent toward higher knowledge of reality: "Give the name dialectician [to one] who is able to exact an account of the essence of each thing [...] striving to examine everything by essential reality and not by opinion" (7.534bc). This instructional *tour de force* presents Plato's tripartite soul theory (4.) as a way for students to govern and order their polis within. They might then understand that to thrive here and hereafter obliges a desire to be wise guardians of their souls. The epic cave allegory (7.514a-518d) counsels against the menace of ignorance, for that which opposes

---

[19] See J.N. Findlay, *Plato: The Written and Unwritten Doctrines,* (London: Routledge, 1974).

[20] Gerasimos Santas, ed., *The Blackwell Guide to Plato's Republic.* (Oxford: Blackwell, 2006), 81.

liberation from misperception and ascent to true Good is evil. The Er myth suggests that *metempsychosis* (transmigration of souls) is possible.[21] Apparently, Plato audaciously advocates the abolition of slavery (4.433d) and gender equality in education (5.451c-457b).[22]

The *Phaedrus* is a tellingly crafted three-part revision of the *Meno*, *Euthydemus*, and *Cratylus*, which elaborates the *Republic's* lesson that rational dialectic founds fruitful discourse. Each dialogue glimpsed here serves sundry pedagogic purposes. However, the *Phaedrus* elucidates the Academy's curriculum and so warrants broader survey. Plato declares his core aim: "The cultivation of his soul (*psychēs paideusin*), that which there neither is nor ever will be anything of higher importance in truth either in heaven or on earth" (241c). Earthly beauty can be a philosopher's reality of divinity. Students have come from the pathos of Socrates's trial and martyrdom in *Apology* to longing for the harmony of their souls, since lovers of wisdom dread its loss. Plato further explains his theory of recollection (cf. *Phaedrus* 71e-72e) and how it enables philosophers' relationship with divinity.

> Recollection of those things which our soul once beheld, when it journeyed with God and, lifting its vision above the things which we now say exist, rose into real being. And therefore, it is just that the mind of the philosopher only has wings, for he is always, so far as he is able, in communion through memory with those things the communion with which causes God to be divine. Now a man who employs such memories rightly is always being initiated into perfect mysteries and he alone becomes truly perfect; but since he separates himself from human interests and turns his attention toward the divine. (249cd)

Socrates's languid pondering on beauty stirs another testimony to the power of rhetoric: "Is not rhetoric in its entire nature an art which leads

---

[21] Stephen Halliwell, "The Life-and-Death Journey of the Soul: Interpreting the Myth of Er," in *The Cambridge Companion to Plato's Republic,* ed. G.R.F. Ferrari (Cambridge: Cambridge University Press 2007).

[22] Respectively: Brian Calvert. "Slavery in Plato's Republic," *The Clssical Quarterly*, 37:2 (1987), 367-372; and Julia Annas, "Plato's Republic and Feminism," *Philosophy* 51 (1976): 307-321.

the soul by means of [persuasive] words" (*psychagōgia*; 261c). Plato then employs an anatomical analogy to explain the unity of worthy dialectic: "Every discourse must be organized, like a living being, with a body of its own, as it were, so as not to be headless or footless, but to have a middle and members, composed in fitting relation to each other and to the whole" (264c). Plato then makes an intriguing assertion about the shock of recognizing mechanical behavior: "There are two kinds of madness, one arising from human diseases, and the other from a divine release from the customary habits" (265a). This type of *metanoia* warrants weightier inquiry. Might Platonic psychagogy purposely rouse vexing moral aporia to induce a cognitive agitation which triggers mind changing reformation?[23] As a necessary condition of philosophical advancement, does Plato primarily use Socratic elenchus to incite unresolved contradictions that encourage students' exercise, or at least increased awareness, of their ethical sovereignty?

Plato reiterates that words themselves do not furnish knowledge, for reality is soul-seeded and self-harvested. He explains: "Words which cannot defend themselves by argument cannot teach the truth effectually" (276c). Yet, as at 261c, some persuasive words can lead the soul. The *Phaedrus* is especially important to Platonic *paideia* as it expresses its method and intent, inspiring students to move beyond Socratic ethics in preparation for the *Parmenides's* tertiary challenges.

The attentively staged *Parmenides* examines Plato's seminal theory of Forms and their particularization. Sagacious Parmenides (and others), wonder whether Forms exist, and if so, how might they participate in sensibles. He remarks to young Socrates:

> If these ideas of things exist and we declare that each of them is an absolute idea … [then] only a man of very great natural gifts will be able to understand that everything has a class and absolute essence, and only a still more wonderful man can find out all these facts and teach anyone else to analyze them properly and understand them. (135ab)

---

[23] Yonezawa, "Aristotle's Testimony," 276-298.

Undaunted, Plato's Socrates presents eight defenses of the Forms, teaching as he learns the practices of dialectic method. Implying that Forms, and perhaps teachers "of very great natural gifts," do exist.

Plato employs his literary genius to produce an epistemological masterwork, the *Theaetetus*. The Academy's more philosophically advanced students, epitomized by the gifted and eager Theaetetus, enjoin an intellectual labor to analyze and understand what knowledge is not, ending in more *aporia* (perhaps forewarning the folly of certainty). As with other aporetic dialogues, here Plato fosters long thought and higher knowledge. Prompting puzzlement can help students realize what they do not know, which can sustain changes of attitudes, opinions, and beliefs. Socrates continues to declare ignorance and, his midwifery having failed to deliver the child,[24] he counsels Theaetetus: If you become "pregnant with better thoughts than these … [for] if you remain barren, you will be less harsh and gentler to your associates, for you will have the wisdom not to think you know that which you do not know" (210c). As this dramatized *paideia* closes, Socrates departs to attend a reading of the charges against him. Theaetetus perhaps masks young Plato, the budding mathematician who had, or knew of, an encounter that ended when Socrates went to face indictment.

The *Sophist* précises Plato's practical and resolute application of philosophy, dare we say masked as the Eleatic Stranger. Plato now favors a more direct protreptic, unrestrained by the questions and answers of Socratic maieutic: "The method of dialogue, Socrates, is easier with an interlocutor who is tractable and gives no trouble; but otherwise, I prefer the continuous speech by one person" (217cd). Plato bids to tidy up some loose pedagogic ends, clarifying false assumptions about "unutterable" non-being (237-239c), encouraging efforts to define philosophy, and deriding eristic as chicanery. He restates the necessity for good *dialektikoi* to know, own, and rectify errors from ignorance.

The *Sophist* necessarily precedes its companion dialogue, the *Statesman*, which is staged the following day. The *Statesman* transitions Platonic politics from the *Republic* to the *Laws* (perhaps being put on

---

[24] Sedley, *Midwife*, 31-33.

wax at the same time). The Stranger's performance of Platonic *paideia* is resolute and studied. This tertiary work of civil education instructs dialectic technique (cf. 285d, 286d–287a) and reaffirms the necessity to know, concede and challenge ignorance. Statesmen must be skillful *dialektikoi* who rationally seek truth if they are to rule wisely.

> The greatest and noblest conceptions have no image wrought plainly for human vision [...] we must therefore endeavor by practice to acquire the power of giving and understanding a rational definition of each one of them; for immaterial things, which are the noblest and greatest, can be exhibited by reason only, and it is for their sake that all we are saying is said. (285e–286b)

We can only wonder what Plato intended to teach in a possibly unwritten companion to these two dialogues, entitled the *Philosopher*.[25]

The *Sophist* and *Statesman* weave together *paideia* threads from the *Parmenides, Phaedo, Republic, Theaetetus*, and other dialogues. Plato's philosophical practice is performed by a stranger who, nonetheless, speaks familiar language. Socrates is moved to the wings, still his elenchus is lauded for facilitating budding philosophers' intellectual purification so they might know what they do not know — ignorance is voluntary.

The *Philebus* elaborates lessons from the *Phaedrus* about the aim and method of using and acquiring knowledge. To realize the true beauty of life, you must know your desires: are you ruled by pleasure-seeking or reason? A well-examined life harmonizes both. Recall the *Protagoras's* exhortation to avoid *akrasia*, "being overcome by pleasure" (*Prt.* 352e). In the *Philebus*, Plato distills the haecceity of his Academy for those able to comprehend:

> The road is easy to point out, but very difficult to follow [...] this is the road I mean. [...] a gift of gods to men [...] the ancients, who were better than we and lived nearer the gods, handed down the tradition that all the things which are ever

---

[25] Dmitri Nikulin, ed., *The Other Plato: The Tübingen Interpretation of Plato's Inner-Academic Teachings*, (New York: SUNY Press, 2012), 81.

said to exist are sprung from one and many and have inherent in them the finite and the infinite (16c).

The *Timaeus*, like the *Parmenides*, begins by revising the *Republic's* lessons. Elder Plato claims lineage from Solon, perhaps to ancestrally dedicate this mystical text. The actor Timaeus proposes a likely and teleologically good account of cosmic origin and humanity's particularization in a cosmos created by what Plato refers to in the *Phaedrus* as "the mind *(nous)* that arranges and causes all things" (97c).

The *Critias* continues the *Timaeus's* progression from divine creation to human conduct, and perhaps was initially part of the latter.[26] We may wonder if this dialogue is named for Plato's notorious second cousin or Critias's great grandfather? Plato again cites descent from Solon, the supposed intermediary of the Atlantis myth from an Egyptian priest to Dropides, who then told it to his son Critias (grandfather of Plato's cousin).[27] This text echoes the *Apology* and the *Republic* in that it is more a "true story" about the need for *aretē* in Athenian politics than Atlantean mythology. The elderly Plato writes: "How gladly do I now welcome my release [...] from my protracted discourse, as a traveler who takes his rest after a long journey" (106a).

Whereas Socrates's tenor choruses the Platonic voice amplified by Parmenides, the Eleatic Stranger, and Timaeus, in the *Laws* Socrates vacates the stage to a solitary Athenian who delivers what in tertiary *paideia* are more didactic lessons, albeit delivered as palatable segments. Plato details the rationale behind his *paideia's* practice:

I term, then, the goodness that first comes to children *'paideia.'* When pleasure and love, and pain and hatred, spring up rightly in the souls of those who are unable as yet to grasp a rational account; and when, after grasping the rational account, they consent thereunto that they have been rightly trained in fitting practices:—this consent, viewed as a whole, is goodness, while the part of it that is rightly trained in

[26] M.W. Haslam, "A Note on Plato's Unfinished Dialogues," *The American Journal of Philology* 97.4. (1976): 336-339.
[27] Oliver D. Smith, "The Atlantis Story: An authentic oral tradition?" *Shima* 10:2 (2016): 10-17.

respect of pleasures and pains, so as to hate what ought to be hated, right from the beginning up to the very end, and to love what ought to be loved, if you were to mark this part off in your definition and call it *'paideia,'* you would be giving it, in my opinion, its right name. (2.653cd)

The *Laws* was, and perhaps remains, Plato's least appreciated work. His concluding class proposes a realistic second-best city, Magnesia, teaching a way for good citizens to traverse life's trials and allures. The *Laws* explores the pragmatism of Realpolitik life to inform and educate. Good citizenship requires temperance and composure. Know this: "Three kinds of force [compel us] to refrain from law-breaking [...] godly fear [...] love of honour, and that which is desirous of fair forms of soul" (8.841d). The Athenian's mention of the explanatory "preludes" that provide the *Laws*'s laws with philosophical context acknowledges the merit of well defended persuasive words.

Let us grant that Plato believed that the *Laws* was his final composition and that he wrote, or at least inspired, its last word, *syllepsomai*. This conscientious teacher, whom Speusippus praised as a quick minded and modest boy, placed carefully chosen words with precision. From *syllambánō*, *syllepsomai's* cognates may mean: to collect and gather together, restore, I take with me and close the mouth of the body.[28] *Syllepsomai* is sympathetically translated by R.G. Bury as "assist you I will" (12.969d). Who other than Plato the benevolent teacher voices this fond farewell? A last word that attests a life dedicated to learning and schooling the wisdom of knowing thyself.

Platonic tertiary education has no closing graduation, wisdom is a lifelong pursuit. True *paideia* sustains an autodidactic learning practice to know the essential reality of self and the world. The capacity to assist self-realization does not necessarily imply a teacher's prior experience of it. It does, however, require a ready student. Plato offers learners' immersion in his teaching to cultivate a self-motivated organic process of soul harmonization. Thus, his *paideia* is an endeavor of challenges and persuasion which elucidates a fundamental premise, good humans can ascend from ignorance to understanding.

---

[28] Henry George Liddell and Robert Scott, *A Greek-English Lexicon* (Oxford: Clarendon, 1940), sv. Συλλαμβάνω.

Conclusion

Philosophical knowledge of true *technē* cannot guarantee virtue. Platonic philosophy teaches protective method against voluntary ignorance. However, it does not presume to impart immunity from folly and iniquity. Plato's pedagogy inspires purposeful, introspective dialogue. He urges students to seek and awaken their elemental need to love the truth of beauty and wisdom. Learners unwilling to moderate the constraints of the sensuality that often determines thoughts and actions cannot know *euetheia*—the truly good and fair disposition of character and mind that follows good speech, good accord, good grace, and good rhythm (*Republic* 3.400de).[29]

I submit that Plato's nascent teaching began with a rudimentary outline of the Academy's curriculum founded on Socratic elenchus and ethics. His dialogues then philosophically evolve to integrate the metaphysics and epistemology of Heraclitus/Cratylus, Pythagoras, Parmenides, and others. The dramatization of the Academy's higher learning was composed over the span of 50 years and inevitably divulges the maturation of Plato's self-knowledge. His teachings thus entail the suppositions from emergent insights, which manifest as the critical analysis that expands the gravitas and scope of Platonic *paideia*. During his philosophical progress Plato's private aim remains constant: better know thyself and learn the practical application of philosophy to live and teach well.

The Delphic maxim *gnōthi seauton* (know thyself) has different meanings. They include know your mortality, know your human limitations, and know that what you do not know bounds your wisdom. Pausanias wrote that there were three inscriptions on the Temple of Apollo's pronaos. After "know thyself" followed "nothing to excess" and "certainty brings insanity."[30] Might we conclude that Plato adopted these Delphic entreaties as his core tenets, and similarly

---

[29] Knowledge and practice of the good is the quintessence of Platonic philosophy: "This reality, then, that gives their truth to the objects of knowledge and the power of knowing to the knower, you must say is the idea of good, and you must conceive it as being the cause of knowledge, and of truth in so far as known" (*Republic* 6.508e).

[30] Pausanias, *Description of Greece*, trans. W.H.S. Jones and H.A. Ormerod (Cambridge, MA, Harvard University Press; 1918), 10.24.1.

beseeches would-be philosophers to know thyself, be temperate and frequently question your beliefs?

Plato employed his literary gifts to teach a philosophical practice that is best understood in the realization of its semantic unity, rather than in the scrutiny of its plurality. His Ariadne thread strives to lead students from the complexity of the cave to the simplicity of coherence. Attentive analysis of individual dialogues and passages is important; however, excessively teasing that thread can unravel and obfuscate the genius of Plato's *paideia* performance.

Mateo Duque[1]
Performing Philosophy:
The Pedagogy of Plato's Academy Reimagined[2]

The overarching question of this paper is "How did Plato teach in his Academy?" I take as an uncontroversial premise that Plato taught the dialogues in the Academy.[3] So, a follow up question is, "How were the dialogues read in the Academy?" The verb "read" can be taken in a figurative sense to mean how the dialogues were interpreted and understood, or it can be taken in a much more basic, and literal sense. I turn to instances of reading in the dialogues in order to begin to answer the question more literally. While admittedly speculative, thinking about the performance of the dialogues in the Academy can help us to think about their *pedagogical* function: "how did Plato use the dialogues to educate?" Drawing primarily on evidence internal to the Platonic dialogues, I will argue that in the Academy the dialogues were probably performed *rhapsodically*, with one speaker reading all the roles, as opposed to performed *dramatically*, with several actors. I propose that the dialogues were read aloud by someone; after which, listener-students could ask that parts be re-read, ask questions about the dialogue, or enter into a discussion about topics discussed in the dialogue. I also contend that the structure of certain dialogues can tell

---

[1] Mateo Duque is an assistant professor of philosophy at Binghamton University. His research focuses on Plato and what he calls "Socratic *Mimēsis*," moments in the dialogues when Socrates relinquishes speaking in his own voice and speaks as another persona. Socrates's dramatic performances are a method for teaching indirectly and it is a necessary complement to his more well-known method of dialectic. He is the co-editor (with Gerald Press) of *The Bloomsbury Handbook of Plato*.

[2] I would like to thank Heather Reid, Susi Kimbell, Darby Vickers, Michał Bizoń, Michael Goyette, John Starks, Mark Ralkowski, Andrey Darovskikh, Tony Preus, William Altman, Jill Frank, Martha Beck, Anne-Marie Schultz, Nikos Charalabopoulos, Michalis Tegos, and the SPEL graduate students who took my "Platonic and Socratic *Mimēsis*" course in spring 2020 at Binghamton University.

[3] William H.F. Altman, "The reading order of Plato's dialogues," *Phoenix* 64.1 (2010): 21; see also William H.F. Altman, *Ascent to the Beautiful* (Lanham, MD: Lexington Books, 2020), xiv.

us about *how* Plato taught, and additionally, *how* Plato's pedagogy may have found its way into the dialogues.

Other views on Platonic pedagogy

I want to acknowledge some alternative methods of answering the question, "How did Plato teach in the Academy?"[4] One can look at the "program of studies" for the education of the philosopher rulers in *Republic* 7: the study of mathematics (arithmetic, plane and solid geometry, astronomy, and harmonics) as well as dialectic. John Burnett defended the pedagogy of the *Republic* as the one Plato practiced in the Academy.[5] Others, like Paul Shorey, add to the "program of studies" from the *Republic* other lessons from other dialogues, like the *Parmenides, Philebus, Sophist,* and *Statesman.*[6] Another possibility is to look at the education of the young in the *Laws.* There are skeptics of these kinds of approaches that try to extract a pedagogy directly from some of the dialogues. For example, Henri-Irénée Marrou argued that the utopian educational schemes in the *Republic* or the *Laws* were not meant for the Academy.[7]

There are others who have offered speculative proposals reimagining Plato as performing the dialogues as theatrical dramas in the Academy. In fact, the theatricality of the *Protagoras* leads William Altman to suggest that the *Protagoras* "was performed as a play, and

---

[4] John Glucker, "Plato in the Academy: some cautious reflections," in *Plato's Academy: Its Workings and Its History,* eds. P. Kalligas, C. Balla, E. Baziotopoulou-Valavani, and V. Karasmanis (Cambridge: Cambridge University Press, 2016), 90-3, identifies three types of answers to what Plato taught in the Academy. The first is some pedagogical program that is described in the dialogues; the second is Plato taught the dialogues themselves as textbooks; and, finally, the third is similar to the second, Plato taught the dialogues as "exercise-textbooks" along with training in Platonic philosophy.

[5] John Burnet, "The Programme of Studies," *Greek Philosophy, Thales to Plato* (London: Macmillan, 1914), 223-9.

[6] Paul Shorey, *What Plato Said* (Chicago: University of Chicago Press, 1933), 29-31.

[7] Henri I. Marrou, *Histoire de l' Éducation dans L' Antiquité,* (Paris: Éditions du Seuil, 1965), 114–16; *A History of Education in Antiquity,* trans. George Lamb (New York: Sheed and Ward, 1956), 102-4.

was staged for what might be called 'the Academy's incoming class,' i.e., for its Freshmen."[8] While I am deeply fascinated by these kinds of proposals—and I would like them to be right—I will argue that evidence from the dialogues seems to suggest that instead of a dramatic reproduction of the dialogues there was a rhapsodic recitation. Furthermore, I do not think that merely reproducing a dialogue as theatrical drama would be sufficient to count as philosophical pedagogy. Similar to the discussion on rhetoric that follows the three speeches of the *Phaedrus*, to properly engage with the dialogues, I believe that the students in the Academy would have to actively interact with them and question them (from within and without). So, even *if* Plato staged the *Protagoras* as a play, *then* Plato's pedagogy was not over when the play was over. The students could not just passively take in the drama of the dialogue, they would have been asked to study it by playing with it.

Before turning to the dialogues, I would like to lay out some of my presuppositions, which are meant to be plausible, but are worth spelling out.

1) Plato was a consummate teacher. For example, as a writer, he tries to teach his listeners/readers even if these lessons are not immediately clear or explicitly didactic.
2) Plato's dialogues are eminently teachable.
3) Plato's dialogue formed the curriculum of the Academy; he most likely taught the dialogues in the Academy. (Plato's teaching was incorporated into the dialogues).
4) A corollary of (3), Plato's dialogues reflect his teaching.[9]

Also, since my view hinges on reading practices in ancient Greece, it is worth explicating what is at stake.

---

[8] Altman, *Ascent to the Beautiful*, 48. On the theatricality of the *Phaedo*, see Nikos Charalabopoulos, *Platonic Drama and its Ancient Reception* (Cambridge: Cambridge University Press, 2001), 66-8 and Gilbert Ryle, *Plato's Progress* (Cambridge: Cambridge University Press, 1966), 23-4.

[9] Although I may have come to some of these points independently, I am deeply indebted to William Altman, and to his presentation of these points in his five-volume work on "Plato the Teacher." For more on Plato the educator, see A.K. Cotton, *Platonic Dialogue and the Education of the Reader* (Oxford: Oxford University Press, 2014).

Reading in ancient Greece

There is a performativity to reading Greek in the 5th and 4th centuries BCE that was determined, in part, by the method of writing that was used. I will discuss the performativity and the materiality of writing in turn. In order to attempt to comprehend the extent of "performance culture" in ancient Greece, I propose a thought experiment.[10] Imagine a world with no recordings of any kind—no cassette tapes, records, movies, DVDs, YouTube, Spotify, Netflix, etc. In the ancient world, if you wanted to recall a piece of media (like a poem, song, or drama), you needed to bring it back from memory, back to life, by performing it and most likely singing it aloud. Performance, memory, and the ability to recall were so important that one historical episode can illustrate this broader experience. Plutarch, talking about the Athenian soldiers captured in the Sicilian Expedition in 413 BCE, writes:

> A few were rescued because of their knowledge of Euripides, for it seems that the Sicilians were more devoted to his poetry than any other Greeks living outside the mother country. Even the smallest fragments of his verses were learned from every stranger who set foot on the island, and they took delight in exchanging these quotations with one another. At any rate there is a tradition that many of the Athenian soldiers who returned home safely visited Euripides to thank him for their deliverance which they owed to his poetry. Some of them told him that they had been given their freedom in return for teaching their masters all they could remember of his works, while others, when they took to flight after the final battle, had been given food and water for reciting some of his lyrics (Plutarch, *Life of Nicias* 29.2-3).[11]

This example makes vivid the stakes of performance and shows how alien that kind of mind and memory are from our contemporary

---

[10] The term "performance culture" is a nod to Simon Goldhill and Robin Osborne, eds. *Performance Culture and Athenian Democracy* (Cambridge: Cambridge University Press, 1999).

[11] Plutarch, and Ian Scott-Kilvert, *The Rise and Fall of Athens: Nine Greek Lives* (Harmondsworth, Middlesex: Penguin, 1960).

world, where if we want to listen to a song, watch a TV show or a movie, all we have to do is pull up a recording on our electronic devices. If we were to be caught in a similar situation, most of us, if we were forced to recall, would not be able to remember—and sing or act out—our favorite media. We might memorize one song or scene, but not entire epic poems and plays, like many of the ancient Greeks did.

Another big difference between us and the ancient Greeks is our writing systems. We do not realize it but the spaces in between words and certain punctuation marks are innovations that have contributed to the ease and spread of literacy. These would not have been available to a reader in the 5th and 4th century BCE Greece. Even many classicists do not pay close enough attention to ancient readers' actual material writing system. How would someone have read a text? It would be through their writing system, which was "scriptio continua." Scriptio continua is a style of writing that forgoes spaces and punctuation marks between words or sentences. The following is an example of the very first line of Hesiod's *Theogony* 1-4 in scriptio continua:

ΜΟΥΣΑΩΝΕΛΙΚΩΝΙΑΔΩΝΑΡΧΩΜΕΘΑΕΙΔΕΙΝΑΙΘΕΛΙΚ
ΩΝΟΣΕΧΟΥΣΙΝΟΡΟΣΜΕΓΑΤΕΖΑΘΕΟΝΤΕΚΑΙΠΕΡΙΚΡΗ
ΝΗΙΟΕΙΔΕΑΠΟΣΣΑΠΑΛΟΙΣΙΝΟΡΧΕΥΝΤΑΙΚΑΙΒΩΜΟΝ
ΕΡΙΣΘΕΝΕΟΣΚΡΟΝΙΩΝΟΣ[12]

With more modern punctuation, the difference in cases between miniscule and majuscule (which was developed later), and line breaks for ease of scansion, the line would appear as:

Μουσάων Ἑλικωνιάδων ἀρχώμεθ᾽ ἀείδειν,
αἵ θ᾽ Ἑλικῶνος ἔχουσιν ὄρος μέγα τε ζάθεόν τε
καί τε περὶ κρήνην ἰοειδέα πόσσ᾽ ἁπαλοῖσιν
ὀρχεῦνται καὶ βωμὸν ἐρισθενέος Κρονίωνος.

And now an English translation by Hugh Gerard Evelyn-White:[13]

From the Heliconian Muses let us begin to sing,
who hold the great and holy mount of Helicon,

[12] This particular example is from "Scriptio continua," *Wikipedia*, June 3, 2022.
[13] Hesiod, *The Homeric Hymns and Homerica*, trans. Hugh G. Evelyn-White (London: Heinemann, 1914), 78-9.

and dance on soft feet about the deep-blue spring
and the altar of the almighty son of Cronos.

This is my attempt to recreate the feel of Scriptio continua in English:

COULDYOUREADTHISEASILYIFYOUWEREFORCEDTO

While this last line is something that a contemporary reader *can* read, it is not a form of writing that comes easily to us because we have become accustomed to the spaces, punctuation, the difference between lower and upper case, and the line and paragraph breaks of our modern writing system.[14] To better understand the contrast, Gregory Nagy, writes that in ancient Greece:

> the text was meant not only for *reading* [...] It was also meant for *performance* [...] The ancient Greeks, including Aristotle himself, regarded *reading* as a *reenactment* of live speech. Such a sense of reenactment was driven by their writing system [...] The experience of seeing words run together in scriptio continua impedes not so much the general process of reading but the specific process of 'silent reading.'[15]

So, while scriptio continua does not facilitate "silent reading"—a kind of reading that is most common in our modern times—it is a writing system that was developed primarily for reading aloud. Scriptio continua is developed and utilized in a society in the crux of

---

[14] For poetry, poetic meter could be helpful in reading scriptio continua, but this technique would not be available in prose writers, such as in Plato, Xenophon, or Thucydides.

[15] Gregory Nagy, "Performance and text in ancient Greece," *The Oxford Handbook of Hellenic Studies*, eds. George Boys-Stones, Barbara Graziosi, and Phiroze Vasunia (Oxford: Oxford University Press 2009): 419-21 (emphasis in original; available online at chs.harvard.edu). Nagy says that when "Aristotle in the *Poetics* (1456b20-38) speaks about syllables and about the consonants and vowels that delimit them [...] he is demonstrating a remarkably accurate linguistic understanding of the sound system or phonology of the Greek language as spoken in his time [...]. Just as remarkable is the phonological accuracy of the writing system inherited by Aristotle and his contemporaries in reproducing the language that went into the texts they produced" (419-20).

converting and adapting from an oral/aural culture to a literary one. So, using some external evidence we can see that when Plato's dialogues were read they were read aloud, and (most likely) as a kind of performance. Furthermore, it is likely that the reader of a Platonic dialogue would want to change his voice, his tone, and also his body, in terms of gestures and facial expressions, to better represent the change in characters in a dialogue. This is so that the different characters can be heard and distinguished by the listeners, and not to fall into a monotonic background where everyone sounds the same.

With these presuppositions in hand, we can turn to look at some of the instances of reading in the Platonic dialogues, which begin to help us answer how they may have been read in the Academy (like a rhapsode, I will argue). I propose to look at evidence from within the dialogues that evoke what Plato may have been doing while teaching in the Academy. I want to read certain scenes with "Plato the teacher" in mind; and to see his dialogues as metatheatrical/metaphilosophical, that is, as Plato possibly commenting on his own methods.[16]

The depiction of reading in the dialogues

Let us reconstruct the possible performance of dialogues in the Academy by examining three instances of reading out loud in the Platonic dialogues themselves.

[1] There is only one instance in the Platonic corpus where a *Socratic* dialogue is read: *Theaetetus*. At the beginning, in the frame narrative of the dialogue (142a-3c), a slave reads aloud a book written by Euclides to both Euclides and Terpsion. The action depicted in the inner frame of the *Theaetetus* is a dialogue that records the conversation that Socrates had with Theaetetus, Theodorus, and another young man also named Socrates who was present as well. Euclides mentions that he cannot recall the conversation from memory, the one that Socrates had with Theaetetus, but that he made some notes immediately after getting home, and then later at his leisure he wrote the things he remembered. We can only assume that because the action does not shift back to the frame narrative—as it

---

[16] For metatheatre in Plato, see Mateo Duque, "Metatheatre," *The Bloomsbury Handbook of Plato*, eds. Gerald A. Press, and Mateo Duque, (London: Bloomsbury, 2022), 287-9.

does, for instance, when Phaedo is recounting Socrates's last day (*Phaedo* 88c-89b; 102a; 118a)—that the slave reads the book all the way through uninterrupted.[17]

From this instance of reading, I reconstruct what a recitation of a Platonic dialogue may have been like in the Academy. Someone, perhaps even a slave as depicted here in the *Theaetetus*, reads the dialogue aloud for a group of listeners. The speaker could also have been Plato or one of his students. It would have to have been someone "musical" enough to read and perform the scriptio continua writing, and to imitate different characters in such a way as to make them distinct from one another when speaking. Imagine what a speaker would have to do for a dialogue like *Symposium,* which calls for twelve different speaking roles: Apollodorus; Glaucon; Appollodorus's friend; Socrates; Aristodemus; Agathon; Pausanius; Aristophanes; a slave; Eryximachus; Phaedrus; Diotima; and Alcibiades.

[2] Another instance of reading in the dialogues is at *Parmenides* 127c-d when Zeno reads his book to a group gathered in Athens. Socrates was quite a young man at the time (around eighteen years old). Socrates and others had been wanting and waiting to hear Zeno's writings, which Zeno had brought to Athens for the first time. Zeno himself read them aloud. After Socrates had heard Zeno read his book, he asked Zeno to read the first hypothesis of the first argument again. After Zeno rereads it, Socrates initiates him in a series of back-and-forth questions (dialectic) about his ideas. From this instance of reading, I reconstruct that a student may have been allowed to ask the reader to go back and re-read portions of the text, as well as to interrogate those earlier portions of the dialogue.

[3] A final instance of reading a text in a dialogue is the *Phaedrus* (there's an irony here because Socrates criticizes writing in the

---

[17] For framing in the Platonic dialogues, see: David Halperin, "Plato and the Erotics of Narrativity," *Oxford Studies in Ancient Philosophy* supplement (1992): 93-129; Anne-Marie Schultz, *Plato's Socrates on Socrates Socratic Self-Disclosure and the Public Practice of Philosophy* (Lanham, MD: Lexington, 2020); Margalit Finkelberg, "Frame and Frame-Breaking in Plato's Dialogues," *Framing the Dialogues: How to Read Openings and Closures in Plato,* eds. Eleni Kaklamanou, Maria Pavlou, and Antonis Tsakmakis (Leiden: Brill, 2021), 27-39.

Phaedrus). Although Phaedrus would love to try to recite Lysias's speech by heart to Socrates, Socrates notices that Phaedrus has a scroll of the actual speech hidden in his cloak. Socrates orders Phaedrus to read Lysias's speech of a non-lover trying to persuade a youth to be with him (230e-4c). Afterward, Socrates gives two of his own speeches; a first speech as the non-lover (237a-41d) and then another speech, the palinode, as the lover (244a-57b). After these speeches, Socrates and Phaedrus turn to discussing rhetoric. This post-performance discussion is *crucial*. The speeches are not allowed to stand on their own and just go uninterrogated.[18] Socrates and Phaedrus examine many topics and themes that are raised by the three previous speeches.

We also see here that Socrates asks Phaedrus to re-read a work that had just been read aloud, like we saw Socrates ask Zeno to re-read the first hypothesis of his work. Socrates twice asks Phaedrus to re-read the beginning of Lysias's speech (262d; 263e-4a). Socrates is making a point about the disordered nature of Lysias's speech and wants Phaedrus to see it. And yet there is a performative contradiction here; if writing continues "to signify [*sēmainei*] just that very same thing forever" (as Socrates claims at *Phaedrus* 275d-e; cf. *Protagoras* 329a), then there would be no use, no purpose, to Socrates having Phaedrus re-read the beginning of Lysias's speech—it would just say

---

[18] While I cannot argue that this was a Socratic innovation, I can contend that Socrates's practice of "debriefing" after speeches was in deep tension with rhetorical practices in other spheres. For example, in Athenian courtrooms cross-examination of witnesses was not allowed, and there was no collective deliberation after the hearing of both sides in a legal case (see Kelly Lambert, "Law and Courts in Ancient Athens: A Brief Overview" at https://kosmossociety.chs.harvard.edu/law-and-courts-in-ancient-athens-a-brief-overview/). Socrates's cross-examination of Meletus in *Apology* 24c-28a seems to be an exceptional circumstance. In addition, in a sympotic setting it was considered bad form/rude to interrupt a speaker or to go back and question a previous speaker. Again, Socrates in the *Symposium* 199b-201c is an exception to this general rule and is granted a *brief* exchange with the previous speaker, Agathon. However, Phaedrus, the symposiarch, calls out Socrates for his crosstalk in between speeches at 194a-d.

the same thing over and over again forever.[19] And yet Socrates wants Phaedrus to see something new, something different, when re-reading those lines that he had previously missed.[20]

So, to recap, I am hypothesizing that in order to educate, a Platonic dialogue would be read aloud in Plato's academy. Who would do the reading? This might be too difficult to say with any kind of certainty. Some possibilities are: (i) a slave (like in the *Theaetetus*), (ii) a student in the academy (but it is hard to say if this would have been a novice or experienced one); (iii) a teacher in the academy (like Aristotle); or (iv) maybe even Plato himself. The number of speakers is unknown. All of the examples from the Platonic corpus are of one person reading aloud, but there could have been various readers functioning as "actors." The polyvocal suggestion leads to a more theatrical or dramatic performance of the dialogues, whereas a monovocal suggestion to the rhapsodic performance.[21] Following the internal evidence gathered so far, after the reading, a student could: ask to have one of the passages reread (like in the *Parmenides* and the *Phaedrus*); ask a question concerning a passage from the text (like in the *Parmenides*); and, finally, enter into a more far-ranging discussion surrounding issues brought up by the dialogue (like the second half of the *Phaedrus*). There Socrates and Phaedrus look back at the three speeches given in the first half of the dialogue especially with an eye to what is a good art of speaking and writing (*rhetorikē*). In order to argue that Plato's teaching informed his writing and rewriting of the dialogues, and vice versa, that Plato's writing informed his teaching, I will first give evidence that Plato was a reviser.

---

[19] Woodruff and Nehamas's translation of the *Phaedrus* in *Plato: Complete Works*. All quotes from the *Phaedrus* come from this translation.

[20] See Mateo Duque, "(Re)-reading without Writing?: A performative contradiction in Plato's *Phaedrus*" (2021 manuscript).

[21] The single rhapsodic speaker seems to be also mirrored in how the dialogues will have only a single narrator. For more on the role of the narrator in Plato, see Anne-Marie Schultz, *Plato's Socrates as Narrator: A Philosophical Muse* (Lanham: Lexington, 2013).

Plato the Reviser

My third presupposition that Plato's dialogues were shaped by his teaching relies, in part, on the premise that Plato revised his dialogues. For some, this point would not even need to be argued for. It would seem evident that the dialogues, as master literary-philosophical works, evince tremendous care and attention to detail that can only come from careful revision. Moreover, we have some ancient testimony of Plato's habit of revising. Jacob Howland has gathered the ancient evidence for Plato as a consummate reviser; and I am indebted to him for the following quotes.[22] Diogenes Laërtius reports that "Euphorion and Panaetius have said that several revisions of the opening of the *Republic* have been discovered" (3.37).[23] And Dionysius of Halicarnassus writes (*On Literary Composition*, 25):

> Plato, even at the age of eighty, never let off combing and curling [*ktenizōn kai bostruxizōn*] his dialogues and re-plaiting [*anaplekōn*] them in every way. Of course, every scholar is familiar with the stories told about Plato's industry, especially the one about the writing-tablet which they say was found after his death, with the opening words of the *Republic* arranged in various orders ("I went down yesterday to the Piraeus with Glaucon the son of Ariston").[24]

There are also references to revision within the dialogues. In the *Theaetetus*, Euclides discusses how he rewrote his dialogue:

> I have not made Socrates relate the conversation as he related it to me, but I represent him as speaking directly to the persons with whom he said he had this conversation […] I

---

[22] Jacob Howland, "Re-Reading Plato: The Problem of Platonic Chronology," *Phoenix*, 45. 3 (1991): 189-214. Another scholar who has collected the evidence for Plato's revision is Holger Thesleff, *Platonic Patterns* (Las Vegas: Parmenides, 2009), 230-5.

[23] This and other quotes from *Diogenes Laërtius* are of Pamela Mensch's translation of *Lives of the Eminent Philosophers*, ed. James Miller, (Oxford: Oxford University Press, 2018).

[24] Dionysius of Halicarnassus: *Critical Essays, Volume I. Ancient Orators. Lysias. Isocrates. Isaeus. Demosthenes. Thucydides,* translated by Stephen Usher, (Cambridge, Mass: Harvard University Press, 1974).

wanted, in the written version, to avoid the bother of having the bits of narrative in between the speeches—I mean, when Socrates, whenever he mentions his own part in the discussion, says 'And I maintained' or 'I said,' or, of the person answering, 'He agreed' or 'He would not admit this.' That is why I have made him talk directly to them and have left out these formulae. (143b-c)[25]

Here, we have Euclides admitting that he has revised his written account in order to take out what we would call 'dialogue tags' and have a more direct narrative, almost like a theatrical or dramatic play. This is something that Plato himself may have done with the *Theaetetus*.[26] One last example is from the *Laws*. It is also interesting, and telling, that within this work that was reported *not* to have been revised, there are at least two mentions of the revision of writing.[27] A necessary corollary of my third presupposition, that Plato integrated particular pedagogical moments from his teaching in the Academy into his dialogues, is that Plato revised his dialogues. I have given external historical evidence as well as internal evidence for this.

Plato's teaching likely informed his dialogues

I want to provide some evidence for my third presupposition, namely, that Plato's teaching could have informed the dialogues. I think Plato wrote and re-wrote his dialogues as he was teaching in the Academy, and as he was teaching earlier versions or drafts of the dialogues. As a result, I think Plato incorporates selected "teachable moments" from his teaching in the Academy into the dialogues. It is highly likely that good points brought up by Plato's students in discussions in the academy may have been written into revised versions of dialogues. Some examples of this are the following.

---

[25] M.J. Levett translation from *Plato: Complete Works*.

[26] Thesleff, *Platonic Patterns*, 207.

[27] For evidence that the *Laws* were not revised, most scholars point to *D.L.* (3.37): "Some say that Philip of Opus transcribed Plato's *Laws*, which were preserved on wax tablets." However, see Howland, "Re-reading Plato," 201-2 for skepticism. For revision of writing in the *Laws* see: "*to d'epaneromenon epirruthmizein*" (802b5-6) and "*epanorthōtea*" (809b5).

(3a) There is an intervention by Clitophon and Polemarchus during Socrates's and Thrasymachus's discussion about justice that talks about rulers in the precise sense at *Republic* 1.340a-1c. The dispute arises from whether or not Thrasymachus thinks that the rulers, the stronger, can make mistakes. That is, are the strong, the rulers, able to enact a law that might actually be detrimental to them, that is, to their *dis*advantage? In order to deal with this problem, Thrasymachus has to stipulate that he means "rulers in the precise sense [*kata ton akribē logon*]," which turn out to be infallible rulers, who cannot make mistakes, and can only pass laws to their advantage. I can imagine students in the Academy reading an earlier draft of the *Republic* and discussing Thrasymachus's proposal that "justice is the advantage of the stronger," and someone questions whether or not rulers might ever err and pass a law that might *not* be to their advantage. Plato likes this line of questioning that complicates Thrasymachus's theory and re-writes it into a revised version.

(3b) At *Euthydemus* 290b-1a, Clinias or someone else distinguishes generalship from the statesman's art, and mathematical arts from the dialecticians' art. The point comes from an earlier analogy, just as hunters and fishermen must hand over their prey to cooks, likewise geometers, astronomers, and calculators must hand over their discoveries, their "prey," to dialecticians. Later the idea is extended to the division of labor between generals and statesmen. The point arises from an exchange supposedly between Clinias and Socrates. However, Crito, who is listening to Socrates recount the conversation of the confrontation with the sophist-brothers Euthydemus and Dionysodorus, does not believe Socrates when he says that it was Clinias who made this point, but thinks it was someone else. Perhaps one of Plato's students used this metaphor in a discussion about the difference between dialectics and mathematics and he liked it so much that he wrote it into the *Euthydemus*. Plato marks off the point in an unusual way (by alluding to some "superior being"), almost seeming to highlight that something special is happening, as if he is quoting.[28]

---

[28] At 290e-1a, the story that Socrates has been telling Crito gets interrupted and Plato returns to the frame with which the dialogue began:

Mateo Duque

In addition to brilliant contributions, Plato could also have included the mistakes or missteps of his students in the dialogues.

(3c) For example, Young Socrates makes a mistake at *Statesman* 262a-3a of not dividing a category (animals) properly (that is, in half). Instead of dividing a class in half, Young Socrates tries to separate off a smaller part, rational animals, from a much larger part, non-rational animals. The *Xenos* compares this kind of lopsided division to dividing up humanity into Greek and Barbarian (262c-d). One of Plato's students may have tried to divide up the kind "animal" into the rational and the non-rational, or the kind "human" into Greek and Barbarian, and Plato catches this mistake, but he still likes it as a pedagogical tool for teaching listeners of his dialogue what not to do, so he writes it into the *Statesman*.

(3d) At *Statesman* 268a-c Young Socrates has problems again, this time in comparing the ruler to a shepherd. As the *Xenos* explains later, the mistake was in having the wrong model, the ruler as shepherd (274e-9a). Instead of excising an entire part of the dialogue because it was operating with a wrong paradigm, Plato instead keeps it as an important lesson for the reader/listener of the dialogue of how one can

---

CRITO: What do you mean, Socrates? Did that boy utter all this?

SOCRATES: You're not convinced of it, Crito?

CRITO: Good heavens no! Because, in my opinion, if he spoke like that, he needs no education, either from Euthydemus or anyone else.

SOCRATES: Dear me, then perhaps after all it was Ctesippus who said this, and I am getting absent-minded.

CRITO: Not my idea of Ctesippus!

SOCRATES: But I'm sure of one thing at least, that it was neither Euthydemus nor Dionysodorus who said it. Do you suppose, my good Crito, that some superior being was there and uttered these things—because I am positive I heard them.

CRITO: Yes, by heaven, Socrates, I certainly think it was some superior being, very much so.

(Quoted from Rosamond Kent Sprague's translation of *Euthydemus* in *Plato: Complete Works*.) Another, less exciting, suggestion is that Plato could instead be referencing himself. Perhaps, all the flourish surrounding this point is just meant to allude to Plato's own discussion of the difference between mathematics and dialectics in the *Republic* 7.

go wrong. We can envision that Plato was perhaps inspired by overhearing one or several of his students using the "bad analogy" of a political ruler as a shepherd, but he thought the error fruitful enough to depict in the *Statesman*.

The structure of dialogues as indication of Platonic pedagogy

I turn from looking at specific passages to the overall structure of some dialogues to consider how (4) Plato's pedagogy in the Academy may be represented in the architectonics of some of the dialogues. One can imagine Plato having had "guest lecturers" that came to speak at the Academy and his students were allowed to ask questions in much the same way that in the dialogues Socrates interrogates traveling sophists (Gorgias, Protagoras, Hippias). Perhaps students or heads of other schools would have come to the academy to present their work and to answer questions on their views. We know of one impromptu "guest lecture" from Diogenes the Cynic via Diogenes Laertius (6.40):

> When Plato had defined man as an animal with two legs and no feathers, and was applauded, Diogenes plucked the feathers from a cock, brought it to Plato's school, and said, 'Here is Plato's man.' (This was why 'having broad nails' was added to the definition).

I love bringing up this (possibly apocryphal) anecdote, which is meant to support the plausible idea that Plato may have had speakers from outside the Academy come and present their views (although in the case with Diogenes the Cynic, he was not invited).

One can also imagine that Plato held "tag-team" philosophical debates. Perhaps he staged two-on-one contests like modern professional wrestling matches. I can see Plato or another instructor at the Academy (such as Aristotle, Speusippus, Xenocrates, or Heraclides of Pontus) holding his own against two alternating bright young students. This kind of two-on-one debate/discussion is similar to the ones represented in the dialogues: Socrates vs. Glaucon/Adeimantus (in the *Republic*); Socrates vs. Cebes/Simmias (in the *Phaedo*); and Socrates vs. Euthydemus/Dionysodorus (in the *Euthydemus*). The very structure of some of the dialogues can also give us insight into how Plato may have taught; I gave the two examples of the guest lecture and the two-on-one tag-team debate.

Plato's broadmindedness, both in and out of the dialogues

An aspect of Plato's pedagogy that is evident both within the dialogues and outside of them is his tolerance for opposing views, or better his "broadmindedness."[29] Plato allowed for diverse viewpoints to flourish within the Academy, often allowing for students to take positions that went against his own teachings. In addition, Plato often represents views that he most likely disagreed with in the dialogues. The most famous examples are: Thrasymachus in the *Republic*; Callicles in the *Gorgias*; Protagoras in the *Protagoras*; and Euthydemus and Dionysodorus in the *Euthydemus*. And within his school,

> general tolerance was one of the chief hallmarks of the Platonic Academy. Eudoxus, Speusippus, and Aristotle, for example, were able to propound teachings in it which were diametrically opposed to those of Plato. Plato expressed objections to these views — on occasion even in his dialogues — but it never occurred to him to ban them.[30]

Plato teaches in two distinct but related ways, first as a writer through the dialogues and second as an educator in the Academy. Plato the writer teaches his listeners through the staging of pedagogical philosophical theater. The internal audience (the interlocutors of the dialogue) often do not learn or recognize this lesson properly, but this heightens Plato's provocation to his external audience, the listeners. Plato does not write in his own voice, but speaks through the characters in the dialogues. Plato the writer hides himself. It is likely that Plato the teacher used a form of mimetic pedagogy in teaching and discussing the dialogues in the Academy. Instead of giving "tyrannical" authoritative readings or interpretations, Plato would call on his students to come up with their own views. Thus, Plato did not hand down his direct teachings. Plato the teacher hides himself.

Plato's openness to various (and often conflicting or competing) views (both within his Academy and in his dialogues) is a kind of

---

[29] For the suggestion that "Plato" (which, regardless is a nickname) means "broadmindedness," see David M. Robinson, "The Greek View of Life," *The Mississippi Quarterly* 7. 1 (1953): 34.

[30] Baltes, "Plato's School, the Academy," 9.

pedagogy on its own. By not trying to merely reproduce partisans of his own views but instead by encouraging others to develop their own ideas (even if they go counter to his own), Plato teaches the proper generosity of spirit that a good educator should have in spurring his students' own projects.

Socratic *mimēsis* as a hint to Platonic pedagogy

Students in the Academy after reading a dialogue may have been called upon to think and play with dialogues. The student would be called to consider things from within the fiction of the dialogue and also from a perspective outside of it. On the one hand, they would have been asked to role-play with the characters in the dialogues. That is, to think from within a character's role in a dialogue *as that character*—to inhabit, take up, and defend that character's point of view. Plato might have asked a student who was role-playing as a character to explain the character's psychology, and the reasons for the character's actions. At *Phaedrus* 271d, Socrates explains how philosophical rhetoric is about directing the soul, and the rhetorician must know: the kinds of soul, their number, of what sort each person is, how individuals have a certain sort and others another sort. Plato is describing the psychology and art of typology, i.e., the ability to understand an individual as a type or as a kind of person. This is the sort of investigation at work in playing with the dialogues.

On the other hand, students may have been asked to take a position outside of the dialogue and to criticize or defend a character's words or actions. That is, the students would be invited to essentially "re-write" extemporaneously a character's lines, to make them say what the students believe to be correct. Plato often has Socrates engage in textual criticism that ignores the possible intentions of the author/poet or even dismisses the motivations of the characters. Plato represents Socrates as instead interested in what is true, in what is really the case.[31] Both of these ways of playing with the dialogues I call pedagogical *mimēsis*.

---

[31] *Charmides* 161c: "the question at issue is not who said it, but whether what he said is true or not." Another example is Socrates's tendentious strong "re-interpretation" of Simonides's poem in the *Protagoras* 339a-347a. Additionally, Socrates will often quote Homer out of context.

These two ways of playing with dialogues are exemplified by phenomena in the dialogues I have called Socratic *mimēsis*. These are moments in the dialogues when Socrates role-plays, when he speaks in another voice as a different persona. In the *Crito*, beginning at 50a, Socrates takes on the role of "the Laws" and performs a play within a play. Socrates acts out a drama between "the Laws" and another character, "Socrates." In performing this vignette, Socrates engages his interlocutor, Crito, in a completely different way than he did previously. Earlier, Socrates was trying to rationally convince Crito that the just and right thing for him to do is to stay in jail rather than escape. At various moments in this scene Socrates draws Crito in by asking him questions about how the character "Socrates" should reply to "the Laws" (50b, 51c, 52d, 54d). Another example is in the *Theaetetus* when Socrates and Theaetetus have been criticizing Protagoras and his *homo mensura* view. At 166a2-168c2, however, Socrates in the so-called "Defense of Protagoras," impersonates Protagoras and defends Protagoras and his views *as* Protagoras. By imitating Protagoras, Socrates is also finally able to bring a reluctant Theodorus into the discussion and get Theodorus to criticize his former deceased teacher.[32]

I want to provide some examples of what this playing with the dialogues may have looked like. I can imagine Plato calling upon one of his students to take on the role of Crito in the *Crito,* and asking the student "why did Crito act and speak the way that he did?" "Why was Crito so silent during the speech of "the Laws"?" Then, Plato may have asked, "How would you have convinced Socrates to escape from jail, if you were called upon for the job?" After reading the *Republic*, Plato may have asked the students, "If you were in Adeimantus's or Glaucon's place, what objections would you have to 'the *Kallipolis*'?" Or another question: "If you were Thrasymachus how would you defend the view that 'justice is the advantage of the stronger" in Book 1 of the *Republic*?" After reading the *Parmenides*, he could ask, "If you were not as tractable as Aristotle in the *Parmenides*, what interventions

---

[32] For a defense and more elaborate treatment of the points in this paragraph, see Mateo Duque, *In and out of Character: Socratic Mimēsis*, PhD diss., The Graduate Center of The City University of New York (CUNY), 2020.

would you make and what questions would you have of Parmenides's deductions in the second half?"

While somewhat speculative, my ideas about Plato's pedagogical performances are not merely theoretical proposals, they are *also* backed up by practice. In Spring 2021 I taught a graduate level philosophy course on Plato called "Platonic and Socratic *Mimēsis*" where I divided the class into groups that would meet outside of the classroom. Each group read aloud various passages from the dialogues (that they had selected) and then they would discuss them before meeting for a discussion with the class as a whole, including me, the instructor. One of the exercises I encouraged was this imaginative role-playing of characters within the dialogues. I asked students to imagine themselves *as* the characters in the dialogue in order to better understand and explore a character's psychology and motivations.[33] I also asked them to imagine themselves in the role of some of the characters that they read. What would they have said or done in the place of those characters?

Conclusion

I used passages from the dialogues (supplemented with some ancient testimonia) to answer the question, "How did Plato teach in the Academy?" My reconstruction of Plato's pedagogy in the Academy is that there was a single person who read the dialogue aloud like a rhapsode (this is in contrast to the dramatic theatrical hypothesis, in which several speakers function as actors in the performance of a dialogue); and after this, students were allowed to ask that portions of the text to be re-read, to ask a question about the text, and were encouraged to enter into a broader conversation about the topic and themes brought out by the text. This later pedagogical method of interrogating and investigating a dialogue is of more importance than the mere reading of a dialogue. I made complimentary claims: that Plato's experiences teaching were woven into some of the dialogues, and that Plato's pedagogy reflects some of the ways that he taught in the Academy. I proposed that excellent points made by students may have been written into revised forms of the dialogue. And not only good points, but also mistakes in reasoning

---

[33] And as Heather Reid reminded me, I am surely not the first to do this.

may have been added into the dialogues. I suggested that the way certain dialogues are organized with "guest lecturers" and "tag-team" philosophical debates reflect Plato's pedagogy in the Academy. Plato's broadmindedness, his openness to various and opposing viewpoints, is also evident from both outside and inside of the dialogue. Lastly, drawing on the idea of Socratic *mimēsis*, I gave a plausible curriculum for how Plato may have used the dialogues to teach them: he had his students "play" with them. Plato may have asked his students to enter into the roles of the characters in the dialogues to better understand them and the type of person they represent. Plato may have also asked students to take over from the position of the character in the dialogue and to suggest a better, truer account of things than what the characters said or did.

Veronika Konrádová[1]
Poetic Enthusiasm and the Perils of Ethical *Mimēsis*[2]

With his writing, Plato enters a field where tradition clashes with the new tendencies of his time. Tradition, broadly conceived, here means above all the culture and educational schemes guided by the oral poetic tradition. Plato actively intervenes in this encounter, offering alternative ways of conducting human life and elaborating a competing system of education. This essay focuses on Plato's polemical interaction with the poetic tradition, targeting its methods and educational impact. The starting point for my survey will be the *Ion*, a dialogue that introduces the theme of philosophical polemics with poetry, and raises the problem of poetic competence. I will then move on to consider some significant aspects of Plato's polemic with poetry as they are discussed in the *Republic*, particularly in Books III and X. My aim is to reveal the educational motives behind Plato's criticism of poetry.

The analysis proceeds in the following steps. First, it illustrates the cultural context of *paideia* in Plato's time, emphasizing the practical-educational dimension of the Homeric epics and their socializing role, implemented through the pervasive phenomenon of poetic performance. Next, I analyze two interrelated aspects of Plato's criticism of the contemporary practice of transmitting and inculcating cultural values. First, I discuss Plato's objections to methods of poetic communication based on inspiration, addressing his elaboration of the concept of *enthusiasm* and its implications for understanding the

---

[1] Veronika Konrádová is Assistant Professor in the Department of Philosophy and Humanities at the Jan Evangelista Purkyně University in Ústí nad Labem, Czech Republic. Her research focuses on ancient philosophy, in particular Plato and Aristotle. Along with political and ethical issues, her research interests cover communication strategies in philosophy, the relationship between philosophy and poetry, and Greek epic and drama. She is the author of the book *Cosmogonic and Theogonic Motifs in Hesiod's Theogony* (2008, in Czech), co-editor of a monograph *For Friends, All is Shared* (2016) and author of articles and chapters on various aspects of Plato's and Aristotle's thought in national and international journals.
[2] This article was supported by research funds for the Faculty of Arts of the Jan Evangelista Purkyně University in Ústí nad Labem for 2022.

educational role of the poet. In terms of poetic competence and expertise, these implications challenge poetry's status as a *technē* (art) and emphasize its non-rational and non-cognitive nature. Second, I elaborate on Plato's questioning of ethical *mimēsis*, examining it from both the ontological-epistemic and psychological-educational perspectives. The latter proves to be particularly relevant because the mimetic character of poetry— considered in its educational aspect—is related to the intense emotional charge of poetic performance, inviting the audience to identify with the experienced narrative and the attitudes of the agents. At the same time, the complementarity of the two perspectives shows the complexity of *mimēsis* set in a robust ontological *and* psychological scheme.

By addressing these issues, this essay aims to reveal Plato's competitive ambition in the sphere of socio-political and educational impact. Plato acknowledges the charm of poetry and its social influence, but at the same time he recognizes the risks of shaping lifestyle patterns according to traditional poetic models. Against this, he raises a new model of education built on intellectual grounding. The interpretation presented here does not assume a straightforward and simple rejection of poetry on Plato's part, and rather admits his multifaceted interaction with the poetic tradition. In this light, it maps the opening phase of this interaction—the phase in which Plato acutely detects the deficiencies of poetry both in terms of the poet's mental state and in terms of the nature of his final product and its effect on the audience.

Homeric *paideia*

Turning to the cultural context of Plato's criticism, let me begin by discussing traditional Homeric *paideia*, especially the three crucial characteristics typical of its communication: orality, performativity, and emotionality. In Plato's time, the mental and speech practices typical of orality overlapped with the newly established domain of literacy and texts. It is important to note what this means for the transmission of knowledge. Whereas in scriptural culture, knowledge is preserved in institutions such as libraries and transmitted through the medium of written production, in oral culture, knowledge survives in the minds of individuals and is communicated through the practice of poetic recitation. Therefore, the Homeric poems had not merely an aesthetic and entertainment function but, more importantly, a practical-pedagogical role, i.e., they enabled people to meaningfully navigate the world and society.[3] As a mediator of knowledge, the poet constructs a shared understanding of the world, of its order, and presents it to his listeners. He depicts the gods as powers embodying the diverse aspects of reality. At the same time, the poet makes visible the complex web of relationships that shape this world: he portrays the interrelationships of the gods, the relationships between the divine and human spheres, and the interrelationships of human beings.[4]

In terms of our topic, it is crucial to note that poetic authority dominated the realm of popular morality, which was shaped by exhorting and praising correct behavior. Poetic speech conveyed the proper modes of behavior by portraying role models and visualizing model situations. When Ion, in the eponymous Platonic dialogue, infers the correct social conduct from knowing "what it's fitting for a man or a woman to say—or for a slave or a freeman, or for a follower or a leader" (*Ion* 540b),[5] he attests the still essentially oral framing of moral education. As Kevin Robb puts it: "To know what to do in an oral society is primarily to know what attitude to take in speech, or what to say to whom and how to say it, and with what degree of deference or abuse."[6]

However, the acquisition of correct behavior in oral cultures does not occur through private intellectual insight. On the contrary, it is linked to the collective experience of public performances. These were firmly integrated into the social life of the Greeks, as they had a fixed place during festivals and a prominent role in public life.[7] So, poetic

---

[3] Eric Havelock, *Preface to Plato* (Cambridge, MA: Harvard University Press, 1963), 61-86, famously speaks about a "tribal encyclopedia" when characterizing the scope and impact of Homeric epic poetry.

[4] Note that this subject's scope corresponds to the specification of the content of a poetical work in the opening passage of the *Ion* (531c-d).

[5] Quotations from Plato are based on John M. Cooper, and J. M. Hutchinson, eds., *Plato. Complete Works* (Indianapolis: Hackett, 1997).

[6] Kevin Robb, *Literacy and Paideia in Ancient Greek* (Oxford: Oxford University Press, 1994), 165.

[7] It is also attested by the dramaturgical setting of the *Ion*, when Ion proudly mentions his victory at the festival of Asclepius in Epidaurus.

work was presented and consumed in the public sphere—in the communicative space opened up between the poet, or rhapsode, and his audience. The format of public presentation also determines the characteristic modes of communication: poetic performances typically employ narrative, visualization, temporal structure, and dramatic plot. Thus, poetry does not proclaim abstract rules but confronts the audience with the particular fates of the heroes, from which good or bad behavior patterns can be deduced.

Moreover, this moral education does not occur in a neutral setting. When a Homeric rhapsode performs a piece of poetry, he evokes a vivid and intensely emotional experience for listeners, who sympathize with the hero whose story is recited. Poetic performance, therefore, excludes a disinterested approach for both the performer and the audience. The text of Plato's *Ion* testifies to such intense emotionality and involvement. Says Ion, "when *I* tell a sad story, my eyes are full of tears; and when I tell a story that's frightening or awful, my hair stands on end with fear and my heart jumps." (*Ion* 535c). Socrates adds: "And you know that you have the same effects on most of your spectators too, don't you?" Ion replies, "I know very well that we do. I look down at them every time from up on the rostrum, and they're crying and looking terrified, and as the stories are told they are filled with amazement" (*Ion* 535d-e).

This emotional imprint is a powerful psychological device for the appropriation of the set of cultural norms mediated by Homeric epic. The observation of Carlotta Capuccino on the effects of poetry aptly foreshadows the issues to which I will return in the following exposition: "poetry persuades by enchanting, i.e., by affecting emotions: through the voice of a rhapsode who declaims his verses, Homer, praiser of heroes, persuades the audience to emulate their actions by involving them, i.e. by giving them pleasure through the expressive means of poetry."[8]

Poetic enthusiasm

Let us elaborate on the mediating role of poetry introduced in the *Ion*. Faced with the appeal of Homeric poetry, Plato in this short

---

[8] Carlotta Capuccino, "Plato's *Ion* and the Ethic of Praise," in *Plato and the Poets*, eds. P. Destrée, and F. Herrmann (Leiden: Brill, 2011), 79.

dialogue reveals the mechanisms of poetry by elaborating a theory of poetic inspiration derived from the Muses. The complex structure of agents involved in the process of poetic creation and consumption is captured by Plato with the familiar image of divine magnetism. Using the analogy of a magnet with the power to draw one iron ring to itself, and through that another and another, Plato's Socrates suggests that a poet is similarly attracted to the Muse—literally "magnetized" by her power which pervades him as well as the other participants in the poetic performance:

> ...it's a divine power that moves you, as a 'magnetic' stone moves iron rings [...] This stone not only pulls those rings, if they're iron, it also puts power *in* the rings, so that they in turn can do just what the stone does—pull other rings—so that there's sometimes a very long chain of iron pieces and rings hanging from one another. And the power in all of them depends on this stone. In the same way, the Muse makes some people inspired herself, and then through those who are inspired a chain of other enthusiasts is suspended. You know, none of the epic poets, if they're good, are masters of their subject; they are inspired, possessed, and that is how they utter all those beautiful poems. (*Ion* 533d-e)

Next, employing a *principle of transitivity* of inspiration, as Carlotta Capuccino puts it,[9] the *Ion* expands the conglomerate of affected

---

[9] In her concise formulation, Capuccino, "Plato's *Ion*," 63–92 summarizes the structure of poetic agency as: "the chain of divine inspiration, which in the way it works resembles a magnetic chain of iron rings attracted by a magnet: just as the magnet itself in virtue of its strength attracts the first ring of the chain and the second one through it, and so on until the last one, so the Muse attracts to herself the inspired poet, e.g., Homer, who in turn attracts the rhapsode, who finally captures the audience, closing the chain of enthusiasm. I.e., every ring turns out to exercise the Muse's power, on her own concession, by a *principle of transitivity* of inspiration borrowed from that of magnetism: the poet is attracted by the Muse and attracts the rhapsode, the rhapsode is attracted by the poet and attracts the audience" (533d ff.).

persons. It completes the image of the chain by linking the poet, performer, and audience, all captivated by the Muse's power:

> And you know that this spectator is the last of the rings, don't you—the ones that I said take their power from each other by virtue of the Heraclean stone [the magnet]? The middle ring is you, the rhapsode or actor, and the first one is the poet himself. The god pulls people's souls through all these wherever he wants, looping the power down from one to another. And just as if it hung from that stone, there's an enormous chain of choral dancers and dance teachers and assistant teachers hanging off to the sides of the rings that are suspended from the Muse. One poet is attached to one Muse, another to another (we say he is 'possessed,' [*katechetai*] and that's near enough, for he is *held* [*echetai*]). From these first rings, from the poets, *they* are attached in their turn and inspired, some from one poet, some from another: some from Orpheus, some from Musaeus, and many are possessed and held from Homer. You are one of *them*, Ion, and you are possessed from Homer. (*Ion* 535e-536b)

The vocabulary of these passages continuously evokes the idea of possession. That is, the state of not being master of oneself but being "possessed" by the Muse. Here we come to the heart of Plato's idea of poetic enthusiasm. It says the poet himself is not the creator of the piece of poetry but a mere mediator, i.e., that it is not man but a god who speaks through the work of art. This idea is repeatedly illustrated by verbal phrases suggesting that the poet literally has "a god within him" (*entheos*, 533e, 534b) and is further enhanced by analogy to the divine obsession of Corybantes and Bacchantes.[10] Like Bacchic frenzy, poetic creativity is driven by a divine presence that puts the person in a state of enthusiasm (*enthusiazein*, 533e).

Invoking the Bacchantes, moreover, intensifies associations that are constitutive of the Platonic model of poetic creation. One possible link between poetic and Bacchic activity is the motif of honey, evoked by the Euripidean image of Bacchantes drawing honey and milk from

---

[10] See also Plato, *Laws* 719c, 790d–e.

rivers (534a-b), and recalling the "honey-sweet" speech with which poets are endowed by divine favor. This is an echo of a Hesiodic motif,[11] which, in the Platonic context, may intensify the moment of ease and relief brought by poetry. Another link between poetry and Dionysus may be suggested by another delicacy, namely wine: the poetic exaltation evoked by drinking is a standard motif adopted in the classical period,[12] and Plato may be alluding to it in relation to the manic nature of the poetry he wishes to emphasize.

Inspired poetry

Let us dwell for a while on the theme of inspiration, which Plato follows up on here. It will become clearer in what respect Plato reinterprets this theme and how this reinterpretation serves his purposes in challenging the status of poets educators. The central concepts for this survey will be the notion of inspiration and its relation to truth and knowledge.

In the pre-Platonic period, poetic self-understanding was determined by the privileged relationship between poet and god, with the divine Muse bestowing the gift of song on her protégé and praiser. This model of poetic inspiration is attested by Hesiod, who portrays himself as a servant of the Muses, chosen to proclaim a divine message (*Theogony* 29-34). Similarly, the Homeric singers Phemius and Demodocus have acquired a permanent gift of eloquence which guarantees the quality of their songs. Through this gift, the poet is able to utter verses and reveal realities otherwise unavailable to mortals. Furthermore, because he speaks from the favor of the deity, he conveys a message that is not his own. In this sense, the poet mediates between the divine and the human world—we might even say that without his mediating role, divine speech would be incomprehensible to men.

---

[11] Hesiod, *Theogony* 81-84, 96-97.

[12] See Cratinus, fr. 199 and Epicharmus, fr. 132. For evidence in Greek lyrics, see Alcaeus, fr. 70; Simonides, fr. 647, 602; Archilochus, fr. 120. For an overview of the metapoetical motifs of honey, water, and wine, including a distinction between types of inspiration among "water-drinkers" and "wine-drinkers," see Hugo H. Koning, *Hesiod: The Other Poet. Ancient Reception of a Cultural Icon* (Leiden: Brill, 2010), 337-38.

It is important to note that this archaic model of inspiration—conceived as a form of divine empowerment—is closely connected to the claim of truthfulness.[13] This connection is explicit in the work of Pindar, who combines the Hesiodic notion of dependence on the Muses with a prophetic status: "give me an oracle, Muse, and I shall be your prophet" (fr. 150). Pindar claims his words to be true precisely because of his close relationship with the Muses, who guarantee his truthful communication of *kleos*.

Shifts in the understanding of inspiration occur in classical and Hellenistic times when the link between inspiration and the content of the message (i.e., its truthfulness) is weakened, and a new accent is placed on the creative process itself. This type of inspiration is reconceived as a momentary outburst of artistic creativity. In its modified form—closer to our modern understanding—inspiration refers mainly to the "non-technical" and airy nature of poetic or artistic creation. Accordingly, the inspired poet or artist is regarded as an author *par excellence*, a creative personality who composes his or her work with the maximum amount of spontaneity and originality. Such creative excitement characterizes the true poet, as is illustrated by the contrast between the poet guided with typical ease by the poetic imagination, and the clumsy writer who toils with rhyme.[14]

Substantial modifications, contributing to the complexity of the ancient interpretation of inspiration, come in the classical period with Plato, who reinterprets inspiration as enthusiastic rapture,[15] and

---

[13] Hesiodic Muses famously proclaim their ability to tell the truth as well as falsehood resembling the truth (*Theog.* 27-28). However, their status as divinities ensures all-encompassing knowledge of things that are, were, and will be. The disturbing reference to deceptiveness may refer rather to the conflicting nature of reality, which the Muse's song captures in its diversity precisely by combining truth and truth-like communication.

[14] On non-technical aspects of poetry, see Ch. Janaway, "Craft and Fineness in Plato's *Ion*," *Oxford Studies in Ancient Philosophy* 10 (1992): 1-23.

[15] Plato is not the first to reflect on the enthusiastic nature of poetic creativity and its dependence on a divine source. Among the philosophical authors for whom we have evidence, it was Democritus that attributed a divine nature to poetic creation (Dio Chrysostom, *Orationes* XXXVI,1 = *DK* 68 B

complements the whole pattern with the notion of poetic madness.[16] As we have seen, the exponent of this mode of poetry for Plato is Homer, in whose person Plato also seeks to discredit the educational ambitions of oral culture.

Before turning to this point, let us note that Plato's path in this direction had already been prepared. In particular, there are subtle metapoetic differences in the assessment of the two great epic poets. From the 5th century BCE, Homer and Hesiod represented opposing styles, with Homer exemplifying the sweet and magnificent distortion of reality, while Hesiod represented the toilsome pursuit of truth with the help of the Muses. That is, unlike the didactic poetry of Hesiod, conceived as a revelatory experience devoted to the transfer of knowledge without pathetic overtones, Homeric poetry gradually became regarded as untruthful, misleading, and focused primarily on an appeal to emotions.[17]

---

21). However, deciding how much Plato was actually influenced by Democritus is too speculative given the lack of extant Democritean material. In the texts of later authors such as Cicero and Clement of Alexandria, Democritus and Plato are jointly cited as proponents of the theory of poetic enthusiasm (Clement of Alexandria, *Stromateis* VI,168 = *DK* 68 A 18). From these brief accounts, however, it is difficult to deduce much about the possible correspondence between Democritus's and Plato's conceptions of enthusiasm. It is at least clear that both agree on the divine nature of poetic inspiration. However, while for Democritus this underlines the high value of poetry, Plato's view of poetry's value is considerably more complicated due to his emphasis on the manic nature of enthusiasm and his emphasis on contrasting *mania* and *technē*. Both seem to be Plato's elaboration of the issue. See Hugo H. Koning, *Hesiod*, 326; Eugène N. Tigerstedt, *Plato's Idea of Poetical Inspiration* (Helsinki: Societas Scientiarum Fennica, 1969), 72-79; Glenn. W. Most, "The Poetics of Early Greek Philosophy," in *The Cambridge Companion to Early Greek Philosophy*, edited by Anthony A. Long (Cambridge: Cambridge University Press, 1999), 332-62; and Suzanne Stern-Gillet, "On (Mis)interpreting Plato's *Ion*," *Phronesis* 49 (2004): 169-201.

[16] The notion of poetic frenzy, *furor poeticus*, further extends this vision.

[17] Hugo Koning, whose analysis I follow here, concludes: "By focusing on Homer, Plato's attack on the poets' status as a teacher and on their

It is evident how Plato builds on these presumptions. He partly adopts the older model of divine inspiration but modifies it with new patterns which serve his critical intentions. In particular, he introduces the idea of divine madness. From this perspective, divine possession and enthusiasm imply the absence of reason.[18] This is emphasized in discussion with Ion, and we are repeatedly reminded that poets are in a state of losing their minds (*úk emfrones*) at 534a and 534b-c:

> ...a poet is an airy thing, winged and holy, and he is not able to make poetry until he becomes inspired and goes out of his mind and his intellect is no longer in him. As long as a human being has his intellect in his possession he will always lack the power to make poetry or sing prophecy. Therefore because it's not by mastery that they make poems or say many lovely things about their subjects (as you do about Homer)—but because it's by a divine gift—each poet is able to compose beautifully only that for which the Muse has aroused him.

The nature of poetic activity is thus characterized by two interrelated moments: the presence of divine power *and* the absence of reason.[19] Characterizing the nature of poetic utterance as a "divine gift" (*theia moira*, 534c) instead of expertise in the sense of rational and cognitive control of one's subject matter has radical implications for the evaluation of the overall status of poetry and its educational relevance. The decisive role plays on the assumption that the poet is not the master of his message and that he acts as a mediator or translator through whom—without his own contribution—divine speech resonates in the human world.[20]

---

reputation for truth and knowledge thus rested on previous views of the poet and built further on them" (*Hesiod*, 328).

[18] Thus, similar to the older tradition, the divine intervention empowering the poet to his performance can be compensated for by another loss – in Homer loses his sight, and the poets in Plato lose their reason.

[19] For similar characteristic of prophecy see Plato, *Timaeus* 71d-72b; *Meno*, 99c-d; *Apology* 22a-c.

[20] Among modern authors, Friedrich Nietzsche subscribes to this mediatory dimension of inspired poetry. See G. Colli, and M. Montinari, eds., *Der*

Poetry without *technē*

The consequence of Plato's conception of poetic enthusiasm is a transformed understanding of poetic competence and expertise. This transformation consists, above all, in challenging the status of poetry as *technē*.[21] More precisely, the question raised in the *Ion* concerns the professional competence of the rhapsode. Within the dialogue, the existence of a rhapsodic *technē* is at first assumed. Ion's expertise, declared at the opening, is shaken when confronted with general claims about the nature of *technē*. According to the dialogue, characteristic features of *technē* are as follows: (1) *technē* is a cognitive activity based on rules and principles that apply throughout its field (532c-e), (2) these principles provide criteria for judging the final product (531d-e), (3) each *technē* has its own subject matter (537c-d), and (4) the expert is able to give an account of this subject matter (542a). This standard model fails to apply to rhapsodic activity.

The first part of the dialogue (531b-533c) problematizes the first two of these points. Here, Ion persistently claims to be a connoisseur and admirer only of Homer, not other poets. This is clarified immediately afterwards by the enthusiastic concept that explains this specialization: each Muse has her poet who is always a specialist in one genre, and each poet, in turn, attracts his admirers. Ion's preoccupation with Homer is therefore not a matter of expertise and lacks the required characteristics of *technē kai epistēmē*—for, in that case, it would have to embrace poetry as a whole—rather, it is the result of the aforementioned enthusiastic influence.

The final section (537a-542a) similarly fails in the search for the proper object of the rhapsodic *technē*. Again, the strategy leading to this failure stems from the inability to fulfil the requirement that rhapsodic activity as a *technē* is able to operate with the general principles applicable to the entire field of poetry. The inevitable consequence is that the discussion fails to locate rhapsodic activity as

---

Fall Wagner. Götzen- Dämmerung. Der Antichrist. Ecce homo. Dionysos-Dithyramben. Nietzsche contra Wagner (München: De Gruyter), 339-340.

[21] This section of the paper partly follows the argument in Veronika Konrádová, "Enthúsiasmos a techné," in *Platónův dialog* Ión, eds. Aleš Havlíček, Jakub Jinek (Praha: OIKOYMENH, 2014), 61-76.

an activity informed by relevant knowledge of its subject matter like other *technai*. The paralyzing effect is produced by Socrates's assumption that the ability of critical judgment stands on the same level as the ability to actually perform those skills depicted in Homer. In fact, the whole strategy of questioning here makes it impossible to arrive at a satisfactory assessment of the subject of rhapsody. Ion correctly suspects that he must defend a holistic claim, and he repeatedly attempts to follow that path despite logical counter-argumentation that he cannot resist. His conviction is thus intuitive, and Ion fails to verbalize or defend it. By exposing this inability, Plato's systematic attack on Ion's competence is accomplished. As a result, poetic recitation is denied a rational and cognitive nature and is revealed as an essentially irrational and emotional matter.

Let us consider the motivation for this attack. Questioning the status of rhapsody as a *technē* can have a twofold disruptive effect: since the poet, like the rhapsode, is part of the same structure of divine influence that denies them both rational and cognitive capacities, it can be assumed that the poet's activity is also devoid of the nature of a *technē*. This, of course, implies a radical shake-up in the traditional educational status of poetry, whose nature, on the contrary, included the interplay between its inspired and technical character; the older tradition assumed that poetic production was carried not only by musical inspiration but precisely by expertise in the sense of a *technē*.[22] Poets were therefore *sophoi* in a double sense: as those who had privileged access to knowledge and as those who had properly mastered their craft. *Sophos* is a term that originally referred to handicrafts. It denotes a capacity in which the theoretical aspect is not separated from the practical one. At the same time, this ability does not preclude divine intervention. On the contrary, craftsmanship is a divine gift standing under divine patronage. By attacking the qualities traditionally associated with poetic creativity, Plato undermines the position of poets as recognized social authorities and educators.

---

[22] It is not easy to determine the exact nature of the Muse's contribution to the creative process. In any case, the dual emphasis on its inspired and technical character of production implies that for the older tradition, poetry is a product not only of divine favor but also of learning.

118

Questioning the professional qualities of the rhapsode aims in the same direction. If the rhapsode proves incompetent to exhibit the qualities of a piece of poetry, the poet himself is discredited through this questioning, or rather the entire cultural tradition in which poetic activity is embedded. This attack simultaneously discredits traditional poetry in its pretension to be an educational authority.

Let us recall the pedagogical mechanisms of Homeric poetry. Homer's verses praise persons and deeds, thereby encouraging imitation so that, in the broadest sense, they present cultural patterns of behavior for various types of everyday situations. In this sense, the rhapsode, whose mission is to manifest precisely this poetic agency, is a mediator of a particular lifestyle determined authoritatively through the persuasive and enchanting effect of poetic words. Plato's criticism aims against this educational practice, determined by the normative status of poetic utterances, and built on the presentation of paradigms, praise, and imitation. If this education consists of passive and unreflective acceptance of the norms for one's own life, it ignores the claim of responsible conduct in accordance with knowledge and reason. Therefore, an effective means of attacking a lifestyle based on poetic authority may be to underscore the irrational nature of the poetic activity and to discredit the professional competence of the exponent of that authority.

Ethical *mimēsis*

I will now briefly sketch how the features of the poetic agency revealed so far relate to the theory of *mimēsis*.[23] Admittedly, there are major differences between the two Platonic theories of poetry, the enthusiastic and the mimetic, and it may therefore be debatable to what extent they are mutually coherent. I suggest, however, that these divergences can be overcome and the common core of both theories can be pointed out. Each approaches the issue of poetry from a different angle, but both converge in their focus on the non-cognitive nature of poetry and its inability to provide a true discourse. While the enthusiastic model targets the deficient cognitive state of the poet, the

---

[23] Various aspects of *mimēsis* are discussed in Destrée and Herrmann, eds., *Plato and the Poets* (Leiden: Brill, 2011).

Veronika Konrádová

mimetic model considers the consequences of poetic ignorance. Let us now take a closer look at the concept of *mimēsis*.

In *Republic*, the discussion of *mimēsis* is set in a ring composition connecting Books III and X. Book III describes one aspect of the poet's mimetic activity—*mimēsis* in narrative *lexis*—and introduces *mimēsis* as appearance-making. The appearance is evoked by the poet hiding himself and giving the impression that it is not he who is speaking but directly one of his characters. This effect is produced not only by lexical means but also by gestures and body posture, as well as by the use of different types of rhythm. On the one hand, the poet or performer thus likens himself to the character being rendered, and in this sense, *mimēsis* can be understood as impersonation: "to make oneself like someone else in voice or appearance is to imitate the person one makes oneself like" (*Republic* 393c). On the other hand, however, he also provokes a particular impression in the audience, and in this sense, *mimēsis* can be broadly understood as appearance-making. To put it more precisely, *mimēsis* is not simply a matter of acting like another person but it primarily involves making an audience believe that they see or hear events on the stage *as if* they are really happening with the agents depicted. In short, Book III grasps *mimēsis* by contrast with making something truthful or real and it seems justified to regard the later discussion in Book X as an amplification of this earlier sketch.

Book X builds on the earlier discussion of the nature and methods of poetry and elaborates it into a more complex account. It defines poetry, and art in general, as mimetic in the sense that it produces images or appearances: "it touches only a small part of each thing and a part that is itself only an image" (*Republic* 598b). A more refined account of the nature of poetic imitation then reads: "all poetic imitators, beginning with Homer, imitate images of virtue and all the other things they write about and have no grasp of the truth" (*Republic* 600e). This formulation incisively captures a deeper level of the problem of poetic *mimēsis*: unlike visual art, poetic image-making depicts not only how people look but, more importantly, how they act and what motivates their decisions. This is where the scheme of imitation becomes multiplied: the problem is not only a faulty or

120

insufficient imitation of external appearance but especially a distorted imitation of intrinsic motivation and virtuous conduct.

Here, *mimēsis* is set in a robust ontological-epistemological framework, and in this context, it is conceived as an imitation of a real being. Plato here outlines a threefold ontological scheme distinguishing the idea, the real thing, and its image, and a corresponding epistemological scale assigning an appropriate degree of epistemological certainty to the degree of ontological reality of the object in question. The deficit of artistic/poetic representation then lies in the fact that it can only present an "imitation of an imitation." Although the risks of poetic influence can be seen precisely in the fact that the encounter with mere imitations makes access to truth impossible, another aspect of *mimēsis* is also crucial. Let us call it ethical *mimēsis*. For the most serious charge against imitation lies in its ethical-psychological impact:

> When even the best of us hear Homer or some other tragedian imitating one of the heroes sorrowing and making a long lamenting speech or singing and beating his breast, you know that we *enjoy it*, give ourselves up to following it, sympathize with the hero, take his sufferings seriously, and praise as a good poet the one who affects us most in this way. (*Republic* 605c-d; my emphasis)

The essence of poetry, then, is captured both by the psychosomatic imitation of poetic action *and* by the intense emotional involvement and delight in watching poetic performances. In the atmosphere of poetic appearance-making, the spectator wants to be deceived, is ready to consent to the common illusion for the moment and accepts that the man with the mask on the stage is a mythical hero. Plato sees a particular risk in the fact that the imitative aspect of poetry concerns not only the performers themselves but also transfers to the audience and has a formative effect on them. The dangers of alternately imitating a variety of characters have already been pointed out in Book III when it stressed the need for cautious imitation of ethically appropriate behavior, precisely in view of the fact that imitation develops a taste for the things imitated. Nothing less than psychological formation is at stake: "Or haven't you noticed that imitations practiced from youth become part of nature and settle into habits of gesture, voice, and thought?" (*Republic* 395d).

Moreover, the adoption of conduct and thought patterns is strongly supported by emotional involvement and pleasure: from enjoying imitation, we come to enjoy really acting and speaking that way (*Republic* 395c). It is not just that one loses rational control over oneself during poetic performances, indulges in strong emotions, and allows oneself to be "deceived" by the story being told. The greatest danger is that one adopts the states fostered by the pleasure one experiences and then habitually acts on them. Socrates says:

> I suppose that only a few are able to figure out that enjoyment of other people's sufferings is necessarily transferred to our own and that the pitying part [of the soul], if it is nourished and strengthened on the sufferings of others, won't be easily held in check when we ourselves suffer. (*Republic* 606b)

The reminder of the structured nature of the soul brings into focus the psychology developed in Books IV and IX.[24] Against this background, it appears that the consequence of experiencing pleasure in poetic performances is twofold. First, indulging in pleasure results in the excessive growth of one part of the soul, the element that is elsewhere labeled as the "appetitive" part: "Hence, we called it the appetitive part (*epithumētikon*), because of the intensity of its appetites for food, drink, sex, and all the things associated with them" (*Republic* 580e). This part of the soul tends toward unlimited growth and uncontrolled dominance, fostering an intemperate and unbridled lifestyle devoted to the unlimited gratification of pleasure. With regard to the internal dynamics of the soul, Lear aptly comments: "The psychological effect of this style of poet which he emphasizes is [...], rather, intemperance, a determination to do as one pleases; an inability or unwillingness to resist the pleasures that conflict with the work one

---

[24] In Book IX, the tripartite structure of the soul is described thus: "The first, we say, is the part with which a person learns, and the second the part with which he gets angry. As for the third, we had no one special name for it, since it's multiform, so we named it after the biggest and strongest thing in it. Hence, we called it the appetitive part." (*Republic* 580d-e).

ought to do. Throughout the *Republic* Plato associates the variety typical of Homeric epic and tragedy with unbridled appetitiveness."[25]

Second, the pleasure of imitating many different characters leads to confusion and disintegration of human nature. One cannot coherently imitate multifarious and conflicting characters. Lear, again, grasps the problem: "the person who imitates a multitude of characters has fun acting in a variety of ways which, taken as a whole, are inconsistent."[26] The inconsistency and ambivalence of poetic paradigms thus make it impossible to follow them coherently.

Finally, taking these criticisms together, it becomes clear that the two aspects of *mimēsis* (the ethical-psychological and the ontological-epistemic) are not separate but closely interrelated. The poet cannot capture the true essence of things, the Form, so he only depicts the multiplicity of its phenomenal manifestations in individual deeds. Nevertheless, these are not only manifold but also mutually contradictory. Therefore, what the poet represents cannot be a reliable guide to a consistent life. In response to these findings, the space is opened for Plato's competing scheme of education and psychological formation based on philosophical examination.

Conclusion

To summarize briefly, we can say that Plato engages in a large-scale project targeting the educational impact of traditional Homeric poetry. He reveals—not only in the *Ion* but throughout his corpus—the corruptive psychological influence of the prevailing practices of poetic education. In particular, he attacks the exaggerated emotionality and, ultimately, the excessive desire for pleasure that poetry evokes. However, Plato does not entirely reject poetry. He interacts tirelessly with poetry throughout his writing, and many parts of his dialogues—on both small and large scales—demonstrate that the reception and transformation of poetic motifs and intertextuality with poetic works is a formative part of his own work. Given this multiformity, we can say that Plato does not simply condemn the

---

[25] Gabriel R. Lear, "*Mimesis* and Psychological Change in *Republic* III," in *Plato and the Poets*, eds. Pierre Destrée, and Fritz-Gregor Herrmann (Leiden: Brill 2011), 214.

[26] Lear, "Mimesis and Psychological Change," 215.

educational use of poetry, but revises it. To put it more precisely, he pursues its philosophical transformation. In this respect, he redefines the relationship between rationality and irrationality, re-evaluating *mania*,[27] and admitting persuasive speech guided by philosophical insight.[28] Finally, pursuing his competitive ambition to have a socio-political and educational impact, he introduces a new hero of philosophical education, Socrates, who offers alternative ways of cultivating the soul.

If we may end somewhat hypothetically, a tentative suggestion might be that a subtle network of allusions implies this role of Socrates in the very opening passage of the *Ion*, which mentions the festival of Asclepius, the god of healing. Yet in the context of other dialogues, Socrates himself is presented as the "physician of the soul." In this medical context, Socrates's therapeutic action replaces the activity of the Homeric rhapsode, who comes from the festival of Asclepius, but without the proper knowledge.

---

[27] See esp. the re-evaluation of divine madness in the *Phaedrus* (244a-245a).

[28] In the political context, see the *Laws*, which highlights legislation as "the best tragedy" (817 b-c).

Michał Bizoń[1]
Plato's Frenmity with the Poets over *Paideia*

But you should also know that hymns to the gods and eulogies to
good people are the only poetry we can admit into our city.

εἰδέναι δὲ ὅτι ὅσον μόνον ὕμνους θεοῖς καὶ ἐγκώμια τοῖς
ἀγαθοῖς ποιήσεως παραδεκτέον εἰς πόλιν.[2]

It is not surprising that this notorious claim lends itself as a prime example of Plato's alleged authoritarian mindset. That it came at the end of a long and meandering reasoning is of no importance. Plato is taken to have sinned against liberal sentiment—both modern and ancient—and transgressed against one of its most hallowed norms: to say what one wants. In what follows, I argue that far from advocating censorship in a sense incompatible with liberalism, Plato's quarrel with the poets is grounded in a view of education—and the written and spoken word in general—that is indeed radically more liberal than many a modern liberal would be willing to accept.

On the face of it, this seems like a fool's errand. Plato's exclusion of the poets is one of the most offensive aspects of his imagined city-state.[3] Throughout the dialogues, one is hard-pressed to see Plato's

---

[1] Michał Bizoń is adjunct lecturer in Philosophy at Jagiellonian University in Kraków, Poland. He has published translations with commentary in Polish of Plato's *Hippias Minor*, Antiphon's *Tetralogies* and sophistic fragments (*Truth* and *Concord*), and is currently translating and commenting on Demosthenes's *Against Leptines*. He works on Greek philosophy of the Archaic and Classical periods, with a focus on Plato's and Aristotle's moral psychology.

[2] *Republic* 10.607a3-5. The Greek text of the *Republic* is taken from Platonis *Rempublicam*, ed. S.R. Slings (Oxford: Oxford University Press, 2003). Translations of the *Republic* are from Plato, *Republic*, trans. G.M.A. Grube, rev. C.D.C. Reeve (Indianapolis: Hackett, 1992). For the *Phaedrus*, I use Harvey Yunis's edition (Cambridge: Cambridge University Press, 2011). All other Greek texts are from *Platonis opera*, ed. Ioannes Burnet (Oxford: Oxford University Press, 1901-1907).

[3] *Republic* 2.369a6-8. The point is salient in light of *Republic* 5.473a1-2: "Is it possible to do anything in practice the same as in theory? Or is it in the

treatment of the poets as less than irreverent. Time and again, he pounces on the great Hellenic literati in a distinctively surreptitious and predatory manner. It often begins with a ruse, the interlocutor lured into the trap by a thinly veiled profession of admiration. Having put the speaker and his poet off guard, Plato proceeds to tear apart the content of the work. Before the victim knows it, he is exploited for ulterior ends, philosophical or otherwise, and his *oeuvre* is left in ruins, picked apart, reinterpreted, subverted. Thus, in the *Protagoras*, the message of Simonides's poem is placed on its head and used to support Socrates's argument that virtue cannot be taught. In the *Hippias Minor*, some of the more memorable passages of the *Iliad* and *Odyssey* are twisted in the service of malicious paradoxes that knowledgeable people are the greatest liars and that good men, if any, do wrong willingly. Last but not least, as part of the *Republic's* opening discussion of the central notion of justice, Plato has the great Sophocles make a cameo with the weighty argument that he is impotent (and good riddance).[4]

And yet, Plato cannot help quoting the poets at practically every opportunity—and from memory at that, as appears from his slips and offhand emendations. Even if he made a sport of mocking and distorting the poets, he clearly knew them intimately well and was rather fond of them. If Plato so feared the noxious content of poetic lore, why did he quote it so copiously, not only in *Republic* Books II-III—where such quotations are arguably necessary to make the point clear—but throughout his writings? Was he not unnerved about the influence such views may inflict on his readers? Perhaps Plato did not intend the dialogues to be read—or heard—by children. But then, his criticism of the pernicious influence of poetry is by no means limited to the young. What is more, at least some expressions of admiration

---

nature of practice to grasp truth less well than theory does, even if some people don't think so?" ἆρ᾽ οἷόν τέ τι πραχθῆναι ὡς λέγεται, ἢ φύσιν ἔχει πρᾶξιν λέξεως ἧττον ἀληθείας ἐφάπτεσθαι, κἂν εἰ μή τῳ δοκεῖ; If there is an essential difference between how something is said and how it is done, this sheds doubt on the exact nature of the "expulsion" of the poets. The disparity of word and deed reappears in the criticism of writing from the *Phaedrus*, discussed below.

[4] *Protagoras* 339a-342a; *Hippias Minor* passim; *Republic* 1.329b-c.

for the poets, i.e., for Sappho, Ibycus, and Anacreon as masters of things erotic in the *Phaedrus*, don't bear any obvious marks of irony.[5] So how do we reconcile the simultaneous malicious caricatures and banishment from the Kallipolis with such professions of admiration? What is with this "frenmity"?

Trying to make sense of Plato's "age-old quarrel" with the poets,[6] it may be natural to focus on reasons that might be called ethical. The key notion here is truth, which trumps any personal admiration of poetry. Says Socrates in the *Republic*:

> I'll tell you, even though the love and respect I've had for Homer since I was a child make me hesitate to speak, for he seems to have been the first teacher and leader of all these fine tragedians. All the same, no one is to be honored or valued more than the truth. So, as I say, it must be told.[7]

---

[5] *Phaedrus* 235c2-4; contrast *Republic* 3.398ab.

[6] See: E.S. Belfiore, "Plato's Greatest Accusation against Poetry," *Canadian Journal of Philosophy* 9 (1983): 39-62; T.V.F. Brogan, "Representation and Mimesis," in *The New Princeton Encyclopedia of Poetry and Poetics*, eds. Alex Preminger and T.V.F. Brogan (Princeton, NJ: Princeton University Press, 1993), 1307-44; Julius A. Elias, *Plato's Defence of Poetry* (Albany: State University of New York Press, 1984); G.R.F. Ferrari, "Plato and Poetry," in *The Cambridge History of Literary Criticism* vol. I, ed. G.A. Kennedy (Cambridge: Cambridge University Press, 1989), 92–148; Hans Georg Gadamer, "Plato and the Poets," in *Dialogue and Dialectic: Eight Hermeneutical Studies on Plato*, tr. P.C. Smith (New Haven: Yale University Press, 1989), 39–72; Jessica Moss, "What is Imitative Poetry and Why is it Bad?" in *The Cambridge Companion to Plato's* Republic, ed. G.R.F. Ferrari (Cambridge: Cambridge University Press, 2007), 415–44; Cathrine Osborne, "The Repudiation of Representation in Plato's *Republic* and its Repercussions," *Proceedings of the Cambridge Philological Society*, 33 (1987): 53–73; Morriss Henry Partee, "Plato's Banishment of Poetry," *Journal of Aesthetics and Art Criticism*, 29.2 (1970): 209–22; J.O. Urmson, "Plato and the Poets," reprinted in *Plato's Republic: Critical Essays*, ed. Richard Kraut, (Lanham, MD: Rowman and Littlefield, 1997), 223–34; Laszlo Versenyi, 1970–71, "The Quarrel Between Philosophy and Poetry," *Philosophical Forum*, 2 (1970-71): 200–12.

[7] Plato, *Republic* 10.595b9-c4.

Poetry however, as Socrates argues, creates appearances that are at a third remove from the truth:

> Then, we must also consider tragedy and its leader, Homer. The reason is this: We hear some people say that poets know all crafts, all human affairs concerned with virtue and vice, and all about the gods as well. They say that if a good poet produces fine poetry, he must have knowledge of the things he writes about, or else he wouldn't be able to produce it at all. Hence, we have to look to see whether those who tell us this have encountered these imitators and have been so deceived by them that they don't realize that their works are at the third remove from that which is and are easily produced without knowledge of the truth (since they are only images, not things that are), or whether there is something in what these people say, and good poets really do have knowledge of the things most people think they write so well about.

> οὐκοῦν, ἦν δ᾽ ἐγώ, μετὰ τοῦτο ἐπισκεπτέον τήν τε τραγῳδίαν καὶ τὸν ἡγεμόνα αὐτῆς Ὅμηρον, ἐπειδή τινων ἀκούομεν ὅτι οὗτοι πάσας μὲν τέχνας ἐπίστανται, πάντα δὲ τὰ ἀνθρώπεια τὰ πρὸς ἀρετὴν καὶ κακίαν, καὶ τά γε θεῖα: ἀνάγκη γὰρ τὸν ἀγαθὸν ποιητήν, εἰ μέλλει περὶ ὧν ἂν ποιῇ καλῶς ποιήσειν, εἰδότα ἄρα ποιεῖν, ἢ μὴ οἷόν τε εἶναι ποιεῖν. δεῖ δὴ ἐπισκέψασθαι πότερον μιμηταῖς τούτοις οὗτοι ἐντυχόντες ἐξηπάτηνται καὶ τὰ ἔργα αὐτῶν ὁρῶντες οὐκ αἰσθάνονται τριττὰ ἀπέχοντα τοῦ ὄντος καὶ ῥᾴδια ποιεῖν μὴ εἰδότι τὴν ἀλήθειαν—φαντάσματα γὰρ ἀλλ᾽ οὐκ ὄντα ποιοῦσιν—ἤ τι καὶ λέγουσιν καὶ τῷ ὄντι οἱ ἀγαθοὶ ποιηταὶ ἴσασιν περὶ ὧν δοκοῦσιν τοῖς πολλοῖς εὖ λέγειν.[8]

---

[8] *Republic* 10.598e4-599a5. Cf. *Republic* 10.599d2-600b3: "Homer, if you're not third from the truth about virtue, the sort of craftsman of images that we defined an imitator to be, but if you're even second and capable of knowing what ways of life make people better in private or in public, then tell us which cities are better governed because of you [...]. Then, if there's nothing of a public nature, are we told that, when Homer was

The argument may go that poets have a deleterious influence on young people by way of their false depiction of gods and heroes. On this view it is the pernicious *content* of poetry that Plato wished to ban from the Kallipolis. According to another argument the problem may reside rather in the *form* of poetry rather than its content. It may be argued that mimetic art inculcates irrational desires and deters young and impressionable souls from the guidance of reason. Whether true or false, poetry develops unreasonable attitudes by influencing the non-rational faculties of the soul by exposing it to the suggestive influence of literary characters. It is less clear how *mimēsis* accomplishes this, whether by imitation, appearance making, or otherwise.[9]

---

alive, he was a leader in the education of certain people who took pleasure in associating with him in private and that he passed on a Homeric way of life to those who came after him, just as Pythagoras did? Pythagoras is particularly loved for this, and even today his followers are conspicuous for what they call the Pythagorean way of life." Ὦ φίλε Ὅμηρε, εἴπερ μὴ τρίτος ἀπὸ τῆς ἀληθείας εἶ ἀρετῆς πέρι, εἰδώλου δημιουργός, ὃν δὴ μιμητὴν ὡρισάμεθα, ἀλλὰ καὶ δεύτερος, καὶ οἷός τε ἦσθα γιγνώσκειν ποῖα ἐπιτηδεύματα βελτίους ἢ χείρους ἀνθρώπους ποιεῖ ἰδίᾳ καὶ δημοσίᾳ, λέγε ἡμῖν τίς τῶν πόλεων διὰ σὲ βέλτιον ᾤκησεν [...]. Ἀλλὰ δὴ εἰ μὴ δημοσίᾳ, ἰδίᾳ τισὶν ἡγεμὼν παιδείας αὐτὸς ζῶν λέγεται Ὅμηρος γενέσθαι, οἳ ἐκεῖνον ἠγάπων ἐπὶ συνουσίᾳ καὶ τοῖς ὑστέροις ὁδόν τινα παρέδοσαν βίου Ὁμηρικήν, ὥσπερ Πυθαγόρας αὐτός τε διαφερόντως ἐπὶ τούτῳ ἠγαπήθη....

[9] On this distinction see Gabriel R. Lear, "Mimesis and Psychological Change in *Republic* III," in *Plato and the Poets*, eds. Pierre Destrée and Fritz-Gregor Herrmann (Leiden: Brill, 2011), 195-217. For Plato's criticism of the poets in the context of Plato's educational project in the *Republic*, see Miles Burnyeat, "Culture and Society in Plato's *Republic*," *The Tanner Lectures on Human* Values 20 (1999): 215-324; Rachana Kamtekar, "Plato on Education and Art," in *The Oxford Handbook of Plato*, 2nd ed., ed. Gail Fine, (Oxford: Oxford University Press, 2019): 605-627; Alexander Nehamas, "Plato on Imitation and Poetry in *Republic* X," in *Virtues of Authenticity. Essays on Plato and Socrates* (Princeton, NJ: Princeton University Press, 1999): 251-279; David K. O'Connor, "Rewriting the Poets in Plato's Characters," in *The Cambridge Companion to Plato's*

While partaking in the truth, both arguments face obvious problems. Plato does explicitly reject some depictions of gods and heroes on the basis of their falsity, yet he himself advocates the use of falsity in the upbringing of the guardians.[10] Also, he avails himself of distortions of myths and of downright fictions in several of his own dialogues, the Noble Lie and the fairy tale of Atlantis are obvious cases in point. In fact, the entire project of constructing a city in words constitutes a *mythos*.[11] As for the second view, Plato makes clear that not all mimetic art is to be discarded. On the contrary, he deems *mimēsis* and non-cognitive expression to be of paramount educational importance.[12] And, of course, the dialogues as literature are anything if not mimetic.

I argue that Plato's disapproval of the poets is primarily concerned neither with the content nor form of their poetry; although I don't suggest that these factors are not at all important. The primary reason for criticizing the poets is grounded in Plato's idiosyncratic notion of paideutic method, which in turn is related to his critical view on writing. Seen in this light, Plato's criticism of the poets appears to be related to that of the sophists, who in the second half of the 5th c. BCE were developing new educational approaches to rival the traditional ones championed by the poets. Plato's quarrel with the poets as well as the sophists is, on this reading, essentially concerned with the way poetry and writing in general ought to be used for the purpose of *paideia*. How mimetic poetry specifically accomplishes its nefarious work is not the crucial factor determining Plato's approach to poetry in the *Republic* and throughout. Instead, I suggest that the

---

Republic, ed. G.R.F. Ferrari (Cambridge: Cambridge University Press, 2007), 55-90; Amélie Oxenberg Rorty, "Plato's Counsel on Education," *Philosophy* 73.284 (1998): 57-178.

[10] *Republic* 3.389bd.

[11] For the uses of falsity in *paideia*, see *Republic* 2.382cd. For the *Kallipolis* as a *mythos*, see *Republic* 2.376d9-10: "Come, then, and just as if we had the leisure to make up stories, let's describe in theory how to educate our men." ὥσπερ ἐν μύθῳ μυθολογοῦντές τε ἅμα καὶ σχολὴν ἄγοντες λόγῳ παιδεύωμεν τοὺς ἄνδρας.

[12] As demonstrated by the important role of music in *paideia*, see especially *Republic* 3.401d-402a.

primary criterion for the detrimental impact of *mimēsis* is essentially related to the subsumption of mimetic art under the genus of play (*paidia*).[13] Using this criterion, I argue that the key mistake of the poets is to attribute an undue degree of authority to their poetic creations, which do not and cannot rise up to that expectation. Therefore, they ought not to be treated seriously. It is not that poetry is false or mimetic. It is that despite being false and mimetic it is taken seriously as an authority. Moreover, education (*paideia*) ought to be, according to Plato, a form of play (*paidia*). So long as poetry does not see itself as a form of *paidia*, it cannot be used for *paideia*.

Freedom

Let us now take a closer look at the method and approach that Plato puts forward in his discussion of *paideia* in *Republic*. We may note at the outset that the ultimate aim of *paideia* is to bring up and educate the young to be free men and women.[14] Accordingly:

> [O]ur guardians must be kept away from all other crafts so as to be the craftsmen of the city's freedom, and be exclusively that, and do nothing at all except what contributes to it, they must neither do nor imitate anything else.

> εἰ ἄρα τὸν πρῶτον λόγον διασώσομεν, τοὺς φύλακας ἡμῖν τῶν ἄλλων πασῶν δημιουργιῶν ἀφειμένους δεῖν εἶναι δημιουργοὺς ἐλευθερίας τῆς πόλεως πάνυ ἀκριβεῖς καὶ μηδὲν ἄλλο ἐπιτηδεύειν ὅτι μὴ εἰς τοῦτο φέρει, οὐδὲν δὴ δέοι ἂν αὐτοὺς ἄλλο πράττειν οὐδὲ μιμεῖσθαι (...).[15]

The term *eleutheros* has a more robust meaning than the modern "free person." The essential notion is political, wherein the *eleutheros* is opposed to a *doulos* (slave).[16] Ideally, an *eleutheros* is subject to no one. This ideal is equally valid in the aristocratic culture going back to the archaic period and in the context of Athenian democracy, where it

---

[13] Plato, *Sophist* 234a; cf. *Republic* 10.602b.

[14] *Republic* 3.395bc; cf. 9.590e-591a.

[15] *Republic* 3.395bc.

[16] On the Greek notions of *eleutheria* and the *eleutheros*, see Kurt Raaflaub, *The Discovery of Freedom in Ancient Greece: Revised and Updated Edition* (Chicago: University of Chicago Press, 2004).

takes on the further dimension of citizenship as opposed to political disenfranchisement. Plato, however, pushes it even further, going beyond the original political and social sense. Ideally one ought not to be in the thrall of anything, be it poet, sophist, or pleasure. Thus, in the *Protagoras* Socrates argues that one ought not—in fact, cannot—be "overpowered" by non-rational factors such as pleasure, but rather is always guided by one's best knowledge. The discussion of *akrasia* in *Protagoras* is part of a larger reasoning on the teachability of virtue, where the same motif of sovereignty and subservience is also at play. The dialogue opens with the young and impressionable Hippocrates eager to learn from the sophist Protagoras, yet Socrates insists that he take his time and consider for himself what the outcome of such education might be. Once they arrive at the house of Callias, Socrates in imperious fashion presents Hippocrates as one who would like to know what he could learn from the sophist. The ensuing discussion on the teachability of virtue could be seen as a prolonged *elenchus* of Protagoras's expertise that would enable Hippocrates to make an informed and sovereign decision as to his choice of teacher.[17]

A parallel attempt at empowerment seems to be at work in the *Phaedrus*. When the eponymous character meets Socrates, he is under the spell not of a sophist but the orator Lysias. By elaborate deconstruction of the orator's art, Socrates tries to subvert Phaedrus's uncritical admiration of Lysias. Having completed his reinterpretation of the speech to Eros, he revealingly invokes pederastic terminology and casts Phaedrus in the role of Lysias's dominant lover.[18] The pederastic theme is reminiscent of perhaps the most famous case of philosophical empowerment, namely the Alcibiades scene from the *Symposium*.[19] Dissembling affection, Socrates manages to develop in Alcibiades an interest in his own person, ultimately reversing their pederastic relation and switching his role from being the active lover

---

[17] So that he is not overpowered by his desire for the sophist's *synousia*, but makes an *hairesis* on the basis of knowledge, cf. *Protagoras* 356c-357e. See also: Charles L. Griswold Jr., "Relying on Your Own Voice: An Unsettled Rivalry of Moral Ideals in Plato's 'Protagoras'," *The Review of Metaphysics* 53.2 (1999): 283-307.

[18] *Phaedrus* 257b1-6.

[19] *Symposium* 212d-222a.

(*erastēs*) to becoming the chased beloved (*erōmenos*). Alcibiades, in turn, goes from being the object to being the subject of their philosophical romance. Empowerment—both against one's own weaknesses and against subjection to external authority—is a prerequisite to freedom.[20]

According to this robust sense of *eleutheria*, in order to be free— an undisputed ideal for any Hellene—one must not be under the domination of pleasure, orators, sophists, or poets. Implicitly, none of these are worthy enough to determine the course of one's life. And yet there are some that treat poetry with the utmost seriousness, to the point of adopting it as a source of authority in the weightiest matters. It is precisely this worry that constitutes the context of the notorious banishment of the poets in Book X of the *Republic*:

> And so, Glaucon, when you happen to meet those who praise Homer and say that he's the poet who educated Greece, that it's worth taking up his works in order to learn how to manage and educate people, and that one should arrange one's whole life in accordance with his teaching [...].

> οὐκοῦν, εἶπον, ὦ Γλαύκων, ὅταν Ὁμήρου ἐπαινέταις ἐντύχῃς λέγουσιν ὡς τὴν Ἑλλάδα πεπαίδευκεν οὗτος ὁ ποιητὴς καὶ πρὸς διοίκησίν τε καὶ παιδείαν τῶν ἀνθρωπίνων πραγμάτων ἄξιος ἀναλαβόντι μανθάνειν τε καὶ κατὰ τοῦτον τὸν ποιητὴν πάντα τὸν αὑτοῦ βίον κατασκευασάμενον ζῆν [...].[21]

Poetry appears here as much more than just *paideia*, in which case it would be possible to downplay its role by seeing it as an educational prop for the facilitation of learning. Far from it, poetry is here the object of great expectations. Indeed, it may be seen as a comprehensive source of normativity (*panta ton hautou bion kataskeuasmenon zēn*) that has direct practical application (*pros dioikēin* [...] *tōn anthrōpinōn*

---

[20] Cf. Alcibiades's slick self-justification in Thucydides, *The Peloponnesian War* 6.92. that he is fighting against his fatherland only to recover it on his own terms, since it has wronged him in his rights as a citizen.

[21] *Republic* 10.606e1-5

pragmatōn). It is to be a source of value and guidance for ordering and conducting one's whole private and—presumably—public life.

For the guardians, however, the source of normativity ought not be a poet or sophist, but reason (*Republic* 10.607a6-7). As free men and women their ideal is not to be subjected to anybody's authority, and until they manage to attain this optimal state, they should subject themselves to the guidance only of one who is him- or herself led by the good.[22] According to Socrates, however, the poets treat their mimetic creations most seriously:

> As for someone who is not of this sort, the more inferior he is, the more willing he'll be to narrate anything and to consider nothing unworthy of himself. As a result, he'll undertake to imitate seriously and before a large audience all the things we just mentioned (...)

> οὐκοῦν, ἦν δ᾽ ἐγώ, ὁ μὴ τοιοῦτος αὖ, ὅσῳ ἂν φαυλότερος ᾖ, πάντα τε μᾶλλον διηγήσεται καὶ οὐδὲν ἑαυτοῦ ἀνάξιον οἰήσεται εἶναι, ὥστε πάντα ἐπιχειρήσει μιμεῖσθαι σπουδῇ τε καὶ ἐναντίον πολλῶν (...)[23]

That distinction, however, ought to belong solely to the truth, as is argued in the context of the Three Waves in *Republic* V. The squeamish may giggle; yet, women ought to train naked alongside men, since:

> [I]t's foolish to think that anything besides the bad is ridiculous or to try to raise a laugh at the sight of anything besides what's stupid or bad; or (putting it the other way around) it's foolish to take seriously any standard of what is fine other than the good.

---

[22] *Republic* 9.590d3-6. "It is better for everyone to be ruled by divine reason, preferably within himself and his own, otherwise imposed from without, so that as far as possible all will be alike and friends, governed by the same thing." ἀλλ᾽ ὡς ἄμεινον ὂν παντὶ ὑπὸ θείου καὶ φρονίμου ἄρχεσθαι, μάλιστα μὲν οἰκεῖον ἔχοντος ἐν αὑτῷ, εἰ δὲ μή, ἔξωθεν ἐφεστῶτος, ἵνα εἰς δύναμιν πάντες ὅμοιοι ὦμεν καὶ φίλοι, τῷ αὐτῷ κυβερνώμενοι.

[23] *Republic* 3.397a1-4

καὶ τοῦτο ἐνεδείξατο, ὅτι μάταιος ὃς γελοῖον ἄλλο τι ἡγεῖται ἢ τὸ κακόν, καὶ ὁ γελωτοποιεῖν ἐπιχειρῶν πρὸς ἄλλην τινὰ ὄψιν ἀποβλέπων ὡς γελοίου ἢ τὴν τοῦ ἄφρονός τε καὶ κακοῦ, καὶ καλοῦ αὖ σπουδάζει πρὸς ἄλλον τινὰ κοπὸν στησάμενος ἢ τὸν τοῦ ἀγαθοῦ.[24]

There is nothing laughable about the good, at least for the guardians.

It is this attitude—of treating seriously and as authoritative that which doesn't merit it—that is unbecoming and indeed deleterious for the guardians. While the good is not laughable regardless of how far it diverges from the prevalent custom, poetry on the contrary ought to be seen as a less-than-serious enterprise. As Socrates argues, it is only when one takes poetry seriously, as an authoritative source of normativity, that it becomes dangerous for the souls of the young:

> If our young people, Adeimantus, listen to these stories without ridiculing them as not worth hearing, it's hardly likely that they'll consider the things described in them to be unworthy of mere human beings like themselves or that they'll rebuke themselves for doing or saying similar thing.

> εἰ γάρ, ὦ φίλε Ἀδείμαντε, τὰ τοιαῦτα ἡμῖν οἱ νέοι σπουδῇ ἀκούοιεν καὶ μὴ καταγελῷεν ὡς ἀναξίως λεγομένων, σχολῇ ἂν ἑαυτόν γέ τις ἄνθρωπον ὄντα ἀνάξιον ἡγήσαιτο τούτων καὶ ἐπιπλήξειεν, εἰ καὶ ἐπίοι αὐτῷ τι τοιοῦτον ἢ λέγειν ἢ ποιεῖν, ἀλλ᾽ οὐδὲν αἰσχυνόμενος οὐδὲ καρτερῶν πολλοὺς ἐπὶ σμικροῖσιν παθήμασιν θρήνους ἂν ᾄδοι καὶ ὀδυρμούς.[25]

---

[24] *Republic* 5.452d6-e2. That the good is the benchmark of the *kalon* is a frequent theme, cf. *Hippias Maior* 290c-291d. It is closely associated with a functional interpretation of the good according to which to be *agathon* means to perform one's *ergon* well. See *Republic* 1.353ce, 10.601d; Xenophon, *Memorabilia* 3.8.5, 4.6.8-10; Rachel Barney, "Plato on the *kalon* and the good," *Classical Philology* 105 (2010): 363-377.

[25] *Republic* 388d2-7. Cf. also *Republic* 3.395a on the idea that one cannot competently engage in many activities. Presumably, one cannot do so if one wants to be serious about them. Mimetic poetry, however, is by its

The problem for Plato is therefore not simply that the young will be exposed to mimetic art, nor even to false myths. The problem is if they might take them seriously. As Plato says, very young children don't have the cognitive capacity to understand allegory (*Republic* 2.387de). Arguably, however, once the young guardians become capable of critical appreciation of poetry there is no obvious limit to what they can enjoy.[26]

Play

Why, however, is a serious approach to poetry a problem? Why couldn't one be at liberty to choose their preferred source(s) of normativity, even to Plato's displeasure? It is because taking poetry seriously engenders a fundamentally mistaken view of the world, wherein that which is most important in life is founded upon what Plato calls "real falseness" (*hōs alēthōs pseudos, tōi onti pseudos*). Falsity in words may be acceptable and can indeed be used for the benefit of the guardians' *paideia*. Treated as such, poetry – and perhaps *mimēsis* in general – is not inherently reproachable. It is only when one mistakes that which exists only in words for reality itself that one falls into the trap of believing a real falseness (*Republic* 2.382bc). It is only when falseness in words is translated into actions that its deleterious impact is manifested. So long as one is not quite serious about poetry – treating it merely as words – one is safe. Once however one accepts its message in all seriousness – not as pastime or allegory – one will be tempted to follow its authority and model one's actions on it.[27] Therefore, a wrong attitude towards poetry is not merely a cognitive mistake, but one that has substantial practical implications. It is

---

very nature multifarious, with the poet and/or performer imitating or impersonating a variety of personas. Accordingly, it ought not and indeed cannot be practiced seriously.

[26] In *Republic* 2.378a Plato suggests that even the revolting myths of Ouranos and Kronos can be appreciated, so long as it is done in private, a small group, and having performed the appropriate offerings to the gods. See also *Republic* 3.396a4-6; cf. 3.397a, where Plato seems to imply that as long as mimetic poetry is merely recounted and not imitated it may be acceptable.

[27] For poetry as influencing words as opposed to actions, see *Republic* 3.389d; for grounding one's beliefs on poetry *Republic* 3.391bd.

nothing less than to espouse a fundamentally mistaken source of normativity, with potentially catastrophic consequences. It is not only that one will profess false beliefs about family traditions, heroes, and gods. Nor is it merely that one will take pleasure in unseemly things. Drawing one's norms from the wrong source has the consequence that one will order one's whole life in a fundamentally mistaken way, namely, by taking seriously that which ought not to be taken seriously:

> What I assert is this,—that a man ought to be in serious earnest about serious things, and not about trifles; and that the object really worthy of all serious and blessed effort is God, while man is contrived, as we said above, to be a plaything of God, and the best part of him is really just that; and thus I say that every man and woman ought to pass through life in accordance with this character, playing at the noblest of pastimes, being otherwise minded than they now are.

> φημὶ χρῆναι τὸ μὲν σπουδαῖον σπουδάζειν, τὸ δὲ μὴ σπουδαῖον μή, φύσει δὲ εἶναι θεὸν μὲν πάσης μακαρίου σπουδῆς ἄξιον, ἄνθρωπον δέ, ὅπερ εἴπομεν ἔμπροσθεν, θεοῦ τι παίγνιον εἶναι μεμηχανημένον, καὶ ὄντως τοῦτο αὐτοῦ τὸ βέλτιστον γεγονέναι· τούτῳ δὴ δεῖν τῷ τρόπῳ συνεπόμενον καὶ παίζοντα ὅτι καλλίστας παιδιὰς πάντ᾽ ἄνδρα καὶ γυναῖκα οὕτω διαβιῶναι, τοὐναντίον ἢ νῦν διανοηθέντας.[28]

---

[28] *Laws* 7.803c2-8, the speaker is the Athenian Stranger. Cf. *Republic* 10.604b7-c1: "The law says, doesn't it, that it is best to keep as quiet as possible in misfortunes and not get excited about them? First, it isn't clear whether such things will turn out to be good or bad in the end; second, it doesn't make the future any better to take them hard; third, human affairs aren't worth taking very seriously […]." λέγει που ὁ νόμος ὅτι κάλλιστον ὅτι μάλιστα ἡσυχίαν ἄγειν ἐν ταῖς συμφοραῖς καὶ μὴ ἀγανακτεῖν, ὡς οὔτε δήλου ὄντος τοῦ ἀγαθοῦ τε καὶ κακοῦ τῶν τοιούτων, οὔτε εἰς τὸ πρόσθεν οὐδὲν προβαῖνον τῷ χαλεπῶς φέροντι, οὔτε τι τῶν ἀνθρωπίνων ἄξιον ὂν μεγάλης σπουδῆς […]. See also *Republic* 8.558ac, where Plato argues that proper *paideia* requires that one starts engaging in noble play as early as possible. In particular, this involves going beyond concerns of political expediency, thus treating present political concerns as truly serious.

Given that Plato took a final opportunity in the *Laws* to snub Protagoras and his "man as the measure" doctrine by claiming that one's measure ought rather to be god, this emphasis on the divine in human life is not unexpected.[29] However, god as such is not of much use for the guidance of life, for knowing him is tantamount to knowing the good. Neither should we expect any substantial revelation to be forthcoming.[30] The salient point of the passage is rather the distinction according to which only the divine is the domain of the serious, while human life is but play. Accordingly, a playful attitude ought to be adopted not only in the context of education, but indeed throughout one's life.

However, a general appreciation of play could be taken as simply a Greek commonplace. Play permeates Hellenic culture, as evidenced by the Dipylon inscription from the mid 8th century BCE, the oldest sample of the Greek alphabet, which kicks off Greek literary culture with a reference to play.[31] It may also be argued that framing *paideia* as a kind of *paidia* is little more than a pun. For Plato also distinguishes between serious lawful play on the one hand and trifling play on the other—siding of course with the former.[32] It could therefore be argued

---

[29] *Laws* 4.716c4-6.

[30] *Republic* 2.382e8-11: "A god, then, is simple and true in word and deed. He doesn't change himself or deceive others by images, words, or signs, whether in visions or in dreams." κομιδῇ ἄρα ὁ θεὸς ἁπλοῦν καὶ ἀληθὲς ἔν τε ἔργῳ καὶ λόγῳ, καὶ οὔτε αὐτὸς μεθίσταται οὔτε ἄλλους ἐξαπατᾷ, οὔτε κατὰ φαντασίας οὔτε κατὰ λόγους οὔτε κατὰ σημείων πομπάς, οὔθ᾽ ὕπαρ οὐδ᾽ ὄναρ.

[31] The fragmentary hexameter verse is inscribed on a vase dated to the mid. 8th c. BCE and reads: "he who among these dancers now plays most gayly to him [scil. will this vessel go]," (in abridged attic form: ὃς νῦν ὀρχεστῶν πάντων ἀταλότατα παίζει/ τοῦ τόδε κλμιν[...]). For the essential presence of play in Greek culture see Stephen E. Kidd, *Play and Aesthetics in Ancient Greece* (Cambridge: Cambridge University Press, 2019), 49-74; Gawin Ardley, Gavin, "The Role of Play in the Philosophy of Plato," *Philosophy* 42.161 (1967): 226-244.

[32] In *Republic* 7.539bd Plato contrasts dialectic as a serious enterprise to eristic as a foolish child's play. See also *Republic* 4.424d-425a for the distinction between play that is *ennomōteros* (more lawful) and that which is

that all this talk of *paidia* is just paying lip service to a Greek expression and perhaps a tinge of Platonic irony, yet the thought remains in essence no-nonsense authoritarianism.[33]

I argue that the *paideia-paidia* juxtaposition is more than a *modus loquendi*. Framing education and indeed life as a kind of play has substantial consequences. For Plato, play is inherently associated with learning.[34] The suggestion that education ought to start as a form of play is not grounded merely in utilitarian concerns facilitating learning for children with a short attention span. The parallels between play and learning go much deeper—they are two sides of one coin. Play is a natural and spontaneous activity for children, which for them has a fundamentally scientific function.[35] Accordingly, knowledge and technical skill should be inculcated through play, during which the young spontaneously manifest their natural interests and discover the means to develop them.[36]

Writing

This understanding of play as inherently scientific connects with Plato's radical reappraisal of writing as a traditional medium for the transmission of knowledge. His view on writing goes radically against the elevated role of poetry that was attributed to it by the poets and

---

paranomos (unlawful), where only the former will produce "ἐννόμους καὶ σπουδαίους ἄνδρας" (lawful and serious-minded men). The dangers of failing to make this distinction are illustrated by the political implications of musical innovation, *Republic* 4.424bc.

[33] *Republic* 7.536e6-537a1: "Then don't use force to train the children in these subjects; use play instead." Μὴ τοίνυν βίᾳ, εἶπον, ὦ ἄριστε, τοὺς παῖδας ἐν τοῖς μαθήμασιν ἀλλὰ παίζοντας τρέφε. This view follows from treating the young guardians as free (*eleutheron*); a similar idea of learning through play is developed in *Laws* 7.819ad. The notion of teaching through play may have been present in the Pythagorean tradition on which Plato drew. According to Aulus Gellius (*Noctes Atticae* 10.12.8-10), Archytas of Tarentum supposedly experimented with constructing interactive toys, and apparently managed to develop a toy steam-powered pigeon

[34] *Republic* 7.536e6-537a1.

[35] Cf. natural curiosity in at least some children, *Republic* 6.487a-c.

[36] *Laws* 1.643bd.

sophists, as well as the ordinary Greek, and that arguably has been attributed to literature ever since. Plato, however, argues that "No discourse that was written, either in meter or without meter, was ever worthy to be taken very seriously."[37] Accordingly, no written word ought or indeed could be the source of authoritative knowledge. It is not only mimetic art but writing in general that does not deserve serious treatment and ought only to be approached in a playful way (when it presumably could reenter the educational curriculum). In particular, the author, if not present, is deprived of any authority. A playful approach to writing implies that it is always deconstructed and reconstructed in the process of interpretation and remains always at the mercy of the interpreter. For this we must turn to live discussion with a responsive sentient being. So, in the *Hippias Minor* Socrates discards Homer and turns to his interlocutor at hand:

> Let therefore Homer be, since it's not possible to ask him any question as to whatever he had in mind when he composed those verses. You however, since you are taking up the mantle, and are of the same mind as you say with what Homer says, do answer both for yourself and for Homer.

> τὸν μὲν Ὅμηρον τοίνυν ἐάσωμεν, ἐπειδὴ καὶ ἀδύνατον ἐπανερέσθαι τί ποτε νοῶν ταῦτα ἐποίησεν τὰ ἔπη: σὺ δ᾽ ἐπειδὴ φαίνῃ ἀναδεχόμενος τὴν αἰτίαν, καὶ σοὶ συνδοκεῖ ταῦτα ἅπερ φῂς Ὅμηρον λέγειν, ἀπόκριναι κοινῇ ὑπὲρ Ὁμήρου τε καὶ σαυτοῦ.[38]

According to this reappraisal, the written word ought not be a source of authority because it cannot be a source of knowledge.[39] And it cannot be a source of knowledge because it cannot engage in a

---

[37] *Phaedrus* 277d6-8: "No statement, either in meter or no meter, was ever written that would be worthy of serious engagement." οὐδένα πώποτε λόγον ἐν μέτρῳ οὐδ᾽ ἄνευ μέτρου μεγάλης ἄξιον σπουδῆς γραφῆναι. Cf. *Phaedrus* 276de.

[38] *Hippias Minor* 365c8-d4.

[39] See S. Halliwell, "The Subjection of *Mythos* to *Logos*: Plato's Citations of the Poets," *The Classical* Quarterly 50.1 (2000): 4-112.

dialectical exchange with the reader, the fundamental mode of learning that is available only to sentient beings:

> For writing, Phaedrus, has this terrific quality, in truth rather like painting. Since also in the latter case its creations are as if alive, yet if one were to ask it something, they are solemnly quiet. It's the same with things written: perchance you think they say something reasonable. Yet if you ask them something, wanting to understand what is said, they always give away one and the same meaning.

> δεινὸν γάρ που, ὦ Φαῖδρε, τοῦτ᾽ ἔχει γραφή, καὶ ὡς ἀληθῶς ὅμοιον ζωγραφίᾳ. καὶ γὰρ τὰ ἐκείνης ἔκγονα ἕστηκε μὲν ὡς ζῶντα, ἐὰν δ᾽ ἀνέρῃ τι, σεμνῶς πάνυ σιγᾷ. ταὐτὸν δὲ καὶ οἱ λόγοι· δόξαις μὲν ἂν ὥς τι φρονοῦντας αὐτοὺς λέγειν, ἐὰν δέ τι ἔρῃ τῶν λεγομένων βουλόμενος μαθεῖν, ἕν τι σημαίνει μόνον ταὐτὸν ἀεί.[40]

In and of itself writing is completely barren and devoid of meaning:

> Afterwards [the adept of rhetoric] must, having considered this adequately, study in action what [the categories of discourses] are and do, and be able to follow them with sharpened senses. Otherwise, he will gain nothing further from having heard the discourses to which he applied himself.

> δεῖ δὴ ταῦτα ἱκανῶς νοήσαντα, μετὰ ταῦτα θεώμενον αὐτὰ ἐν ταῖς πράξεσιν ὄντα τε καὶ πραττόμενα, ὀξέως τῇ αἰσθήσει δύνασθαι ἐπακολουθεῖν, ἢ μηδὲν εἶναί πω πλέον αὐτῷ ὧν τότε ἤκουεν λόγων συνών.[41]

Writing is always in need of an interpreter. This could be another person, even an orator or poet. The best option, however, would be to become the interpreter oneself. For Plato, this is a tall order ultimately requiring mastery of dialectic—which, as he argues in *Republic* 7.539ab, itself originates in a kind of serious play. Such mastery is an ideal that few are likely to attain. What is available for all is to follow

---

[40] *Phaedrus* 275d4-9.
[41] *Phaedrus* 271d6-e3.

the clear-headed empirical methods of Greek rational medicine. So Socrates says:

> Consider now what concerning the study of nature says Hippocrates and the true discourse. Ought we not thus analyze any nature whatsoever: firstly, determine whether that in which we wish to be master craftsmen and make others such is simple or of many forms. Next, if it be simple, consider what ability it has by its nature, in itself and relatively, for acting upon things, and what ability for being acted upon by something. Again, if it has many forms, count them up, and like in the case of a unity, see for each by what quality does it do what according to its nature and by what quality is it acted upon by something.

> τὸ τοίνυν περὶ φύσεως σκόπει τί ποτε λέγει Ἱπποκράτης τε καὶ ὁ ἀληθὴς λόγος. ἆρ᾽ οὐχ ὧδε δεῖ διανοεῖσθαι περὶ ὁτουοῦν φύσεως: πρῶτον μέν, ἁπλοῦν ἢ πολυειδές ἐστιν οὗ πέρι βουλησόμεθα εἶναι αὐτοὶ τεχνικοὶ καὶ ἄλλον δυνατοὶ ποιεῖν, ἔπειτα δέ, ἂν μὲν ἁπλοῦν ᾖ, σκοπεῖν τὴν δύναμιν αὐτοῦ, τίνα πρὸς τί πέφυκεν εἰς τὸ δρᾶν ἔχον ἢ τίνα εἰς τὸ παθεῖν ὑπὸ τοῦ, ἐὰν δὲ πλείω εἴδη ἔχῃ, ταῦτα ἀριθμησάμενον, ὅπερ ἐφ᾽ ἑνός, τοῦτ᾽ ἰδεῖν ἐφ᾽ ἑκάστου, τῷ τί ποιεῖν αὐτὸ πέφυκεν ἢ τῷ τί παθεῖν ὑπὸ τοῦ;[42]

The proper method for acquiring knowledge is an engagement with the physical world that is systematic, empirical, and—arguably—practice-oriented.[43]

Conclusion

I therefore propose a reading of Plato's theory of education wherein all tradition embalmed in hallowed writing is relegated to a subordinate and less than serious role deprived of any authoritative import. Indeed, it appears that Plato's views on this matter steadily grew more radical throughout his life. One may think that tradition and received morality would be all the more obstinately advocated by

---

[42] *Phaedrus* 270c8-d7.

[43] This is of course not to downplay the crucial role played by theoretical knowledge of the Forms.

cantankerous old men wishing to control the bodies of their frisky daughters, and by sanctimonious old women wishing to control the bodies of their cantankerous men. A progression from a stricter to more liberal outlook might appear particularly inappropriate for Plato given he is more often than not seen as a conservative thinker, championing aristocratic values against the novelty of democracy. And yet there is a conspicuous progression as regards the significance of play from the *Republic* to the *Laws*. Perhaps it is the Greek or the child in him that came around.

That the salutary Hellenic genius may be at work is not implausible if one thinks of a modern self-professed nemesis of Plato, who shared with his opponent more than he himself was willing to admit. A classicist and philosopher, Nietzsche began his career as a rather cringy and slavish admirer of the conceited Wagner, believing him to incarnate at Bayreuth the pinnacle of authoritative poetry of the Second Reich. Yet he promptly became disillusioned, ditched the old codger and went his own Dionysian way of the self-rolling child. It may be this aspiration that Plato expressed in the words he attributes to an aged Egyptian priest in the *Timaeus*, who says to the bewildered Solon:

> 'You Hellenes are always children, and no Hellene is ever an old man.' Hearing this, I asked 'what is it you mean by that?' 'Young of soul you are, all of you. For within them you harbor no ancient opinion of old hearsay nor any teaching greyed by time.'

> λληνες ἀεὶ παῖδές ἐστε, γέρων δὲ Ἕλλην οὐκ ἔστιν.' ἀκούσας οὖν, 'πῶς τί τοῦτο λέγεις;' φάναι.' 'νέοι ἐστέ,' εἰπεῖν, 'τὰς ψυχὰς πάντες: οὐδεμίαν γὰρ ἐν αὐταῖς ἔχετε δι᾽ ἀρχαίαν ἀκοὴν παλαιὰν δόξαν οὐδὲ μάθημα χρόνῳ πολιὸν οὐδέν.'[44]

---

[44] *Timaeus* 22b4-8. A kindred thought may be expressed by Aeschylus in the Agamemnon with which we began this symposium. In the parodos the argive elders, deeply troubled by the situation in the city and the uncertain news, reassure themselves that after all: "The old have ever

And yet there is a deeper, more subversive dimension to Plato's reassessment of the paideutic role of poetry and writing. For a Greek the generic term for the normative is *kalon*. And it is poetry that tells us what the *kalon* is. Yet according to Plato the *kalon* is itself in need of a benchmark. This benchmark is the *agathon*. So far as *agathon* pertains in particular to functionality, its essence is discoverable only through empirical, interactive, and systematic practice. Like poetry, writing may at best serve as a prop, at worst a hindrance to cognitive performance. To discover the *agathon* we must play — seriously — with the world, not least through the highest kind of serious play, dialectic. We thus ought to be the *homines ludentes* that Johann Huizinga argued we evolved to be.[45] Or, to draw from another tradition, be people not of a book — any book — but of the word.

---

youth in them to learn well." ἀεὶ γὰρ ἥβη τοῖς γέρουσιν εὖ μαθεῖν (Aeschylus, *Agamemnon* 584).

[45] Johan Huizinga, *Homo Ludens* (London: Routledge & Keegan Paul, 1949).

Kristian Sheeley[1]
Philosophical Rhetoric as *Paideia* in Plato's *Phaedrus*[2]

Plato's dialogues prompt us to question whether Socrates intends to "persuade" (*peithein*) his interlocutors, and if so, we might wonder what benefit should come from such persuasion. If there is an important distinction between persuasion and education (*paideia*),[3] where the latter emphasizes coming to see the truth for oneself, then we might expect that Socrates's goal is to "teach" his interlocutors as much as possible. However, Plato clearly takes the role of persuasion in human life seriously, as evidenced by his substantial discussions of rhetoric. In addition, Socrates sometimes explicitly states that he is trying to "persuade" his interlocutors[4] to adopt particular views rather than using terms related to teaching or education, and he often displays magnificent rhetorical skill. One of Plato's most well-known discussions of rhetoric is, of course, in the *Phaedrus*, which contains insights about the potential pedagogical benefits of rhetoric, especially in the realm of moral education. This essay argues that the *Phaedrus* presents a pedagogically valuable type of rhetoric not only through its explicit analysis of the "art" (*technē*)

---

[1] Kristian Sheeley is a PhD candidate and instructor in philosophy at the University of Kentucky. He is currently writing a dissertation on ethics in Plato's *Gorgias* and *Phaedrus*. He has published two peer-reviewed articles on ancient philosophy in the interdisciplinary journal *Religions* as well as a book review in *Ancient Philosophy*.

[2] I am indebted to my dissertation committee (Marina McCoy, Valerio Caldesi-Valeri, David Bradshaw, Brandon Look, and especially my chair, Eric Sanday) for the thoughtful and challenging questions that inspired this paper. I thank Colin C. Smith and Peter Moore for their guidance and friendship at the *Fonte Aretusa* conference in Siracusa, where I first presented this paper, and I am grateful to have met the organizers and presenters at this conference, especially Paloma Betini.

[3] In passages such as *Republic* 518b-d, *Timaeus* 51d-e, and *Phaedrus* 277b, Plato clearly distinguishes teaching from persuasion.

[4] For example, see *Gorgias* (493d, 494a, 527c) and *Symposium* 212b, where Socrates says explicitly that he is trying to persuade his interlocutor to accept his views about virtue and love, respectively. Further, Socrates claims in the *Apology* that he has "never been anyone's teacher" (33a).

of rhetoric (257b-274b), but also through Socrates's *performance* of this rhetoric throughout the entire dialogue.[5] The goal of (what I call) Socrates's "philosophical rhetoric" is guiding the soul (*psychagōgia*) toward a virtuous, philosophical way of life,[6] and it uses a combination of speeches, myth, philosophical dialogue, and flirtation to guide Phaedrus's reason and non-rational desires toward this end. While other scholars have provided illuminating discussions of *psychagōgia* and the pedagogical context of the *Phaedrus*,[7] my analysis shows that, over the course of the entire text, Socrates performs philosophical rhetoric with the aim of guiding Phaedrus toward the project of self-cultivation.

---

[5] Werner says it is possible to view rhetoric as "enacted" only in the first half of the *Phaedrus* through the three speeches and "expounded" in the second half. Daniel Werner, "Plato's *Phaedrus* and the Problem of Unity," *Oxford Studies in Ancient Philosophy*, 32 (2007): 99. Similarly, Rowe argues that the palinode is Socrates's only demonstration of the true art of rhetoric. C. J. Rowe, "The Argument and Structure of Plato's *Phaedrus*," *The Cambridge Classical Journal*, 32 (1986): 106-125. I contend that Socrates performs philosophical rhetoric throughout the *Phaedrus*.

[6] As Pierre Hadot shows, philosophy for Plato (and for other ancient philosophers) is "a certain way of life and existential option which demands from the individual a total change lifestyle, a conversion of one's entire being, and ultimately a certain desire to be and live in a certain way." Plato's Socrates exemplifies the philosophical life through his love of wisdom, his moral virtue, and his lifelong search for the truth about the nature of reality. Pierre Hadot, *What is Ancient Philosophy?* (Cambridge: Harvard University Press, 1995), 3.

[7] Harvey Yunis and Jessica Moss highlight the dramatic and pedagogical context of the dialogue—specifically, Socrates's goal of guiding Phaedrus toward a better way of life—in their interpretation of its content and the unity of its various themes. Jessica Moss, "Soul-Leading: The Unity of the *Phaedrus*, Again" *Oxford Studies in Ancient Philosophy*, 43 (2012): 1-23, and Harvey Yunis, *Plato*: Phaedrus (New York, Cambridge University Press, 2011), 6-7. Marina McCoy also rightly emphasizes that Socrates's rhetoric aims to direct Phaedrus's love toward the forms, so that he will continue to try to understand them in the future. Marina McCoy, *Plato on the Rhetoric of Philosophers and Sophists* (New York: Cambridge University Press, 2008), 167.

As the name suggests, philosophical rhetoric is characterized by the love of wisdom, and Socrates uses it for the sake of leading Phaedrus toward a life dedicated to wisdom and the rest of virtue. The pedagogical context of the dialogue strongly influences the topics Socrates chooses to cover, as well as the approach he uses to discuss them. Both rational thinking and non-rational desires influence an individual's decisions about what he will care about most, so Socrates seeks to be as persuasive as possible by appealing to both of these aspects of Phaedrus's soul. Philosophical rhetoric therefore combines argumentation, which is meant to address the listener's reasoning, with rhetorical techniques that aim to affect his non-rational desires. The philosopher uses his knowledge of his speech's subject matter (such as love or virtue) and the dialectical art of rhetoric to "plant" a speech in the soul of his listener (276e-277a), which will (ideally) benefit the listener for the rest of his life. The kind of persuasion that Socrates tries to produce is therefore a crucial step in Phaedrus's ethical and pedagogical development.

In the first section, I explain how the *Phaedrus* depicts philosophical rhetoric both through Socrates's analysis of rhetoric and his exemplary performance of it. The second section examines passages in the *Gorgias* and *Republic* pertaining to virtuous and pedagogical uses of *logos*, since they help to deepen our understanding of the *Phaedrus*'s parallel discussions of these topics.[8] Here I discuss reasons why Socrates's rhetoric apparently succeeds in motivating his interlocutors to pursue virtue in some cases and why it fails to do so in others. In the third section, I discuss in greater detail the potential educational benefits of philosophical rhetoric according to the *Phaedrus*, and I conclude this section by supporting the view that Phaedrus's interest in both philosophy and rhetoric contributes to understanding the unity of the dialogue.[9]

---

[8] I do not claim that Plato has a uniform theory of philosophical rhetoric throughout the dialogues. I am simply using passages from the *Gorgias* and *Republic* to shed light on the philosophical rhetoric in the *Phaedrus*.

[9] Scholars have been particularly interested in how the *Phaedrus'* analysis of rhetoric relates to the wide range of other topics that the dialogue

The nature of philosophical rhetoric according to the *Phaedrus*

While Socrates criticizes the popular use of rhetoric in the *Phaedrus*, he also gives detailed suggestions about how to use it virtuously and philosophically. Importantly, Socrates refers to rhetoric as a *technē* in the *Phaedrus*, even though he argues that it is not in the *Gorgias* (462b-466a). Shortly after the palinode, Socrates defines rhetoric: "Isn't the art [*technē*] of rhetoric, taken as a whole, a certain guiding of souls through words [*psychagōgia tis dia logōn*] not only in the law courts and other places of public assembly, but also in private?" (261a-b).[10]

If rhetoric is a *technē*, one can develop some degree of precision in classifying different rhetorical techniques (265d), the kinds of effects they produce on certain kinds of people, and so on, as Socrates and Phaedrus do later in the dialogue (266c-271c). The concept of "guiding"[11] or leading is also important, because it suggests that

---

touches on, such as love (*erōs*), virtue, interpersonal relationships, and the soul. Publications on the unity of the *Phaedrus* that deal with this question thoroughly include Moss, "Soul-Leading;" 1-23, Yunis, *Plato: Phaedrus*; Werner, "Plato's *Phaedrus* and the Problem of Unity," 91-137; Franco Travigno, "Putting Unity in Its Place: Organic Unity in the *Phaedrus*" *Literature and Aesthetics* 19 vol. 1 (2009): 153-82; Tushar Irani, *Plato on the Value of Philosophy* (Cambridge: Cambridge University Press, 2017), 111-193, and Charles Griswold Jr., *Self-Knowledge in Plato's* Phaedrus (New Haven: Yale University Press, 1986), 157-165. My aim here is not to engage in this debate—rather, my interpretation of the philosophical rhetoric and its role in moral education supports points that others have made in explaining the unity of the *Phaedrus*.

[10] Plato, *Phaedrus*, trans. Stephen Scully (Indianapolis: Hackett, 2003). All *Phaedrus* passages are quoted from this translation.

[11] Interestingly, the closely related term "lead" (*proagō*) appears repeatedly throughout the dialogue (see 227c, 230a, and 261a as just a few examples). At the beginning of the dialogue, Socrates physically leads Phaedrus toward the Ilissos (227c-229a), which symbolically mirrors Socrates's act of leading Phaedrus's soul toward vitue and philosophy. At 271d, Socrates repeats that "the capacity of speech [*logou dynamis*]" is to "guide the soul [*psychagōgia*]." Jessica Moss argues that *psychagōgia* is the primary topic of the *Phaedrus*, and that it helps to explain the unity of the dialogue. Moss, "Soul-Leading," 3.

rhetoric can influence, but not force, others to act or think a certain way. Phaedrus at first doubts that rhetoric can be practiced privately, saying that it is typically only used in law courts and the public assembly "in speech form," and that he has "not heard the term used more widely" (261b). Like most people, Phaedrus conceives of rhetoric as a public performance that one gives to a large group. However, Socrates demonstrates how to perform rhetoric privately in his very conversation with Phaedrus, even if Phaedrus does not realize it. Rhetoric is, most essentially, the guidance of another person's soul, so all the types of *logos* Socrates uses to guide Phaedrus toward philosophy and virtue, including speeches, myth, and philosophical dialogue are important components of philosophical rhetoric. By using these different types of *logos* in a private setting to guide Phaedrus toward genuine self-cultivation, Socrates displays a rhetorical *technē* (for Phaedrus as well as the reader) that is new to the intellectual sphere of ancient Greece.

To distinguish philosophical rhetoric as a new kind of *technē* even more clearly, Socrates identifies the effects often caused by the common use of rhetoric in Greece during his lifetime. He states:

> So, when a rhetorician who is mindless of good and evil encounters a city in the same condition and attempts to persuade it, not by praising a mere shadow of an ass as if it were a horse, but by praising evil as good, and by carefully studying public opinion, he persuades the city to do evil things rather than good ones.... (260c)

The average rhetorician lacks knowledge of the difference between what is really best for a city and what merely appears best for it (and the latter is often most advantageous for the rhetorician himself, as well), and he therefore causes many kinds of "evil" in the political realm.[12] However, one need not use rhetoric in this destructive way, a point that Socrates makes by personifying rhetoric:

---

[12] Compare this point to *Gorgias* 517a-c, where Socrates says that Athenian politicians traditionally give the city only what it "desires," and the popularity they gain from doing so brings them power and other

Lady Rhetoric might reply perhaps: 'Astonishing fellows, what nonsense you speak. I never required anyone to be ignorant of the truth when he learns to speak, but—if my counsel means something—to master the truth and then take me up. But I do make one major claim: without me, in no way will a man who knows the truth be able to persuade with art.' (260d)

The ultimate end of philosophical rhetoric is the cultivation of wisdom and the rest of virtue, while common uses of rhetoric (in most cases, at least) aim for popular acceptance, and, consequently, power and pleasure for the orator. Ideally, one learns the truth regarding the matters about which he wishes to speak before using rhetoric to influence the lives of others. In this case, one's knowledge of the truth (and what is truly good) sets the ends toward which he tries to persuade others. For these reasons, Socrates tries to persuade Phaedrus that "unless he loves wisdom [*philosophēsē*] sufficiently, he will never become a competent speaker about anything" (261a). At the same time, Socrates emphasizes how necessary it is to learn the art of rhetoric—if the philosopher wishes to "persuade with art," he must understand rhetoric and learn to use it for philosophical ends.

Moreover, Socrates and Phaedrus discuss how one can use rhetoric "dialectically" (276e), which involves matching a certain kind of speech to the kind of soul that will find it most persuasive (271b). Socrates calls this method "dialectical" because it requires that we understand the similarities and differences between all the kinds of speeches and souls. Or, to use the butcher analogy, dialectic allows us to divide speeches and souls according to their "natural joints" (265e). After the philosopher has "classified" each kind of speech and soul, he must match the appropriate speech to a given soul and be able to explain "the reason why one soul is necessarily persuaded by speeches of a certain sort and another is not" (271b).

---

rewards. By contrast, the "true [*alēthinos*] art of rhetoric" (517a) consists in "leading desires in a different direction and not yielding, persuading and forcing them toward a condition in which the citizens were to be better..." Plato, *Gorgias*, trans. James H. Nichols Jr. (Ithaca: Cornell University Press, 1998). All *Gorgias* quotations are from this translation.

Thus, if the philosopher understands what kind of speech causes each kind of soul to become persuaded of a given view (and she can explain why), then she possesses the "dialectical art" of rhetoric (276e). Possessing the dialectical art of rhetoric increases the pedagogical potential of the philosopher's *logos*, because through it she can persuade her listener more effectively. I use the term "philosophical" instead of "dialectical" to describe the genuine philosopher's kind of rhetoric according to the *Phaedrus*, because it is possible that a person could possess the dialectical art of rhetoric without having the philosopher's characteristic love for wisdom and virtue.[13] In this case, the person using the dialectical art of rhetoric could lead her listeners toward self-serving ends that do not improve their souls. The philosopher who possesses the dialectical art of rhetoric, on the other hand, knows what is most pedagogically and ethically beneficial to her listener as well as the most effective means for facilitating such benefit.

Gorgias and *Republic* passages relevant to philosophical rhetoric

Philosophical rhetoric aims to influence more than just the listener's reason; it carefully aims to affect non-rational desires as well. As I will argue in the third section, Socrates tries to influence Phaedrus's desires, but it will be helpful to first examine an illuminating passage in Plato's *Gorgias* pertaining to the relationship between persuasion and desire. At 493a, Socrates compares the soul to a jar, and he says that a soul with inordinate "desire" (*epithumia*) for conventional goods such as wealth, pleasure, power, and so on is like a jar with large holes. Significantly, he says that *epithumia* is the most "persuadable" aspect of the soul: "[...] and this part of the soul in which the desires [*epithumiai*] exist happens to be such as to be persuaded [*anapeithesthai*] and to change around up and down."[14] In

---

[13] McCoy, *Plato on the Rhetoric*, 167-96 describes Socrates's rhetoric as "Socratic rhetoric" or simply "good rhetoric," though she also uses the term "philosophical rhetoric" at times. All three labels are certainly appropriate, but I think the term "philosophical" best captures the point I aim to make in the context of this project.

[14] The word "part" does not appear in the Greek. Socrates simply uses "this" (*touto*) to refer to whatever aspect of the soul has non-rational desires.

the context of the *Gorgias*, Socrates aims to redirect Callicles's intense non-rational desire away from his current primary goal (excessive amounts of pleasure, power, etc.) and toward the pursuit of wisdom, courage, moderation, and justice. In other words, Socrates works toward the pedagogical and ethical benefit of his interlocutor, just as he does in the *Phaedrus*. In addition to arguing that these virtues promote happiness, a healthy soul, and an overall good life, Socrates aims to influence Callicles's *epithumiai* as well. For example, comparing Callicles's conception of the good life to a leaking jar and the life of a catamite (494e) are rhetorical techniques that might help Callicles feel "shame" (*aischros*) about his current way of life, which could in turn help motivate him to restrain his desires for conventional goods. Socrates's defense of virtue in the *Gorgias* thus appeals to both Callicles's reason and his non-rational desires, since his account must address both aspects of Callicles's soul in order to have the greatest possible chance to persuade him to care for virtue.

Philosophical rhetoric is thus an important tool for the project of "turning" the soul, otherwise known as protreptic education, that Plato discusses in the *Republic* and elsewhere.[15] The *Phaedrus*'s and *Gorgias*'s concern with influencing multiple aspects of the soul, such as reason and non-rational desires, is also reflected in the famous cave image in *Republic* VII:

> 'But the present argument, on the other hand,' I said, 'indicates that this power is in the soul of each, and that the instrument with which each learns—just as an eye is not able to turn toward the light from the dark without the whole body—must be turned around from that which is coming into being together with the whole soul until it is

---

[15] There are also rich passages pertaining to protreptic education in Plato's *Euthydemus* (especially 278c-282d), where Socrates explicitly says that he is trying to "persuade" Clinias "to devote himself to wisdom and virtue" (278d). For an illuminating analysis the theme of turning the soul toward philosophy in Plato (and the way that his dialogues can do this to the reader), see Jill Gordon, *Turning Toward Philosophy: Literary Device and Dramatic Structure in Plato's Dialogues* (University Park: The Pennsylvania State University Press, 1999).

able to endure looking at that which *is* and the brightest part
of that which *is*.' (518c)[16]

Rather than pouring water from a full cup into an empty one
(*Symposium* 175d) or "putting sight into blind eyes" (*Republic* 518c),
protreptic education involves the "turning" or transformation of the
student's "whole" soul such that he can see reality for himself. If
turning the whole soul symbolizes the acquisition of virtue, then this
process requires a reorientation of one's reason and non-rational
desires such that wisdom and the rest of virtue become his top
priorities. Philosophical rhetoric can help to catalyze this change in
the soul by helping one's interlocutor to perceive his own ignorance
and the flaws in his conception of the good life, which in turn
motivates him to seek a better alternative through philosophy.
However, the process of turning the whole soul will take further
effort and habituation on the student's part, since getting adjusted to
the light outside the cave is gradual (516a-c), and one will only be
able to "endure" the sight of Being after he has become virtuous. It is
likely that Plato depicts Socrates using philosophical rhetoric in an
attempt to begin and sustain this process of soul-turning with many
of his interlocutors, such as Phaedrus, Callicles, Glaucon, and
Adeimantus, as I will discuss further below.

Further, toward the end of the *Gorgias*, Socrates identifies love
(*erōs*) as another important aspect of the soul that his words aim to
influence, since *erōs* is the attraction that the soul feels toward
whatever appears best to it.[17] Callicles remarks that although
Socrates's words "seem good" to him, he "suffers the experience of
the many" and is "not altogether persuaded [*peithomai*]." Socrates's
response sheds light on the reason why he uses philosophical
rhetoric to influence Callicles's *erōs*: "Yes, for love [*erōs*] of the people,
Callicles, which is present in your soul, opposes me. But if we
investigate these same things often and better, perhaps you will be

---

[16] Plato, *Republic*, trans. Allan Bloom (New York: Basic Books, 1968). All
Republic passages are quoted from this translation.
[17] In the *Symposium*, for example, Diotima calls love a "leader" [*ho hēgoumenos*] (210a) of the soul that compels it toward whatever appears
to it as best and most beautiful (205d-206a).

153

persuaded" (513c-d). In addition to addressing Callicles's reasoning and non-rational desires, Socrates must also influence Callicles's *erōs* if he hopes to have any impact on him. If, by the end of their conversation, the primary object of Callicles's *erōs* is still the people of Athens (and everything he gets by pleasing them), then he will persist in his current way of life no matter how well Socrates refuted his arguments. Socrates aims to (at least) incite desire in Callicles to habitually examine the ethical and political questions they have been discussing. Only by doing so will he become fully persuaded of Socrates's views, which would help him develop the desire to leave behind his current way of life and instead cultivate virtue. A strictly rational defense of virtue stripped of any rhetorical elements would likely not accomplish the task of influencing Callicles's *epithumia* or *erōs*, and so such a defense would not fit Socrates's goal of motivating Callicles to begin the process of self-cultivation. He instead provides the appropriate degree of refutation and argumentation, and he rhetorically packages it in a way that will be most impactful.

Callicles's remark about being unpersuaded raises important questions about whether (or how often) Socrates's philosophical rhetoric succeeds in helping his interlocutors gain wisdom or virtue. If Socrates attempts to persuade his interlocutors to pursue the philosophical life in many dialogues, then he often fails to achieve this goal. Some of Socrates's interlocutors, of course, lived infamously until the end, such as Alcibiades, Meno, and Critias, to name only a few.[18] By contrast, there is at least one interlocutor who benefitted from his association with Socrates, namely Theaetetus, who lived and died nobly as the frame dialogue of the *Theaetetus* makes clear (142b-c).[19] In other cases, it is difficult to be certain about

---

[18] On the biographies of Plato's characters, see Debra Nails, *The People of Plato: A Prosography* (Indianapolis: Hackett Publishing, 2002).

[19] At the end of the *Theaetetus*, Socrates states the ways in which Theaetetus has benefitted from their conversation: "And so, Theaetetus, if ever in the future you should attempt to conceive or should succeed in conceiving other theories, they will be better ones as the result of this inquiry. And if you remain barren, your companions will find you gentler and less tiresome; you will be modest [*sōphronōs*] and not think you know what you don't know" (210b-c, trans. M.J. Levett).

what impact Socrates's conversation had on his interlocutors, since neither Plato nor historical records give us information about the remainder of their lives. For instance, we do not know what became of Callicles, though he is clearly resistant to Socrates's arguments in the *Gorgias* given the passage mentioned above. Phaedrus falls into the category of interlocutors about whom we cannot be sure. He appears to be persuaded by Socrates at the end of the dialogue, but we also know that he was accused of profaning the Eleusinian mysteries in 415, and the dramatic date of the *Phaedrus* is probably only a few years before this accusation.[20] This fact may suggest that Phaedrus never became a virtuous person, but in my view, it is ultimately unclear whether Socrates succeeds or fails in turning Phaedrus toward philosophy and virtue, since the dialogue does not say enough about Phaedrus's future to give a definitive answer.

Although it is true that Socrates does not persuade all of his interlocutors to turn toward philosophy and virtue, in my view we should not see this as *his* failure. Plato shows us that Socrates creates the best possible conditions for another individual to morally improve himself, but also that cultivating wisdom and the rest of virtue requires one's own habitual choice and effort. There is only so much that Socrates (or anyone) can do to help another person undertake this task. Each interlocutor must decide if he will accept Socrates's guidance and decide to live philosophically. Socrates replies to Callicles's remark about being unpersuaded by saying that "if we investigate these same things often and better, perhaps you will be persuaded" (513c-d), a statement that emphasizes the need for habitual effort and cooperation from Socrates's interlocutor. As Socrates says in the *Symposium*, wisdom is not "like water, which always flows from a full cup into an empty one when we connect them with a piece of yarn" (175d).[21] He cannot simply pour his own wisdom or virtue into the mind of his interlocutor in one conversation. So, when Plato depicts Socrates earnestly trying to give guidance to interlocutors who subsequently refuse it, he suggests

---

[20] Nails, *The People of Plato*, 314.

[21] Plato, *Symposium*, trans. A. Nehamas and P Woodruff (Indianapolis: Hackett, 1989). All *Symposium* quotations are from this edition.

they are to blame for their own vice, not Socrates. Or, another possibility is that Plato is painting more tragic portraits of these of interlocutors by suggesting that their souls were already too corrupted by society or their upbringing, such that their overly intense, misdirected desire (*epithumia*) or love (*erōs*) prevents Socrates's *logos* from having any benefit. Indeed, as I indicated above, Socrates explicitly states that Callicles's "love [*erōs*] of the people" prevents him from being persuaded (513c). Perhaps Callicles, Alcibiades,[22] and others like them are examples of the souls that the *Gorgias's* myth of the afterlife calls "incurable," and we, the readers, are like the souls who benefit by learning from their errors (525c).

So, while it lies beyond the scope of this paper to fully explore the reasons why Socrates's philosophical rhetoric often fails to persuade his interlocutors to pursue philosophy and virtue, I suggest that Socrates does everything in his power to achieve this end. It is fitting that Socrates tries to persuade his interlocutor to accept certain views, to develop a desire for the virtues, and to pursue them habitually, because he recognizes that he cannot simply transmit all of his wisdom about the good life in one conversation. However, if he can rid his interlocutors of their erroneous opinions through refutation, make them aware of their own ignorance or other imperfections, and use strong argumentation to persuade them of the view that, for example, the virtues are worth pursuing because they lead to happiness, then he will have created the best possible conditions (at least in the span of one conversation) that one could have to begin the process of gaining wisdom and virtue. Still, there is always the possibility that the interlocutor will simply go back to his old ways, and apparently this was often the case. Socrates does not corrupt the youth of Athens, but instead displays how one can

---

[22] In the *Symposium*, Alcibiades appears to have the same problem that Socrates points out about Callicles at *Gorgias* 513.c. That is, Alcibiades acknowledges that Socrates is correct when they discuss what way of life is best, but then he "caves in" to his "desire to please the crowd," and so reverts to his old, vicious habits when he is not with Socrates (216b). In other words, both Callicles and Alcibiades have inordinate desires for conventional goods that prevent them from being fully persuaded to live a philosophical and virtuous way of life.

use *logos* as effectively as possible to help another person gain knowledge and virtue.

Pedagogical benefits of philosophical rhetoric in the *Phaedrus*

To gain a clearer sense of how Socrates performs philosophical rhetoric and its potential effects in the *Phaedrus*, we must understand the type of soul that Phaedrus typifies. After all, using rhetoric dialectically requires its practitioner to address a particular type of soul with the type of *logos* that is more persuasive for it. I interpret the character Phaedrus not only as Plato's depiction of a historical person, but also as a symbol for a certain universal type of person. Phaedrus represents those who are not yet committed to a given set of values and way of life, but who are tempted to adopt conventional ways of life centered around the pursuit of goods such as pleasure, wealth, power, and good reputation. Phaedrus's obsession with Lysias's speech signals his temptation to pursue this sort of life. Many people—including many of Plato's readers—find themselves at such a crossroad at some point in their lives. In the dialogue named after him, Phaedrus is in his mid-twenties,[23] he is amorous, and he is very interested in the topics of love and sex, as evidenced by his interest in Lysias's speech (234c). John Sallis paints a helpful portrait of Phaedrus's important qualities based on his appearances in the *Symposium* and *Protagoras*: "[...] Phaedrus is one who associates with physicians and sophists, who has some interest in investigations of nature, and who draws heavily upon mythical things. These characteristics are confirmed in the *Phaedrus*."[24] Socrates remarks that Phaedrus is "going in two directions"—referring to his interests in both rhetoric and philosophy—and Socrates seeks to "turn him toward a love of wisdom" (257b). So, Socrates's speeches and discussion with Phaedrus cater to these characteristics of Phaedrus's soul, especially those pertaining to his interests in love, rhetoric, and myth. In the "palinode" speech, for example, Socrates shows that directing one's *erōs* (or "erotic madness") toward good ends is a

---

[23] Nails, *The People of Plato*, 232.

[24] John Sallis, *Being and Logos: The Way of Platonic Dialogue* (Pittsburgh: Duquesne University Press, 1975), 106.

crucial step in the quest for wisdom, the rest of virtue, and the good life more broadly.

Further, it is no accident that Socrates flirts with Phaedrus as they trade speeches and leisurely recline in a picturesque natural setting. When Socrates flirts with Phaedrus throughout the dialogue (frequently calling him "my dear," and so on), this is not a dramatic detail that Plato adds superfluously. Rather, Socrates's flirting is an important component of philosophical rhetoric that influences the non-rational aspects of Phaedrus's soul. Although not a rhetorical technique strictly speaking, flirting in this context is a pedagogical technique that increases the persuasive power of Socrates's arguments, and so is a component of philosophical rhetoric's project of influencing both rational and non-rational aspects of the interlocutor's soul. Given that Phaedrus is an amorous young man who is interested in the topics of love and sex, Socrates's flirting will ideally capture his attention and help him grow more interested in the topics they discuss together. As Charles Kahn points out, Plato often discusses desire and *erōs* as if they were bodies of water that can be redirected through reason, habit, or persuasion.[25] Moreover, as we know from Alcibiades's speech in the *Symposium*, those who grow erotically interested in Socrates often grow interested in philosophy as well (218b), so it is likely that Socrates's purpose in flirting with young men in general is to get them interested in philosophy. Similarly, Phaedrus's obsession with Lysias's speech is evidence that he is keenly interested in rhetoric and speeches, so this is why Socrates tries to turn him toward philosophy by giving his own speeches and by exploring the best ways to use rhetoric. Socrates's flirting works in tandem with the content of the conversation to show Phaedrus the goods (especially happiness and a rewarding relationship) toward which the *erōs* he already feels can lead him if he channels it in a way that will help him pursue wisdom.

---

[25] Charles H. Kahn, "Plato's Theory of Desire," *The Review of Metaphysics* 41.1 (1987): 77-103. For example, Plato uses this simile in *Republic* VI: "[...] when someone's desires incline strongly to some one thing, they are therefore weaker with respect to the rest, like a stream that has been channelled off in that other direction" (485d).

Of course, Socrates provides arguments that aim to influence his interlocutors' reasoning as well, but he recognizes that reason is not the only aspect of their souls that helps to determine what they consider as top priorities. Phaedrus has little experience with philosophical discussion, so Socrates engages in argument with him as far as possible given his abilities, but his use of argument is more limited than it would be with an interlocutor who has more training in philosophical argumentation. At the start of the dialogue, Phaedrus's desire to practice rhetoric and obtain the rewards it brings prevent him from truly considering the philosophical life as a better alternative to his current way of life. So, Socrates's primary aim in his conversation with Phaedrus is to persuade him, as opposed to offering a comprehensive, strictly rational demonstration about the topics they discuss. Therefore, he shapes his accounts of virtue, love, the soul, and other issues to fit this end. Likewise, Socrates frequently uses images and myth in these discussions, because Phaedrus is already interested in mythology (229c-230a), and he can more easily understand the points Socrates is making through images. In this way, Socrates's use of myth and images are effective rhetorical tools for turning his interlocutor toward the pursuit of virtue and the philosophical way of life. Philosophy itself is a kind of love, or a way of life shaped around the desire for wisdom, so Socrates wants to redirect rational and non-rational desires of his interlocutors in any way he can toward philosophy and virtue. If Socrates is successful, Phaedrus will then go on to examine such matters more often and thoroughly (*Gorgias* 513c-d) and eventually become a virtuous philosopher who sees the truth for himself. Part of this task is refuting Phaedrus's current views and defending alternative views through rational argumentation, and the other part is influencing his non-rational desire using rhetorical means throughout the course of the conversation.

Socrates then uses an analogy of planting seeds to explain the pedagogical power of philosophical rhetoric. Regarding the speeches of those using philosophical rhetoric, he states: "These speeches are not fruitless but bear seed from which other speeches, planted in other fields, have the means to pass this seed on, forever immortal, and to make the person possessing them as blessed as is humanly possible" (276e-277a). The person using philosophical rhetoric uses his knowledge of his speech's subject matter (such as love or virtue), as well as his dialectical art of rhetoric, to "plant" a speech in the soul of someone else. Ideally, the person who hears the speech will continue to think about the speech he hears (i.e., it will "grow" in his mind) until he gains true insight into whatever subject the speaker discussed. Once the person who hears the speech gains such insight, it helps to improve his life (it makes him "blessed"), and he may even learn to use philosophical rhetoric to cause the same effect in others. By performing this very task with Phaedrus throughout the entire dialogue, Socrates sets a concrete example of philosophical rhetoric in practice. Socrates plants *logoi* in Phaedrus's soul in an attempt to guide him toward a devotion to philosophy, virtue, and "wisdom-loving speeches" (257b). Again, I only aim to shed light on Socrates's pedagogical strategy, and I do not claim that he succeeds, since the dialogue does not say enough to give a definitive answer.

An important example of a "seed" that Socrates plants in Phaedrus pertains to the difference between genuine virtue and flawed, conventional notions of virtue, especially in the case of moderation (*sōphrosunē*). At the beginning of the dialogue, Phaedrus is enamored with both the style and the content of Lysias' speech, which one can use to seduce "non-lovers" and thus maximize one's own sexual pleasure (230e-234c). Lysias depicts the non-lover as more self-restrained and therefore more prudent than the lover when it comes to sexual relationships (231a, 231d), and this view supports his speech's thesis that one should give sexual favors to a non-lover instead of a lover. The conception of self-restraint in Lysias's speech is a representative example of the way people conventionally conceive of moderation, both in antiquity and in the present day. In response, Socrates emphasizes that genuine virtue does not simply amount to restraining some desires for the sake of fulfilling others, a characteristic that Socrates refers to as "mortal moderation" and "slavish economizing" (256e),[26] nor can it be reduced to obeying a set

---

[26] This inferior form of moderation is also discussed in *Republic* VIII (553e-554e) and *Phaedo* (68c-69c), and in both passages Socrates remarks that this trait merely "seems" to be moderation to the majority of people.

of predetermined rules. Instead, the *Phaedrus* shows us how to move past slavish economizing toward insight into true beauty and the sources of being (the forms) through "erotic madness," which helps us to actualize our potential for self-knowledge, self-actualization, happiness (*eudaimonia*), and eudaimonic relationships.[27] While there are more "seeds" about virtue that Socrates plants in Phaedrus, so to speak, this is one of the most central ones. Socrates thus helps to initiate Phaedrus as well as the reader into a deeper, more comprehensive understanding of virtue.

Finally, it lies beyond the scope of this essay to fully address the frequently discussed question of the unity of the *Phaedrus*, but an understanding of philosophical rhetoric may shed light on one facet of the answer. Since Phaedrus has an interest in both philosophy and rhetoric—and is therefore "going in two directions"—Socrates covers both topics in a way that will persuade Phaedrus to pursue philosophy, to cultivate virtue, and to use rhetoric in the service of these two ends. Socrates's analysis of both the philosophical life and rhetoric seek to pull Phaedrus away from the path laid out before him by rhetoricians like Lysias, who use rhetoric in the traditional, self-serving manner. Lysias's speech at the beginning of the dialogue clearly exemplifies this way of using rhetoric, as the goal of the speech is to help the person delivering it to maximize his own sexual pleasure. However, Socrates appeals to Phaedrus's interests in rhetoric, philosophy, and love in order to influence him toward the other "path," namely Socrates's own philosophical way of life. The wide variety of topics concerning sex, love, virtue, the soul, the nature of reality, rhetoric, and dialectic, therefore, fit together when

---

[27] The *Phaedrus* highlights an important link between self-knowledge and intimate relationships. Socrates foreshadows this theme in the opening discussion of the dialogue with the following remark: "Phaedrus, I know you as well as I know myself; and if I don't know Phaedrus, I've forgotten myself also." (228a). Later, in the palinode, the philosophical intimate relationship helps one "see himself as though in a mirror" (255d). It is worth noting that this mirror analogy also appears in *Alcibiades I*, where Socrates claims that a close friend is like a mirror in which we can better see ourselves, just as getting physically close to someone allows us to see our reflection in his or her pupils (132a-133c).

considered from the perspective of the pedagogical dynamic between Socrates and Phaedrus. Socrates leads the conversation in a way that will personally engage Phaedrus and make him think carefully about his own life. Hence, I agree with Yunis and Moss in holding that the pedagogical context of the dialogue helps to explain the unity of the *Phaedrus*.[28] My interpretation of philosophical rhetoric as *paideia* simply emphasizes that Socrates unites the various themes of the dialogue through his performance of philosophical rhetoric and his goal of helping Phaedrus take a crucial step in his ethical development.

Conclusion

Given the analyses of philosophy and rhetoric in the *Phaedrus*, it follows that the philosopher must be committed to rhetoric insofar as it is a tool to promote virtue and the practice of philosophy in others. One way to exercise virtue is to help foster virtue in others so far as possible. To use the language of the cave image in *Republic* VII, the philosopher, for Plato, aims to descend back down into the cave to free those who are still imprisoned. The philosopher reaches others through words, and rhetoric helps to give his words as much power as possible to influence others toward virtuous ends. As Socrates says in the *Gorgias*, "rhetoric, and every other action, must be used always for what is just" (527c). So, instead of being a haphazard combination, Plato's choice to pair discussions of philosophy and rhetoric in the same dialogue is fitting. Any philosopher interested in helping others see the value of virtue and philosophy must gain enough mastery in rhetoric to make them question their current commitments and reveal the possibilities of virtue to them in a compelling manner. With enough cooperation on the part of the listener, philosophical rhetoric can be an invaluable guide toward a better life.

---

[28] Yunis, *Plato*: Phaedrus, 6-7; Moss, "Soul-Leading," 3.

Colin C. Smith[1]
Performativity and the Vitality of Discourse in Plato's *Phaedrus*[2]

In this essay, I aim to speak to a neglected aspect of an important passage in Plato's *Phaedrus* (264c2-5) that helps us to understand the connection between performance and education in Platonic philosophy. The *Phaedrus* is a dialogue about discourse (*logos*), method (*methodos*), and love (*erōs*). In it, Plato has his characters, Socrates and Phaedrus, exhibit a series of discursive methods in such forms as speechmaking, myth, rhetoric, and dialectic to show the natures of these methods and the preponderant amount of quasi-erotic care for the listener's soul entailed in each. The passage on which I will focus is Socrates's assertion that good discourse must be a compositionally unified whole of well-measured parts. Here, Socrates offers an analogy between discourse and a healthy animal (*zōon*) that is such a whole of parts, as follows:[3]

> All discourse (*panta logon*) like a living animal (*hōsper zōon*) should be put together with its own body (*sōma*) so that it is not without a head (*akephalon*) or without a foot (*apoun*) but has a middle (*mesa*) and extremities (*akra*), written in such a way that its parts fit together and form a whole. (264c2-5)[4]

Most of Plato's modern commentators who have discussed this passage have focused on the view of Platonic mereology that this

---

[1] Colin C. Smith is an Assistant Teaching Professor of Philosophy at Pennsylvania State University. He has published in *Ancient Philosophy, Classical Philology, History of Philosophy Quarterly,* and elsewhere.

[2] I am grateful to the organizers and participants in the 2022 Fonte Aretusa conference on *Paideia* and Performance for discussion that did much to shape this paper. I owe several points to Peter Moore and Kristian Sheeley, and give thanks to the volume editors for helpful feedback.

[3] More precisely, evidence in Herodotus and Aristotle suggests that "*zōon*" means "that which is animate," of which the animal is a non-exhaustive instance. See Aryeh Kosman, *The Activity of Being* (Cambridge, MA: Harvard University Press, 2013), 5.

[4] *Phaedrus* translations are from Stephen Scully, *Plato's Phaedrus* (Newburyport, MA: Focus, 2003), modified. I follow the Greek of John Burnet, *Plato, Opera* (Oxford: Clarendon Press, 1901).

indicates, including the questions it raises concerning the due measure of parts within wholes and the relationship between such a view and structuring principles for good writing, discoursing, and philosophizing.[5] Here I want to focus instead on a different aspect of the passage: the metaphor concerning the lifelike vitality of good discourse, which I will call the "vitality metaphor."[6] When comparing discourse to the living animal and doing so by drawing upon bodily images of head, foot, midsection, and extremity, Socrates tacitly calls us to think about discourse's character as something possessed of qualities analogous to life, breath, soul, and a body governed by normative standards of health.

My argument is that the vitality of discourse concerns its educative power of performativity through the dialectical exchange between speaker and audience stemming from its performance. By "performance," I mean only the instantiation of discourse in space and time (as opposed, e.g., to written discourse), which can—but need not—entail a sense of a "dramatic rendering." Performance, furthermore, is something that can be done well or poorly relative to principles we will consider throughout. And performance can yield the educational result that I call "performativity," that is, genuine insight dialectically arising from an enactment of discourse between speaker and audience that exhibits the need to change how one thinks, lives, and cares for community and world.

The vitality metaphor is at play throughout the dialogue. A major theme emerging in the text overall is discourse's performative capacity, the numerous forms this can take, and the ways in which a given type of discourse exhibits its nature to communicate, educate, and engage upon its enactment. I argue that this is evident in all seven parts of the *Phaedrus* as I will here divide it:[7]

---

[5] See, e.g., Franco Trivigno, "Putting Unity in Its Place: Organic Unity in Plato's *Phaedrus*," *Literature and Aesthetics* 19.1 (2009): 153-182, and the representative bibliography at 179n3.

[6] "Vitality" entails both (i) life force itself and (ii) a strong, healthy, or otherwise good instantiation of this life force. We find this double sense, descriptive and normative, in the discussion of living discourse.

[7] This division is in the service of my argument, not a claim about exactly how Plato would have us understand the composition of the text.

i. The dramatic frame (227a1-230e5)
ii. Lysias's speech delivered by Phaedrus (230e6-234c5) and Socrates's subsequent critique (234c6-237b1)
iii. Socrates's first speech on love (237b2-241d1) and its afterword (241d2-243e8)
iv. Socrates's palinode (243e9-257b6)
v. The discourse on rhetoric (257b7-274b1)
vi. Philosophical dialectic and "good" (= true and knowing) rhetoric (261a3 ff.)[8]
vii. The critique of writing (274b2-278b5) and conclusion (278b6-279c8).

When considering these passages, I will address performance and performativity in several related senses, including the demonstration of various philosophical concepts and the pedagogical function that it plays. My argument will deviate from those commentators who have understood this dialogue as split between an "enacted" stretch (covering the first three speeches) and an "expounded" stretch (beginning with the passages on rhetoric).[9] Instead, I will argue that the entire dialogue is both a discussion *and* performative enactment of discourse, bringing about a unity of discourse and deed.[10]

I proceed as follows. In the first section, I discuss the first three speeches to reflect on the initial foundation for the vitality metaphor. Next, I consider the discussions of rhetoric and dialectic, focusing on the ways in which these are spoken of in connection to educative performativity and furthermore performed by Socrates. Here I argue that the vitality metaphor ultimately must be understood with close

---

[8] Here, I follow Jenny Bryan, "*Eikos* in Plato's *Phaedrus*," in *Probabilities, Hypotheticals, and Counterfactuals in Ancient Greek Thought*, ed. V. Wohl (Cambridge: Cambridge University Press, 2014), 30-46 in taking the discussion of rhetoric as untangling separate senses of "good" (e.g., true and dialectical) and "bad" (e.g., false and manipulative) rhetoric. Cf. Scully, *Plato's 'Phaedrus,'* 52n119 (especially concerning 266b3-c1).

[9] See Daniel Werner, "Plato's *Phaedrus* and the Problem of Unity," *Oxford Studies in Ancient Philosophy* 32 (2007): 99 for discussion of this view.

[10] For more on the unity of discourse and deed in the *Phaedrus*, see Werner, "Plato's *Phaedrus*," 123-4.

Colin C. Smith

reference to the account of philosophical dialectic in the *Phaedrus* (esp. 261a4-266c1, drawing also on *Sophist* 218b6-c5). In the next section, I use these points to consider the critique of writing (274b2-278b5) and its analogies concerning the vitality of discourse. I then conclude by discussing some connections between the theme of performativity and love in the sense of *erōs*. I will suggest that this offers resources for those who have sought an account of both the unity of the dialogue,[11] and the educational connection between discourse and love that the dialogue makes manifest.[12]

Unhealthy discourse and the turn to myth (227a1-257b6)

I aim to show how the normative force of the vitality metaphor as it concerns the educative performativity of good discourse is at play throughout the *Phaedrus*. I begin with brief considerations of some ways this theme arises in the dramatic frame and first three speeches, that is, in Lysias's speech related by Phaedrus about loving the non-lover,[13] in Socrates's speech on the same subject, and in Socrates's palinode.

An early use of the metaphor of measure-unto-health comes at 229b1, where Socrates describes the "well-measured breeze" (*pneuma metrion*, 229a8) mediating between the shade of the plane tree (*platanos*) and the grass to receive the interlocutors (229a8-b2). Exhibiting his considerable literary power, Plato has his characters invoke an image of a space drawing together sky, earth, and air,

---

[11] The question of the *Phaedrus*'s unifying "scope" has been debated since the 5th c. CE commentary by Hermias of Alexandria. See Harvey Yunis, *Plato, 'Phaedrus'* (Cambridge: Cambridge University Press, 2011), 1n3; and Jessica Moss, "Soul-Leading: The Unity of the *Phaedrus*, Again," *Oxford Studies in Ancient Philosophy* 43 (2012): 1n1. On the history of this question, see Werner, "Plato's *Phaedrus*," 91-137.

[12] On the function of *erōs* in the dialogue and its connection to philosophical discourse, see G.R.F. Ferrari, "The Unity of Plato's *Phaedrus*: A Response," *Dialogos* 1 (1994): 24-5, and Moss, "Soul-Leading," esp. 1-2.

[13] Many have debated whether this speech was indeed written by the historical orator Lysias, or whether it is instead Plato's mimicry. For an overview of the debate and endorsement of the latter view, which I find compelling, see Jenny Bryan, "The Role of Lysias' Speech in Plato's *Phaedrus*," *Cambridge Classical Journal* 67 (2021): 1-24.

which jointly form something of an oasis that offers relief and nourishment amid a hot summer day. The elements of the atmosphere will work together organically to form the conditions that create space for the discourse that is to follow. Discourse is something enacted and hence alive in a sense, and it thus requires a system of nurture such as a healthy environment derived from such mutually co-constitutive elements as shade, grass, and breeze in which it can flourish.[14] By having his interlocutors gesture at the conditions of environmental health that allow for their own discourse, Plato slyly has the dramatic setting anticipate a major philosophical theme that will follow.[15]

But the initial discourse on offer, Lysias's speech via Phaedrus, decidedly lacks both measure and vitality. The speech, notoriously, entails an argument for love—which can, but need not, be understood in the sense of sexual favors—from non-lovers.[16] It is a dense, confusing, and monotonous speech, to say the least. Socrates will critique the speech's lack of measure explicitly later in the dialogue, arguing that the parts (i.e., assertions) in the speech were arranged arbitrarily and could have been arranged in any other way (see especially 264a5-264c2). The nonlinear claims are also repetitive,

---

[14] For a detailed analysis with many great insights into the relationship between the dramatic frame and the philosophical content in the *Phaedrus*, see G.R.F. Ferrari, *Listening to the Cicadas: A Study of Plato's 'Phaedrus'* (Cambridge: Cambridge University Press, 1987), 1-36.

[15] Cf. Scully, *Plato's 'Phaedrus,'* 4n13.

[16] This opens onto the question of whether the *Phaedrus* depicts a literal or figurative seduction. For the former, see Martha Nussbaum, *The Fragility of Goodness* (Cambridge: Cambridge University Press, 1986), esp. 229. For the latter, see Moss, "Soul-Leading," 6-12. I argue that sexuality is implied as a theme, but remain agnostic concerning the relationship between Socrates and Phaedrus. I am, in any case, very skeptical of Gregory Vlastos's well-known and controversial claim that Platonic lovers "control this desire [for physical intercourse] and transmute it into a passion for common study" in *Platonic Studies* (Princeton: Princeton University Press, 1981), 22-23. Instead, I argue the *Phaedrus* concerns philosophy on the model of erotics without necessarily rejecting the satisfaction of bodily desire.

as Socrates notes (235a3-8), and frequently self-refuting. The self-refutational character of Lysias's speech is exemplified, for example, when Lysias defends two contradictory arguments, first advocating benefitting the needy instead of the privileged, and then benefitting the privileged instead of the needy (233e1-234b1). These sorts of argumentative thickets seem designed to confuse the audience and amuse the speaker by demonstrating alleged cleverness without imparting any actual knowledge. The speech's form thus depicts metaphorically its theme of unidirectional sexual gratification.[17]

Furthermore, as translator and commentator Stephen Scully has noted,[18] Lysias uses only the second-person singular and the impersonal, generalizing plural, while markedly refusing (in stark contrast with the speeches to come) to address the listener in the vocative. This gives "the impression that the speech could be said by anyone to anyone," and therefore lacks attention to the specific character of the audience and hence the audience's educational needs. I submit that these problems taken together indicate the poor quality of the speech as a performance, acting as an exercise in mere self-amusement with disregard for the listener in a way that formally reflects self-satisfaction at the negligent expense of one's partner for which the speech's contents entail an argument.[19] Lysias's speech is not a healthy whole of parts, but instead a heap of claims that emphasize self-centered pleasure for the speaker over contributing to the health of the listener through educative instruction. It is, therefore, a precise instance of performance without performativity. While Lysias puts on an amusing show by dramatically rendering this controversial set of claims regarding love, the discourse yields pure inactivity from the audience.

---

[17] David Halperin, "Plato and Erotic Reciprocity," *Classical Antiquity* 5 (1986): 60-80, shows both that Plato intends to depict sexuality in the *Phaedrus* as mutually satisfying (like philosophical dialectic), and that this was against the Athenian customs of Plato's day.

[18] Scully, *Plato's 'Phaedrus,'* 7n20.

[19] I focus here on the need for interest in the *interlocutor's* nature as a condition of good discourse. On good discourse's need for interest in the *self*, see Christopher Moore, "How to Know Thyself in Plato's *Phaedrus*," *Apeiron* 47.3 (2014): 390-418.

Socrates begins to address some of these concerns in the dialogue's second speech, in which he is tasked with giving his own defense of Lysias's strange thesis. Shortly before beginning, he indicates that "one must not praise the discovery of the argument but its arrangement" (*diathesis*), which Phaedrus endorses as a "duly measured" (*metrios*) statement (236a3-b7). Socrates begins this speech by covering his head (237a4-5), which suggests that his dramatic performance will entail distance between his own identity and the claims he will make. But Socrates also uses the speech to begin setting the groundwork for the vitality metaphor, while demonstrating some aspects of the principles of vital discourse in both negative and positive senses.

Early in his speech, Socrates makes explicit some foundational principles of good discourse:

> Above all else, my darling boy [*ō pai*], there is only one way to begin [*mia archē*] if someone means to deliberate successfully. By necessity [*anankē*], he must know what he is deliberating about or he will miss the mark completely. Most people, however, don't realize that they do not know the true essence [*ousian*] of an argument. Because they have not reached an agreement [*diomologountai*] at the beginning [*en archē*] of an investigation, they proceed as if they know, resorting to what seems plausible [*to eikos*], when they have agreed [*homologousin*] neither with themselves nor with others. [... Hence,] we should agree upon [*homologoia*] a definition [*horon*] of love, showing what it is [*ti esti*] and what power it has. (237b7-d3)

This passage is important in the present discussion both for its making explicit principles of well-composed discourse and indicating precisely what is deficient in the speech Socrates is about to give. Positively, the speech begins by addressing its listener in the vocative (*ō pai*, 237b7) and hence exhibits deeper engagement with the audience than did Lysias's disengaged and impersonal speech.[20]

---

[20] On Socrates's diction as opposed to that of Lysias's speech, see Karl Mras, "Platos *Phaedrus und die Rhetorik, II*," *Wiener Studien* 37 (1915): 88-97.

Furthermore, it indicates the need to begin from a "definitional" (*horon*, 237d1) understanding of the "true essence" (*ousian*, 237c3) of the subject itself (*ti esti*, 237c8). Importantly for our purposes, this definition must not be solipsistic, but instead the product of an agreement with others, and the language of "speaking together" (*homologeō*) arises three times in this passage (at 237c3, c5, and d1). In addition to beginning from a definitional account of the thing itself at issue, discursive deliberation thus entails a kind of collective effort between multiple parties, which is what Lysias's speech lacked in both form and content.

But here in his second speech, Socrates tellingly fails to enact these principles insofar as he does not actually reach agreement with an interlocutor. Instead, he simply asserts that love is a form of desire (237d3-4), in a move that he will later criticize (explicitly at 242d11-243a2, and implicitly throughout the palinode). While this satisfies the condition of a definition as a starting point for discourse, it has not been arrived at through any kind of agreement and instead is asserted dogmatically. Socrates's speech, therefore, performatively demonstrates the necessary unidirectional character of this kind of monological speech, showing by deed that the method cannot meet the standards of good, healthy discourse due to its lack of dynamic engagement with another. Surely Socrates was aware of this, and we can understand why he covered his head to signal that such a performance is demonstrative but not something he himself endorses either as a true and complete account or as a method of educating the audience.

In the transition between his first and second speeches, Socrates states that he will become "possessed from within" (*enthousiasō*, 241e5) by the inspirational Nymphs upon Phaedrus's suggestions for the speech's improvement (241d4 ff). The notion of being "possessed from within" by a god will recur throughout Socrates's subsequent speech (through the language of *enthusiazō* at 249d2, 249e1, 253a3, and 263d2)[21] and resolve itself later when, during the critique of writing, Phaedrus describes a certain type of speech as "ensouled"

---

[21] See Scully, *Plato's 'Phaedrus,'* 21n55.

(*empsuchon*, 276a8, echoing Socrates in the palinode at 245e6).[22] We should note that the theme of possession from within arises upon Phaedrus's contribution to the discussion and demonstrates the role of shared, dialectical engagement in the vital "ensoulment" of discourse. This is, I submit, a development of the theme of performativity, insofar as it indicates the role of dialectical engagement that will be developed in what follows; but, tellingly, it begins here through the mythic analogy of divine possession, anticipating the turn to myth that the dialogue will soon take.

This sets the stage for the dialogue's third speech, which is Socrates's arresting and memorable palinode. There is, of course, much of interest in this speech in which core elements of Platonic philosophy are depicted through mythic imagery, but here I limit myself to a few observations relevant to the theme of vital *logos*. The turn toward understanding the soul (beginning at 245c5) is no accident, as the Lysias speech and first Socrates speech had entailed conceiving of the other simply as a body; the consideration of soul thus contributes to the text's upward movement, which ultimately concludes in a discussion of the metaphorical "ensoulment" of good discourse. Relatedly, the soul's power (*dunamei*, 246a7) is said in a well-known metaphor to be like (*eoiken*, 246a5 and *eoiketō*, 246a6) a winged team of horses and a charioteer (246a6-b1). Socrates makes explicit that this is not a complete account of the soul, but instead a likely (*eoiken*) tale that will suffice for present purposes. When dividing the soul into the "noble" and "ignoble" horses that must be overseen by the charioteer, Socrates makes a move similar to his recognition in his first speech of human nature as composed by the conflicting desire for pleasure and the pursuit of the best (237d5-e1). While also capturing a sense of conflict within the human being, the horse metaphor here in the palinode allows Socrates to describe these forces on the model of powers (*dunamin*, 246c4) specifically related to the animalistic embodiment represented by the horses. In other words, while the initial metaphor of conflicting desire suggests a relatively simplistic mechanism of attraction that we might imagine as something like a magnet attracting metal (to borrow an image

---

[22] Here Socrates addresses ensouled bodies as those capable of self-motion.

from Plato's *Ion*), the horse metaphor by contrast invigorates this image in embodied entities driven either by hunger and sexual lust or the pursuit of nobility and health.

The theme of embodiment persists throughout the myth, arising in contexts like the body's necessary subjection to such conditions as the heaviness of weight (247b3-6) and the need to consume food (248b3-5). These are further developed within the description of the two metaphorical horses in bodily terms (beginning at 253d1), and through the numerous subtle references to sexuality as bodily urges.[23] As Socrates indicates at the speech's conclusion (257a5-6), the approach was delivered "poetically" (*poiētikois*) since it was for the sake of Phaedrus and the "psychagogic" care of his soul.[24]

In summary, we have considered some ways in which the movement of the first half of the *Phaedrus* anticipates the vitality metaphor that will arrive shortly after its midway point. The stage was set by some dramatic details and then Lysias's speech, a performance lacking performativity characterized in both form and content as non-dialectical and hence "unhealthy" discourse that offers no educative value to the audience whatsoever. In his first speech, Socrates criticized this approach both positively through his assertions and negatively through demonstration before turning to myth in the palinode, through which a different approach to discourse was exhibited. The myth further developed the theme of embodiment and demonstrated a psychagogic (as well as pedagogic) approach to speechmaking that contrasts with the selfishness of the first two speeches, and introduces the dynamic interaction of parties through the mythic analogy of possession. But still does not reach the level of discursive engagement between participants that will be found in dialectic. In the next section, we will consider the interlocutors' turn to rhetoric and, subsequently, dialectic, the

---

[23] See Halperin, "Plato and Erotic Reciprocity," 62-68 and Scully, *Plato's 'Phaedrus,'* 31-34 for some examples and discussion.

[24] On the psychagogic function of the palinode, see Marina McCoy, *Plato on the Rhetoric of Philosophers and Sophists* (Cambridge: Cambridge University Press, 2007), 167-96, and Moss, "Soul-Leading," esp. 12-14 and 19-22. See also Elizabeth Asmis, "*Psychagogia* in Plato's *Phaedrus*," *Illinois Classical Studies* 11 (1986): 153-72.

vitality metaphor itself, and the senses in which the text continues to exhibit performance and performativity in its discussion.

Vitality in rhetoric and dialectic (257b7-274b1)

We are now prepared to turn to the extended discussion of rhetoric, that art (if it is indeed an art) of speaking persuasively that concerns the dialogue's second half beginning at 257b7. The vitality metaphor arises as one of many points in response to Socrates's question, "How, then, do you write well or poorly?" (258d7), which sits near the dialogue's center and motivates the latter half of the discussion. In response, the interlocutors discuss a host of issues, drawing tacitly on contemporary rhetoric books and introducing the method of philosophical dialectic as a contrasting and, in some senses, complementary notion.[25] But the vitality metaphor occupies a special place, given its implications for our understanding of the structure of discourse.

In this section, I have two aims. The first is to show that this stretch of the dialogue is not merely "expounded" as some have suggested, but is performed, in both the senses of a dramatic rendering and a dialectically "alive" discourse.[26] An "expounded" text would entail mere statement of doctrine, whereas a "performed" text entails an instantiation of discourse with some amount of dialectical engagement and hence educative performativity. My second aim is to speak to Socrates's performance of healthy discourse and its function in understanding philosophical dialectic's role in the vitality metaphor, two notions crucially intertwined.

Concerning the first point, we should note that Plato has Socrates "bring to life" the various rhetoricians and historical figures whose views he discusses, hence the rhetoric section (from 257b7-274b1) is as much a performance as is the first half of the dialogue.[27] Socrates here discusses the nature of rhetoric and ultimately concludes that its successful execution entails understanding both the soul of the audience and hence their educative needs, and the

---

[25] See, e.g., R. Hackforth, *Plato's 'Phaedrus'* (Indianapolis: Bobbs-Merrill, 1952), 155 for more on Plato's use of the rhetorical theory of his day.

[26] See Werner, "Plato's *Phaedrus*," 99.

[27] I am indebted to Yunis, *Plato, 'Phaedrus,'* 21, for several of these points.

ways to divide and collect the various phenomena of life according to their sameness and difference (see especially 271c9-272b2).[28]

In the discussion, Socrates not only names but also reinvigorates the thinking of various historical and mythical figures, engaging dialectically with them in invoked form and using their points to develop his own conclusions. For instance, the reference to "a certain Palamedes from Elea" that Socrates introduces (261d6) is apparently a reference to the Eleatic Zeno widely remembered for his paradoxes,[29] whose invoked voice brings the relations of "like and unlike, one and many, [and being] at rest and in motion" into the account of rhetoric's power (261d6-8). The point, which invokes Zeno's writing directly,[30] is that entities bear relations to one another such as similarity and dissimilarity, wholeness and diffuseness, and change and its lack. One central power of discourse drawn upon by rhetoricians is that of identifying these relations by exhibiting multiple subjects and speaking in ways that demonstrate to the audience the similarities and dissimilarities between the subjects,

---

[28] Socrates summarizes as follows: "Until someone knows the truth about each of the things he discourses (*legei*) or writes about and is able (*dunatos*) to define (*horizesthai*) everything according to itself (*kat' auto te pan*) and, having defended it, knows how to cut it up again according to forms until it has come to the state where it can be cut up no more; and until that person sees thoroughly into the nature of the soul (*psuchēs phuseōs*) according to these same principles, discovering the form that most fits each nature, and accordingly makes (*tithē*) and arranges (*diakosmē*) his discourse, supplying intricate or multi-colored discourse, covering all the harmonic modes for an intricate or multi-colored soul and supplying simple discourse for a simple soul—only then will he be able to manage the class of discourses artfully, to the degree that it is within its nature to be artful, either with respect to teaching (*didaxai*) or persuading something, as the entire earlier discussion revealed to us" (277b5-c6).

[29] This is the majority interpretation; cf. Scully, *Plato's 'Phaedrus,'* 46n109 and Yunis, *Plato, 'Phaedrus,'* 21. For detailed discussion of the debate concerning the identity of this "Palamedes of Elea," see Francesco Ferro, "The Eleatic Palamedes: Zeno's Defence of the Eleatic Doctrine of the One-All in the *Phaedrus,*" *Méthexis* 34 (2022): 1-23.

[30] Cf. Ferro, "The Eleatic Palamedes," 5n25.

and the ways in which they do or do not change (i.e., are in motion or at rest) depending on context. This process, of course, can be done well or poorly.

Identifying these philosophical distinctions allows Socrates to define rhetoric thereafter as discourse (*legomena*, 261e1) that "enables someone to make everything similar to everything else, provided that things are comparable and able to be compared and, when someone else makes these similarities but hides the fact that he is doing so, to bring this to light" (261e1-4). This distinction concerning likeness, unlikeness, and rhetoric's power to exploit these qualities is thus a result of Socrates's dialectical exchange with the invoked Zeno, and a set of relations that Socrates will need to clarify as distinct from the notions of sameness and difference on which the dialectician draws in response to Zeno's provocations.[31] In other words, by speaking in Zeno's voice, Socrates indicates the difficulties we find when considering the natures and relationships of entities engaged in such dyads as same-different, like-unlike, and rest-motion in the Zenonian spirit, thereby giving himself and Phaedrus the task of untangling their meaning.

Socrates will make similar moves throughout the rhetoric section, invoking the voices of Pericles (269b4-c4), Tisias (273d3-274a5), and even a personified version of sophistical rhetoric itself (260d3-8) to describe challenging notions that will allow for positive conceptual progress and help the interlocutors give shape to the account of rhetoric as it develops. This stretch of the dialogue is itself dialectical, as the product of a living engagement with historical thinkers and views. As such, it entails performative enactment and hence demonstrates a kind of vitality that was lacking, for instance, in Lysias's speech.

---

[31] This is often taken to be critical of Zenonian thinking; see, e.g., Ferro, "The Eleatic Palamedes." I suspect, however, that there is more kinship between Zenonian philosophy and Platonic views than is typically thought; for a defense of such a view in the context of the *Parmenides* see Eric Sanday, "Eleatic Metaphysics in Plato's *Parmenides*: Zeno's Puzzle of Plurality," *Journal of Speculative Philosophy* 23.3 (2009): 208-26.

Most significantly for our purposes, the exchange with the invoked Zeno allows Socrates to develop an account of philosophical dialectic itself, which represents the culmination of the theme of discursive methods evident throughout the dialogue in the moves from speeches and myth into rhetoric. The notion of philosophizing is (arguably) first indicated at 261a4, when Socrates describes the need for loving wisdom (*philosophēse*) on the part of the good rhetorician. Although Socrates mentions this merely instrumentally and in passing,[32] it foreshadows the unpacking of distinctions between likeness, unlikeness, sameness, and difference that will be necessary as Socrates describes philosophical dialectic in the context of seeking the nature of rhetoric.

His description of this method is diffuse and scattered through several stretches of text, but we can gather a central sense from three sets of claims (indicated with my Roman numerals). First, Socrates tells us that dialectic entails "...sight that [i] can bring into a single form (*mian ... idean*) things that have previously been scattered in all directions so that by defining (*horizonmenos*) each thing, [iii] he [the dialectician] makes clear (*dēlon poiē*) any subject he ever wants to teach (*didaskein*) about" (265d4-6). Second, Socrates describes [ii] "the power to cut up a composition, form by form according to its natural joints and not to try to hack through any part as a bad butcher might" (265e1-266b2). Finally, he summarizes:

> I myself am certainly a lover, Phaedrus, of these processes
> of division and collection, so that I may have the ability to
> speak and think. If I believe that someone else has the
> capacity (*dunaton*) to see into a single thing and to see the
> natural outgrowth from a single thing toward many things,
> I pursue him [...] I have been calling those who have the
> capacity to do this 'dialecticians.' (266b4-c1)[33]

---

[32] Cf. Yunis, *Plato, 'Phaedrus,'* 184.

[33] On the central importance of this passage, see Hackforth, *Plato's 'Phaedrus,'* 136. On the relation between division in the *Phaedrus* and other dialogues, see Jens Kristian Larsen, "What Are Collections and Divisions Good For? A Reconsideration of Plato's *Phaedrus*," *Ancient Philosophy* 40.1 (2020): 107-33

Thus, we arrive at discourse in its "dialectical" (*dialektikos*, 266c1) sense. The dialectician is that individual who can (i) track genuine sameness and differences across instances, (ii) divide an entity by its "natural joints" to understand its parts, and (iii) make clear (*dēlon poiē*, 265d4) via teaching (*didaskein*, 265d5) the relations of sameness and difference (as in [i]) and part-whole complexity (as in [ii]).[34]

We should note the several ways in which this represents a culmination of the themes of educative performativity, dialectical engagement, and vitality. Socrates describes this process of division and collection as an *activity* that extends from a developed capacity (*dunaton*, 266b5), as the dialectician must engage in an active process of collecting (*sunagōgē*) and dividing (*diairesis*, 266b4). This process is not merely for the dialectician's sake; instead, it is for the sake of making something clear so as to teach. Hence, we should understand dialectic as primarily a kind of *activity*, not merely as the *result* of such an activity (e.g., as it might be laid out in a proof), and one concerning either sameness and difference or mereology (or both) that might have an explanatory or pedagogical function.

I submit that we find a complementary account in Plato's *Sophist*. Here, the anonymous Eleatic Stranger, who acts as primary interlocutor, describes a similar dialectical method of division that he employs throughout and into the sequel dialogue, the *Statesman*. When introducing it to the young mathematician Theaetetus with whom he will converse, he describes the method as a "common" (*koinē*, *Soph.* 218b6 and 218c2) inquiry made by interlocutors to determine a definitional account. Since his points will help us to tie together several key concepts in the *Phaedrus* concerning dialectical engagement, we should consider the Eleatic Stranger's description of division in full (*Soph.* 218c1-5):

> You [Theaetetus] are to [join with me as we] search for and make apparent whatever he [the sophist, the subject of the dialectical inquiry] is. For right now you and I have only the

---

[34] The roles of "making clear" and "teaching" indicate that we must not understand dialectic purely on the model of technical mastery of nature, but instead to have a pedagogical function; cf. McCoy, *Plato on the Rhetoric*, 167.

name in common [*koinē*] about this fellow; but each of us may have, for ourselves, a private notion of the job we call by the name. But we must always and about everything be in agreement [*sunōmologēsthai*] with each other about the thing itself [*to pragma auto*] through discourse [*dia logōn*] rather than the name alone apart from discourse. [35]

If we are justified in taking the Eleatic Stranger's points about dialectic in the *Sophist* to bear on the *Phaedrus* discussion, we will find the re-emergence of an issue discussed in the previous section. Recall Socrates's imperative for "speaking together" (at *Phaedrus* 237c3, c5, and d1) to yield a "definition" (*horon*, *Phaedrus* 237d1) of the subject of the discourse that is derived from collective effort (which, of course, Socrates knowingly fails to do in his monological discourse). Dialectic in the *Sophist* and *Phaedrus* has shown itself to be a method of reaching agreement (*sunōmologēsthai*, *Sophist* 218c5 and echoing the language of *Phaedrus* 237c-d) collectively, resolving this problem that Socrates had indicated previously concerning monologues.[36]

While there is much to say about the function of Platonic dialectic broadly, for our purposes we should note that dialectic has shown itself as a most "vital" kind of discourse. By aiming at the level of the "common" and defining so as to reach an agreement, discourse achieves the kind of activity that Socrates describes in the vitality metaphor. Throughout the subsequent stretch of the *Phaedrus* (particularly 266d1-274b1), Socrates will consider rhetoric and its health or lack thereof with respect to its dialectical engagement with

---

[35] *Sophist* translations are my modifications of Eva Brann, Peter Kalkavage, and Eric Salem (trans.), *Plato, 'Sophist,' The Professor of Wisdom* (Newburyport, MA: Focus Publishing, 1996).

[36] Scholars debate whether division entails discovery or demonstration, that is, whether the primary interlocutor *searches with* the interlocutor(s) for the notion at issue or instead merely *demonstrates* a lesson to a passive interlocutor. My endorsement of the former is Colin C. Smith, "The Method of Bifurcatory Division in Plato's *Sophist*," *Elenchos* 42.2 (2021): 229-60. Here I add that this is one of the lessons of the *Phaedrus*: dialectic is not merely a filling of the ears of passive students, but a quasi-erotic engagement with the other, although the exact nature of this will vary based on the maturity of the secondary interlocutor.

the other in a manner that entails either care for or neglect of the educative needs of the audience. For instance, at 272d7-e2, Socrates criticizes those in the law courts for valuing persuasiveness while neglecting notions of goodness, justice, human nature, and the best ways to raise children, thereby failing to care for the souls of the audience on the model of dialectic. This kind of "unhealthy" discourse marks a partial return to the speech of Lysias, insofar as it entails the desire to persuade in the absence of care. I submit that we should understand the vitality metaphor as finding its full exposition through the notion of philosophical and educational dialectic.

Writing vs. ensouled discourse (274b2-279c8)

This brings us, ultimately, to the well-known critique of writing (274b2-278b5) with which the *Phaedrus* concludes following a brief dramatic resolution (278b6-279c8). The subject of writing in the *Phaedrus* has been thoroughly discussed,[37] and Plato makes its connection to the notion of vital discourse apparent through the interlocutors' vocabulary. The passage thus will resolve the vitality metaphor and its implications about performance and education.

Socrates's critique of writing concerns the written word's inability to address the soul of a given reader directly. Instead, written words are like paintings that "stand there as if alive," but, when questioned, "remain in complete and solemn silence" (275d5-6). Incapable of defending itself or clarifying its meaning, the written word thus represents a kind of static, passive, and inert discourse, always "needing the help of its parent" (275e3-5) to respond to any further inquiry. In summary, writing cannot choose its audience, respond to questions, or control the ways its contents are taken up.[38]

---

[37] See especially Ronna Burger, *Plato's 'Phaedrus': A Defense of a Philosophical Art of Writing* (Tuscaloosa, AL: University of Alabama Press, 1980) and Ferrari, *Listening to the Cicadas*, 204-22.

[38] Socrates's critique is in fact more complicated, involving further criticism for writing inhibiting memory, creating incomplete or false semblances of knowledge, and the illusion of permanence. See Drew Hyland, "Why Plato Wrote Dialogues," *Philosophy and Rhetoric* 1 (1968): 39-40, Jan Zwicky, "Plato's *Phaedrus*: Philosophy as Dialogue with the Dead,"

To understand this, the interlocutors juxtapose writing with "a different kind of discourse" (*horōmen logon*, 276a1), as follows:

> Socrates: [By this I mean] one written with knowledge [*epistēmēs*] in the soul [*psuchē*] of one who understands [*manthanantos*]; this is able [*dunatos*] to defend itself and it knows [*epistēmōn*] when and to whom it should discourse [*legein*], and when and to whom it shouldn't.

> Phaedrus: You are discoursing about the kind of discourse from the person who knows, discourse living [*legeis zōnta*] and ensouled [*empsuchon*], the written version of which would justly be called the image. (276a5-9)

This passage indicates the contrast between the soulless written word and vital discourse, clearly pointing back to the vitality metaphor via the notion of discourse that possesses life (*zōnta*, 276a8) and furthermore adding the term "soul" (*empsuchon*, 276a8). Socrates thus establishes here that the antithesis of the sort of vital discourse at issue in the vitality metaphor is the written word, which precisely lacks "life" and "soul." Nevertheless, he and Phaedrus leave open the possibility that some writing might serve as the *image* of vital discourse, were it to have been written by one who understands and writes with knowledge into souls.

Socrates further unpacks this distinction through the metaphor of sowing seeds (276b1-e3). He compares the able gardener's use of fertile soil to the writer who has knowledge and thus is capable of writing discursive reminders concerning things like the just, beautiful, and good. But Socrates contrasts this kind of writing with the living, enacted use of dialectic (*dialektikē*, 276e5) to sow discourse knowingly into souls, that is, into other interlocutors. By taking root in others and continuing to grow and flourish, this discourse yields insights that will allow the interlocutor to bear further fruit through further discourse in yet others, thereby achieving a kind of "deathlessness" (*athanaton*, 277a2). In other words, the interlocutor who sows discursive seeds properly in the souls of others does so in

---

Apeiron 30 (1997): 24-27, and Doug Al-Maini, "Collection and Division in Plato's Critique of Writing," *Ancient Philosophy* 35.1 (2015): 41-62.

such a way as to allow those seeds to flourish into further, living discourse that can reproduce in future generations as well. Performance, thus, culminates in an educative process for the betterment of the educated that allows for its own reproduction.

The seed metaphor thus represents a final development of the vitality metaphor: just as discourse is alive, so too does it have the power to produce further discursive lifeforms if properly "planted." Discourse in this sense has the same powers (*dunata*) as life, insofar as it could in principle reproduce itself indefinitely, were each generation able to find conditions in which its offspring could grow. In this sense, discourse and life both partake of potential "deathlessness." Life entails mortality, but living things possess the power to produce something alike in kind upon finding the right conditions in which to do so. In this way, both living things and discourse partake of their modest shares of the divine.

I submit that we must understand in this passage's reference to dialectic an explicit connection between the vitality metaphor and dialectic as considered above. We have seen that living discourse is best represented through communal, disciplined investigation into sameness-difference, likeness-unlikeness, and motion-rest among interlocutors. The discussion both entails agreement between participants and guidance from the "primary" interlocutor in allowing the audience to consider these issues in an educative way. And to understand discourse's potential deathlessness, we must return to the notion of dialectic and its distinct ability to offer nurturing conditions to its interlocutors, just like shade of the plane tree, grass, and measured breeze.

Conclusions: performance and *erōs*

We have seen that the notion of discourse as something "alive" permeates the *Phaedrus*. We began with Lysias's unhealthy discourse before Socrates exhibited the constrained power of monological discourse to communicate truths, albeit non-dialectically. Socrates then demonstrated the psychagogic power of myth, which later showed itself to be less vital than rhetoric and, finally, philosophical dialectic. By tracking this permeating theme, our discussion thus has offered perspective on the perennial question of the unity of this seemingly heterogeneous text.

181

From this perspective, the vitality metaphor in the discussion of philosophical dialectic draws together the other parts of the dialogue. Discourse is most "alive" when enacted, and we can understand this enactment as a kind of educative performance. The "primary" interlocutor must exhibit a way of being to guide the becoming of the "secondary" interlocutor in a way that allows the secondary interlocutor not merely to imitate, but to *become* the philosopher. Simultaneously, dialectic calls for genuine, caring communion between interlocutors, not the model of active and passive participation tacitly endorsed by Lysias. Instead, the interlocutors must reach a kind of shared agreement that is mutually beneficial, albeit in a way that reflects their differing levels of maturity and their respective educational needs.

I conclude by suggesting that this might give some insight toward understanding why Plato chose to use the *Phaedrus* as an occasion to consider both discourse *and* love in the sense of *erōs*. Discourse is a kind of mutual engagement between speaker and listener, and this aspect of discourse is well-captured by the notion of erotic love (which could, but need not, be understood sexually). The vitality metaphor thus is in partial service of developing the larger erotic theme: *erōs* is both a *bringer* of life and an *expression* of life. In other words, *erōs* is a function of living through which the very quality of living is enacted, and, at least under the right conditions, in such a way as to allow further life to flourish. *Erōs* hence is paradigmatic in our understanding of vitality itself. And thus, by exhibiting the subject of living discourse within a vital discussion of *erōs*, Plato has educationally achieved a unity of discourse and deed.

Audrey L. Anton & Erika N. Brown[1]

Vicious Art or Vicious Audience?
Tragic Moral Education in Aristotle's *Poetics*

The dominant interpretation of Aristotle's *Poetics* maintains that, for Aristotle, tragedy can be morally instructive if managed correctly.[2] This qualification—correct management of tragedy's instructive capacity—must be critically reviewed through the lens of Aristotle's moral psychology. In this paper we analyze tragedy's effects on the moral psychology of persons of differing moral knowledge. We find that two groups of people who lack keen moral perception—young children and vicious people—*prima facie* pose a unique challenge to the efficacy of moral education through tragedy. Since such agents lack moral knowledge, and because tragedy educates implicitly, youths and vicious people are at a disadvantage for learning the moral of a story. We answer this challenge (on Aristotle's behalf) with the following solution: tragedy can be morally instructive to morally ignorant subjects only if it is performed live before an audience largely comprised of viewers with moral knowledge. Through investigating challenges to the interpretation that tragedy is morally educative, we show that *what*

---

[1] Audrey L. Anton is an Associate Professor of Philosophy at Western Kentucky University. Her research areas include ancient philosophy, ethics, and philosophical gerontology. Erika Brown is a Ph.D. candidate in the Department of Philosophy at Villanova University. Their research areas include women of color and feminist theory.

[2] For an "anticognitivist" take, see J. Lear, "Katharsis," in *Essays on Aristotle's Poetics*, ed. A.O. Rorty (Princeton, N.J: Princeton University Press, 1992), 315–40. For more accounts arguing that Aristotle believed tragedy is morally instructive, see L. Golden, "Mimesis and Katharsis," *Classical Philology* 64.3 (1969): 145–53; H. House, *Aristotle's Poetics: A Course of Eight Lectures* (Greenwood Press, 1978); M.C. Nussbaum, *The Fragility of Goodness: Luck and Ethics in Greek Tragedy and Philosophy* (Cambridge: Cambridge University Press, 2001); S. Halliwell, "Tragic Pity: Aristotle and Beyond," in *The Aesthetics of Mimesis: Ancient Texts and Modern Problems* (Princeton University Press, 2002), 207–33, and M.M.C.O. de Landázuri, "Aristotle and the Pedagogic Function of Aesthetic Pleasure," *Comprendre* 15.2 (2013): 23–34.

and *how* tragedy teaches viewers depends entirely on the current moral condition of the viewer's soul.

Tragedy and moral character

Tragedy is a mode of imitation (*mimēsis, Poet.* 1447a15-17), which has six parts (*Poet.* 1448a1-4), the most important of which is plot. The plot's events are structured to imitate the types of actions that elicit pity and fear (*Poet.* 1452a38-1452b1), which is the goal of tragedy (*Poet.* 1450a22-23). While the qualities of specific characters can differ within a tragedy, Aristotle thinks the protagonist must be slightly morally better than the average person (*Poet.* 1453a8-10, 1454b9-11) for at least two reasons: 1) so viewers can identify with them and 2) so that their downfall may be feared and pitied.

The protagonist commits a moral error (*hamartia*) that is neither vicious nor purely accidental (*Poet.* 1453a15-17). The *hamartia* cannot be vicious since audience members can only pity *undeserved* misfortune, and the vicious deserve all they get. The error cannot be accidental, since it must reflect on the protagonist as something for which they are, at least in part, responsible.[3] Since the error leads to grave consequences for the protagonist, viewers fear a similar fate if they behave similarly.[4]

Viewers witness a *discovery* when a character comes to learn something about the consequences of their actions (*Poet.* 1452a30-1452b3). While the character of the protagonist is important, it illustrates more the type of action that is to be avoided, since the purpose of an action determines its quality (*Poet.* 1449b37-1450b8), and one's character determines one's purpose (*NE* 1114b1; *Poet.* 1454a18-19). Furthermore, as actions ultimately lead to the formation of a certain type of character (*NE* 1103a15-20; *EE* 1220a36-1220b4), which affects an agent's wellbeing, actions are of great consequence for whether one achieves happiness (*eudaimonia*) (*Poet.* 1450a15-20).[5]

---

[3] On the tension between suffering *undeservedly* but also due to an act for which one is responsible, see C. Witt, "Tragic Error and Agent Responsibility," *Philosophic Exchange* 35.1 (January 1, 2005): 69–86.

[4] See I. Smithson, "The Moral View of Aristotle's Poetics," *Journal of the History of Ideas* 44.1 (1983): 14.

[5] Smithson, "The Moral View" 7.

Aristotle describes four kinds of acquired human character. The virtuous person knows the good, does what is right, and feels appropriately towards the good. Only the virtuous see the highest good perfectly (*NE/EE* 1144a34).[6] The virtuous flourish (i.e., achieve *eudaimonia* (*NE* 1098a16-17)) when they possess sufficient external goods (*NE* 1099a31-2). The most common types of character are continence, incontinence, and those in-between. The continent know the good and typically follow that knowledge (*NE* 1104b28, 1105a15; *NE/EE* 1145b9-14; *EE* 1220a36, 1221b34-37). Since they have base desires, they can perform base acts voluntarily (*NE/EE* 1146a10-17, 1151b35-1152a2). Incontinent people also know the good and have strong base desires; however, they routinely fail to act according to their best judgment. Aristotle tells us that, "incontinence and continence are about what exceeds the state of most people; the continent person abides [by reason] *more than most people* are capable of doing, the incontinent person less" (*NE/EE* 1152a25-26).[7] Necessarily, there exists a spectrum between these two types of character, which is why Aristotle adds, "the state of most people is intermediate, even if they lean more towards the worse [i.e., incontinence]" (*NE/EE* 1150a15).[8]

Since the virtuous, continent, incontinent, and people in-between all know the good, let us call them *morally knowing subjects*.[9] While this conglomeration surely includes the vast majority of humanity, it does not include every human being. Two additional types of people—children and vicious persons—do not know the good. For Aristotle, both moral knowledge and character develop over time; no one is born with a moral character (*NE* 1103a12-23).[10]

---

[6] Passages from the three common books of *Nicomachean Ethics* (*NE*) and *Eudemian Ethics* (*EE*) are cited with both abbreviations (*NE/EE*).

[7] Irwin's translation, with our emphasis added (Aristotle, *Nicomachean Ethics*, trans. T.H. Irwin, 2nd ed. (Indianapolis: Hackett, 1999).

[8] Anton, trans.

[9] These shall also be referred to as knowing subjects/viewers.

[10] Natural character is distinct from Aristotle's notion of moral character (i.e., a *hexis*). Natural character consists of the initial characteristics one has at birth. Unlike moral character, these are not chosen. We follow

Young children are pre-rational (*NE* 1111a25, 1111b7-9; *Pol.* 1260a12-14; *EE* 1224a25-29; *MM* 1206b23), therefore, they cannot be morally knowing subjects since one must possess a developed reason to possess such knowledge. On the other hand, vicious persons have developed reason (*NE/EE* 1150a1-2), but they too are morally ignorant (*NE* 1110b28-1111a2). What's worse, they are not aware of their own ignorance (*NE/EE* 1150b36), and they cannot be reasoned with (*NE* 1095b3-8; 1179b4-31). Let us call the pairing of these types of subjects *morally ignorant subjects*.

Moral education

For Aristotle, tragedy educates "not through reporting, but instead through demonstrating by means of pity and fear ending in the catharsis of the sufferings (*pathēmatōn*) of those emotions [i.e., pity and fear]" (*Poet.* 1449b24-27).[11] Good tragedy achieves this result through imitation, as "imitating comes naturally to human beings from childhood [...] and it is through *mimēsis* that he develops his earliest understanding" (*Poet.* 1448b4). That learning itself is enjoyable is evident to Aristotle, since "we enjoy contemplating the most precise images of things whose actual sight is painful to us, such as the forms of the vilest animals and of corpses" (*Poet.* 1448b10-11). So enjoyable is the experience of learning that it can overcome the pain the objects of learning cause, rendering the experience on the whole attractive. Aristotle exalts the pleasure of learning superlatively when he writes, "to be learning something *is the greatest of pleasures* not only to the philosopher but also to the rest of mankind, however small their capacity for it" (*Poet.* 1448b 13-15, our emphasis). Thus, through imitation, tragedy has both an educative

---

M. Leunissen's interpretation that, for Aristotle, natural characteristics change more easily than acquired character states. See M. Leunissen, "Aristotle on Natural Character and Its Implications for Moral Development," *Journal of the History of Philosophy* 50.4 (2012): 524 as well as M. Leunissen, *From Natural Character to Moral Virtue in Aristotle*, (New York, NY: Oxford University Press, 2017).

[11] Anton, trans. Subsequent passages quoted from *Poetics* come from S. Halliwell, *Aristotle: Poetics; Longinus: On the Sublime; Demetrius: On Style* (Cambridge, MA: Harvard University Press, 1995), 1-141.

and an aesthetic value (*Pol.* 1341b38-39). Tragedy is *morally* educative because the imitations in the performance reflect moral actions of good and bad characters (*Poet.* 1448a 1-2), which enables viewers to identify appropriate actions to imitate.

But if tragedy is morally educative, what exactly does tragedy teach? Because poetry, which includes tragedy, focuses on a universal and idealistic plot, "poetry is something more philosophic and of graver import than history, since its statements are of the nature rather of universals, whereas those of history are singulars" (*Poet.* 1451b 5-7). Poetry illustrates how the world ought to be structured, while history recounts how things have already occurred (*Poet.* 1451b 25-26).

The universals taught by tragedies are not universals of nature (e.g., human nature versus dog nature), nor are they universal principles such as cause and effect (e.g., if X is heated, X ignites in flames). Indeed, such universals, much like facts of history, describe how things are and not necessarily how they ought to be. Tragedy teaches *moral* universals, showing viewers "what such and such a kind of man will probably or necessarily say or do" (*Poet.* 9, 1451b8-9). A good man will likely say and do good things, and a bad man will say and do the opposite. Through what transpires for each type of man, Aristotle aims to educate the audience of the good and bad consequences that may follow good and imperfect behavior (respectively).

Tragedy illuminates for viewers why (all things considered) dishonesty is bad, intemperance ought to be avoided, and people ought to keep their promises. Protagonists who fall short of these moral truths suffer greatly. It is through observing their suffering and responding with pity and fear that viewers learn moral truths. However, viewers must first identify which characters are morally worthy of imitation in order to be properly affected by a tragedy.

A new Meno problem

That tragedy teaches moral universals can seem problematic. *Morally knowing subjects* grasp *the that* of practical thought (*NE* 1095b2-13), which is the basic moral universal notions constituting moral common sense.[12] *That* stealing, lying, cheating, etc. are bad, and *that* temperance, bravery, and generosity are good is easily grasped by all knowing subjects. But if these subjects already know such things, how does tragedy teach universal concepts to them?

On the other hand, *morally ignorant subjects* don't grasp such moral universals, and they seem the least poised to learn how through tragedy, since tragedy does not explicitly state who the bad and good people are; the tragedian must *show* them to be as such (*Poet.* 1449b24-27).[13] For example, consider Euripides's *Medea*.[14] Medea's husband, Jason, is unfaithful and betrays her. She, in turn, murders their children. Morally knowing subjects will easily identify the moral universals violated in each person's actions, and they could easily rank the gravity of each moral offense. However, children might not know that adultery or filicide are bad. Therefore, they are ill-equipped to identify with the appropriate characters and actions in the play. Such characters and actions are supposed to imitate real life (*Poet.* 1454a33-37), thus conjuring in the viewer a

---

[12] See M.F. Burnyeat, "Aristotle on Learning to Be Good," in *Essays on Aristotle's Ethics*, ed. Amélie Oksenberg Rorty (Berkeley: University of California Press, 1980), 71-72, 88n3.

[13] See P.A. Taylor, "Sympathy and Insight in Aristotle's 'Poetics,'" *Journal of Aesthetics and Art Criticism* 66.3 (2008): 267.

[14] While Aristotle does criticize Euripides's *Medea* (*Poet.* 1454b1*ff*), scholars argue that he need not have done so. For example, H. Bilgili argues using Aristotle's own criteria that Aristotle misjudged the play's quality as having an immoral plot ("A Critique of Aristotelian Evaluation of Euripides's Medea," *Kaygı. Uludağ Üniversitesi Fen-Edebiyat Fakültesi Felsefe Dergisi* [2020]: 239–61). B. Asaro argues that, had Aristotle been able to reason past his sexism, he would have seen Medea as a fitting heroine ("A Female Hero and Male Antiheroes: An Investigation of the Tragic Hero and Gender Roles in Euripides' *Medea* According to Aristotle's *Poetics*," in *UCLA Thinking Gender Papers* (Los Angeles: California Digital Library, University of California, 2010), 1–8. Against Aristotle's disdain for the *Deus ex machina*, I. Worthington defends Euripides's choice of ending in "The Ending of Euripides' Medea," *Hermes* 118.4 (1990): 502–5. We use *Medea* as an example since it illustrates how morally ignorant subjects could misunderstand and, therefore, mis-prioritize the various harms visited upon characters.

memory of some prior concept. But Aristotle says that, if we see a thing (for example, a painting) for the first time, and we are pleased by it, it "will not be in the picture as an imitation of it" that we are pleased, but rather due to the "execution or coloring or some similar cause" (*Poet.* 1448b18-20). Therefore, the first time a child witnesses the bad deeds of characters in *Medea*, instead of recognizing the imitation for what it is, they will—at most—delight in the poetic elements *not* as imitations, but rather as purely aesthetic stimulations. On the other hand, a vicious person might think adultery or filicide are perfectly acceptable. Indeed, a vicious person might identify with the scorned Medea, thinking her heinous behavior was justified given Jason's provocation. For morally ignorant viewers, this tragedy could confuse their moral understanding, or worse, confirm their false moral assessments.

Herein lies the difficulty. If the knowing subjects already know what they are learning, how can tragedy morally educate them? On the other hand, if the morally ignorant subjects don't know moral universals, how will they take away the correct moral messages from the plot? After all, the plot conveys these messages through imitation. But if they cannot see imitation for what it is, how can they benefit from the moral education of tragedy?

How moral education works: the spectator problem

A second problem arises when we consider what Aristotle says about moral education. Unlike the content of intellectual virtues, which can be learned via instruction (requiring experience and time only; *NE* 1103a14-18), agents must perform good actions to acquire moral virtues (*NE* 1103a27-1103b25). This is, in part, because moral virtues are excellences of the appetitive part of the soul in conjunction with reason, and the appetitive part of the soul includes feelings, such as emotions (*NE* 1102b25-1103a5; *EE* 1221b31-1222a5). Feelings can be conditioned to be one way or another, but such conditioning requires repetitive action (i.e., habit). Therefore, one might argue, no one learns moral content from tragedy, as moral content requires action, and audience members are passive. Let us call this *the spectator problem*.

This objection conflates the requirements of moral virtue with those of moral knowledge. While Aristotle does suggest that virtue can only be won through repetitive action, nowhere does he say that moral knowledge of any sort can only be achieved via repetitive action. Indeed, the fact that he ascribes moral knowledge to even the akratic agent suggests that Aristotle maintained moral knowledge to be attainable *even if* one acts contrary to it *more than most people.* As Anton has argued elsewhere, moral knowledge is certainly enhanced by repetitive behavior in accordance with it; nevertheless, basic moral knowledge seems attainable even without regular good behavior.[15] Indeed, if we consider the *archai* of practical thought — the *that* of what is good — it is possible that one may come to grasp unsophisticated moral knowledge in any number of ways.[16]

As one needn't be virtuous to have some moral knowledge, we maintain, one needn't be virtuous to identify the good in a tragedy. But the objection is not completely answered. For a modified version could still rear its head: even if one can acquire the *archai* of practical thought passively, why should we believe that one could enhance one's understanding passively through tragedy?

This modified objection raises a fair point. Aristotle certainly would not abide an interpretation of his view that leaves open the possibility of a virtuous couch potato. Nevertheless, while being an avid lover of tragedy is certainly insufficient for developing virtue, it does not follow that there is no psychological or educative benefit to increasing one's awareness of and facility with one's own moral knowledge. We shall return to this suggestion; but first, let us consider Aristotle's target audience of tragedy as well as a defense of the educative interpretation of Aristotelian poetry. Only then will we be able to understand the solution.

---

[15] See A.L. Anton, "Virtuous and Imperfect Moral Knowledge in Aristotle's Ethics," in *Aretē in Plato and Aristotle*, eds. R.M. Brown and J.R. Elliott (Siracusa: Parnassos Press, 2022), 253–84, as well as P. Gottlieb, *Aristotle on Thought and Feeling* (Cambridge: Cambridge University Press, 2021) for accounts that Aristotle maintained that knowledge and feeling affect one another.

[16] For example, see J.R. Elliott, "Aristotle on the *Archai* of Practical Thought," *Southern Journal of Philosophy* 56.4 (December 2018): 448–68, for an account of different ways in which different characters may have first acquired *the that* of moral knowledge.

Who is tragedy for?

We may infer that Aristotle intended his audience to be non-virtuous but morally knowing subjects from his instructions to the tragedian. Aristotle insists that since *we* must be able to relate to the tragic hero, he must be "a man not preeminently virtuous and just," but also, he cannot be the sort of man who behaves with "vice and depravity" (*Poet.* 1453a8-10). On the other hand, Aristotle does encourage some embellishment. For he advocates portraying the character as slightly better than average (*Poet.* 1454b9-11), and actions in good tragedy are *elevated.* However, Aristotle carefully qualifies that protagonists should be only *slightly* better than average, and we believe this is the case for two main reasons. First, if we are to learn from tragedy, we must be able to identify with the moral message. We can only do this if we can identify with the character. Few people are truly virtuous (*NE* 1108b30, 1109a30; *NE/EE* 1156a26; *MM* 1186b36-1187a4), and the rest of us (i.e., those in need of moral education) will have difficulty relating to such people. Furthermore, truly virtuous people would never commit base acts voluntarily (*NE* 1100b34-1101a3), for they do not have base desires (*NE* 1102b26-28; *EE* 1222a18).

Second, we believe that the slight embellishment aids the viewer in relating to the protagonist. While Aristotle is not explicit in why this must be the case, we surmise that such elevation is useful since humans are prone to overestimate the quality of their own moral characters, "because men are bad judges where they themselves are concerned" (*Pol.* 1280a20).[17] Therefore, the protagonist and their actions must be similar enough to the average person's character to be relatable, while erring on the side of our better natures. Aristotle elaborates that we "should follow the example of good portrait-painters, who reproduce the distinctive features of a man, and at the same time, without losing the likeness, make him handsomer than he is" (*Poet.* 1454b9-11). That way, we will identify with them, as we overestimate our own moral character and theirs is (in fact) slightly better than ours.

---

[17] Most quoted passages are based on Aristotle, *Politics*, trans. H. Rackham (Cambridge, MA: Harvard University Press, 1932).

Apt pity and fear

In addition, only a protagonist who is slightly better than average renders apt pity possible. For example, Aristotle condemns a plot in which a good man transitions from happiness to misery (*Poet.* 1452b34). In such instances, says Aristotle, neither pity nor fear are elicited, but instead repugnance (*miaron; Poet.* 1452b35). This seems odd initially, as "pity is occasioned by undeserved misfortune" (*Poet.* 1453a5), and the virtuous would be least deserving of such a fate. However, such events elicit a response too strong to constitute pity. Aristotle tells us that the horror (*deinon*) that affects us personally "pushes out" (*ekkruō*) sympathy (*to eleos; Rhetoric* 1386a22-24). If so, perhaps such injustice is so outrageous that it stifles pity altogether.

Furthermore, such a spectacle would be very discouraging. If the virtuous cannot escape a dismal fate, why suppose we could? Since we likely recognize that virtue is difficult (*NE* 1106b31-33, 1109a24-29, 1109b14-16), and in our current non-virtuous state we are not motivated by the fine (*to kalon*) but, instead, the pleasant (*NE* 1095b16, 1151b21-22), witnessing the undeserved downfall of a virtuous person could destroy one's motivation to emulate them.

The audience must be able to identify with the protagonist in another way—their poor choices. For Aristotle is clear that the protagonist must make an error in judgment (*hamartia*), which leads to negative consequences.[18] But this error must teeter between an utter mistake and an action for which the agent is responsible.[19] The

---

[18] There is a surfeit of literature on the nature of Aristotelian *hamartia*. For a recent and thorough review of this literature, see H. Vinje, "The Beauty of Failure: *Hamartia* in Aristotle's Poetics," *Classical Quarterly* 71.2 (2021): 582–600, esp. 582-589. Vinje's position is that *hamartia* is a character flaw she calls *qualified akrasia*, which she takes to be motivated by *thumos* (via temper or a pursuit of good desirable things).

[19] This is one disagreement we have with Nussbaum's account in *Fragility of Goodness*. According to Nussbaum, Aristotle intends viewers to learn from tragic poetry that "having a good character or being in a good condition is not sufficient for the fullness of good living" (380) because "luck is a serious influence in the good life..." and "the good life is

protagonist must be "one who falls into adversity not through evil and depravity, but through some kind of error" (*Poet.* 1453a8-9, Cf. 14-15). The consequences of the protagonist's error must naturally follow from such behavior by men of similar character (*Poet.* 1454a33-37), and "there should be nothing improbable among the actual incidents" (*Poet.* 1454b 6-7). The incidents in the performance cannot occur due to luck, for the audience must identify the protagonist as the cause of their own suffering.

In his discussion of justice (*NE/EE* V), Aristotle distinguishes between an unjust vicious person who chooses to act badly with malice aforethought, and the incontinent person who merely acts unjustly (1134a17-23). Likewise, typical non-virtuous morally knowing subjects are liable to err, and they do so without malice aforethought. Nevertheless, Aristotle holds incontinent people (for example) accountable for acting akratically.[20] Similarly, the *hamartia* that predictably precipitates the downfall of the protagonist, though an error lacking vicious intent, is one for which the agent is

---

vulnerable and can be disrupted by catastrophe." (322). While this is likely true (as Aristotle indicates frequently through examples such as Priam (*NE* 1100a4-9, 1101a6-11), we doubt that Aristotle intended this to be the lesson of tragedy; that bad things can happen to good people seems obvious. Nussbaum also maintains that Oedipus was a good person who committed a justified, blameless act "through no fault of his own" (380). But as Sophocles's text indicates, Oedipus confesses that when the man at the crossroads "tried to thrust me by force from the path...*in anger* I struck the one pushing me aside, the driver, and when the old man saw this, he watched for the moment I was passing, and from his carriage, brought his double goad full down on my head. Yet he was paid back with interest: with one swift blow from the staff in this hand, he rolled right out of the carriage onto his back. I slew every one of them" (805-813). While Oedipus was provoked, it can hardly be said that his response was blameless. At the very least, it was an overreaction regardless of the identities of his combatants.

[20] Indeed, Aristotle states that when an unjust act is performed voluntarily, the agent is blamed (*NE/EE* 1135a21-24), even if it was done voluntarily but not deliberately (*NE/EE* 1135b8-11). Aristotle adds that "we do not forgive vice, nor any other blameworthy quality" (*NE/EE* 1146a1-5), and incontinence is blameworthy (*MM* 1188a35, 1202b5).

accountable. We pity such persons not because they deserve no consequences for their actions, but rather because they suffer greatly out of proportion with their moral failings.[21] For example, in *Medea*, Jason errs in betraying Medea. His actions realistically precipitate a negative reaction from his wife. However, her reaction and the punishment she visits upon Jason is wildly out of proportion with his offense (indeed, innocent people are punished for his offense). Likewise, Oedipus did commit a *hamartia*; he lashed out in rage during a confrontation at a crossroads and killed those he encountered. While we surmise that he should not have responded as he did, it hardly seems fitting that his entire community should suffer a plague as a result.

Oedipus also serves as an excellent example of the need to monitor one's own moral progress. For it is unlikely that anyone decides to be vicious, as Aristotle insists that nobody aims at what they think is bad (*EE* 1223b7; *Rhet.* 1369a3). Instead, people slip into vice through careless incontinent behavior (*NE* 1114a13-22). Nevertheless, becoming vicious is as voluntary as becoming virtuous, since it was in one's power to do so and only through multiple deliberate actions does one achieve such a permanent state of character (*NE* 1110b13-16, 1111a27-30, 1114a30-1114b25; *EE* 1223a19-20, 1223b15-16). Therefore, we are to blame for becoming vicious even if our doing so escaped our notice. Oedipus is clearly concerned that this may have occurred when, after learning that he likely did slay his biological father and wed his biological mother, he

---

[21] Vinje maintains that the protagonist is responsible for an initial bad character flaw (which has consequences), and the consequences of *that* initial flaw are greater than and too far removed from the agent to be rightly attributable to her. See Vinje, "The Beauty of Failure," 590-91. Vinje also notes that similar suggestions can be traced back to at least as early as Stinton, who suggested the protagonist deserves partial blame if her act causes misery disproportionate to her responsibility See T.C.W. Stinton, "*Hamartia* in Aristotle and Greek Tragedy," *Classical Quarterly* 25 (1975): 229-30. In a similar vein, we contend that anyone less-than-virtuous could misjudge the seriousness of their error (voluntary though it may be).

inquires out loud and with trepidation, "Am I now *kakos*?!"[22] His fear and dismay are as surprising to him as they are dreadful. When he killed Laius, he likely considered himself justified, as he was blinded by anger and an inflated sense of righteous indignation. After the event was over, he might have admitted being slightly hot-headed— but understandably so! Perhaps he overreacted...but who wouldn't under such provocation?! Only now, when Oedipus grasps the enormity of the consequences of his actions, does he consider whether he has become vicious.

By focusing on an error that is neither entirely innocent nor vicious, the poet helps the audience to identify with the protagonist in ways that elicit the appropriate fear. Since such errors are easy for non-virtuous persons to make, the audience member could fear erring similarly. The non-virtuous knowing subjects are reminded to be mindful in avoiding such errors; for they may be far greater blunders than they initially appear. In fact, the fates might punish one far more than one deserves, rendering an imperfect person utterly wretched. Furthermore, as the proximal cause of the events which unfold, we fear being responsible for our own misery, since as knowing subjects, we are capable of great regret (*NE/EE* 1150b30, *NE* 1166b25). But regret renders us curable (*NE/EE* 1150a22-23), and so we would be wise to heed tragedy's warnings. Our happiness depends on our attention to avoiding such mistakes.

Against the anticognitivist

It is through feeling pity and fear that viewers of tragedy learn to be mindful not to make careless moral errors; but "pity and fear are unadulterated pains."[23] When Aristotle discusses the pleasurable *mimēsis* of poetry, he insists that we are pleased *because* we are learning when we recognize *mimēsis*. It is perhaps for this reason that some scholars identify tragic learning with *katharsis*[24]—the outcome

---

[22] Sophocles, *Oedipus Tyrannus*, 823.

[23] Lear, "Katharsis," 328. See also *Rhet.* II.5 (on fear) and II.8 (on pity).

[24] It is unfortunate that Aristotle does little in the extant part of his *Poetics* to inform us of the nature of *katharsis*—an apparently crucial part of the tragic experience. In *Politics* at 1341b39-41, Aristotle notes that "the

of tragic pity and fear—for *katharsis* is undoubtedly pleasurable. We argue that this is a mistake.

Considering *katharsis* the instructive part of tragedy only leads scholars to question the obvious educative value of tragedy. For example, in a seminal paper, Lear argues that tragedy *cannot* be educative precisely because *katharsis* is not. But it is perfectly consistent with everything Aristotle says to consider *tragedy* to have morally educative value while denying that the educative value lies in *katharsis*. Aristotle is clear that "the events and the plot are the goal of tragedy, and the goal is the most important thing of all" (*Poet.* 1450a22-23), and these events "yield either pity or fear, just the type of actions of which tragedy is taken to be a *mimēsis*" (*Poet.* 1452a38-1452b1). While it is true that the aim of tragedy is to evoke pity and fear in members of the audience through portrayal of actions and events, and it is also true that experiencing pity and fear ultimately ends in the *katharsis* of these emotions,[25] it does not follow that

---

term *katharsis* we use for the present without explanation...," and promises that "...we will return to discuss the meaning we give to it more explicitly in our treatise on poetry." However, no such discussion appears, and commenters such as H. Rackham (*Poetics*, 671n.a) suggest that, if such explanation existed, it occurred in the lost book of *Poetics*.

[25] When Aristotle first defines tragedy (*Poet.* 1449b26ff), he says it is a *mimēsis* of an action that causes pity and fear *ending* (*perainousa*) in a *katharsis* of the suffering of those emotions. The verb, *perainō*, is usually translated as "accomplishing" or "achieving," which leads readers to imagine that the whole point of tragedy is to achieve *katharsis*. On the contrary, as we note above, Aristotle is explicit that the *telos* of tragedy is the actions that produce pity and fear. Therefore, a better translation would be "bringing to an end" (LSJ 1) or "putting a limit on" (LSJ 2) the suffering of the pity and fear, as these are equally viable translations, which make far more sense (See περαίνω, LSJ 1, 2.). It is preferrable to say that the suffering of pity and fear is limited or concluded via *katharsis* than to say that we aim for the *katharsis* of the pity and fear, since we intentionally conjured the pity and fear in the first place. The latter interpretation supposes we aim to solve a problem that we voluntarily create and could just as easily have avoided. This type of thinking leads to the *purgation* interpretation of

---

katharsis itself is the exclusive and primary aim of tragedy (or, alternatively, that for tragedy to be educative the cathartic experience must be). On the contrary, *katharsis* is the natural closure of having conjured such emotions in audience members. We are pleased not only to be free of the painful emotions of fear and pity, but also because we were able to learn their lessons "the easy way." Instead of learning "the hard way" (i.e., suffering harm in real life), we can learn vicariously through the tragic hero. Still, it is through experiencing pity and fear that members of the audience learn.

As Lear notes, pity and fear are decisively painful emotions. And while Aristotle highlights the connection between imitation, learning, and pleasure in *Poetics* (even going so far as to say that learning is the *greatest* pleasure known to man), readers must not conclude that learning is pain-free. In fact, we often do learn from pain—especially *moral* lessons. In fact, Aristotle also states that when learning is difficult, it is very painful, and this alone could deter us from doing the activity that causes us to learn (*NE* 1175b15-21). Therefore, the pleasure that is endemic to *katharsis* acts as an incentive to go through the pain of feeling pity and fear. We do not learn through *katharsis*. *Katharsis* is the prize for enduring the lesson.

Much of the dispute centers on a key passage in *Politics*, which begins (1341b33-1342a4):

> And since we accept the classification of melodies made by some philosophers, as ethical melodies, melodies of action, and passionate melodies […] and as we say that music ought to be employed not for the purpose of one benefit that it confers but on account of several (for it serves the purpose

---

katharsis. See J. Bernays, "Aristotle on the Effect of Tragedy," in *Articles on Aristotle Vol. 4: Psychology and Aesthetics*, ed. J. Barnes, M. Schofield, and R. Sorabji (New York: Bloomsbury, 1979), 154–65 wherein *katharsis* is characterized as cleansing of something bad. But the pity and fear were not there before engaging with the poetry, and—as Lear ("Katharsis," 318) points out—it is not wrong to feel them (i.e., they are not pathological). Instead, we argue that feeling pity and fear are necessary for learners, but *katharsis* is the pleasant way that such lessons come to an end.

both of education and of *katharsis*)[26] [...] and thirdly it serves for amusement, serving to relax our tension and to give rest from it), it is clear that we should employ all the harmonies, yet not employ them all in the same way, but use the most ethical ones for education, and the active and passionate kinds for listening to when others are performing...

Here Aristotle lists three benefits: *education, katharsis,* and *amusement.* He notes that we ought to employ all types that confer these benefits, provided we do not employ them the same way. But this does not mean that only one type can appear in a single tragedy. In fact, different types of melodies and harmonies are employed at opportune moments in a tragic performance. Further down Aristotle clarifies:

...but for education, as has been said, the ethical class of melodies and of harmonies must be employed [...] but we must also accept any other mode that those who take part in the pursuit of philosophy and in musical education may recommend to us. (*Pol.* 1342a29-33)

If tragedy is to educate *through music,* it must employ melodies and harmonies of the ethical type. However, it is more likely that tragedy educates through its plot, as Aristotle states clearly that this is the most important element of tragic poetry. Therefore, any tragedy can employ melodies "of action" and "passionate melodies" while still educating the audience.

Tragic poetry, like much of art, is layered. Certain aspects of one layer of a work of art may speak more directly to certain viewers than others. For example, in the same discussion in *Politics* VIII.7, Aristotle also writes:

---

[26] Some wrongly translate this line as indicating that tragedy serves the purpose of education through *katharsis.* In the Greek, the construction within the parentheses is: *kai gar paideias heneken kai katharseōs;* the *kai...kai* construction renders education and *katharsis* syntactically equivalent—each is a distinct benefit as *katharseōs* is *not* in apposition to *paideias.*

...for any experience that occurs violently in some souls is found in all, though with different degrees of intensity—for example pity and fear, and also religious excitement; for some persons are very liable to this form of emotion, and under the influence of sacred music we see these people, when they use tunes that violently arouse the soul, being thrown into a state as if they had received medicinal treatment and taken a purge; the same experience then must come also to the compassionate and the timid and the other emotional people *generally in such degree as befalls each individual of these classes...* (*Pol.* 1342a5-14, our emphasis)

Single tragic elements can be employed universally despite affecting different people differently. Admittedly, Aristotle does declare *katharsis* to be something everyone can enjoy (*Pol.* 1342a15-16). Still, the fact that all may enjoy *katharsis* does not mean that everybody learns from tragedy.

The virtuous do not need to learn from tragedy, and certain vicious people might be beyond hope for learning directly from tragedy. Both, it would seem, can enjoy *katharsis*.[27] Perhaps this is why Aristotle allows poets to cater to the tastes of *hoi polloi*. Poets are encouraged to cater to the masses despite the fact that "their souls are warped from the natural state..." (*Pol.* 1342a22) and, therefore, what appeals them will be "deviations" (*Pol.* 1342a26-27). Lear concludes that Aristotle allows for such lowbrow kowtowing because "it's too late. Aristotle contrasts two types of audience: the vulgar crowd [...] and those who are free and *have already been*

---

[27] Even the virtuous can enjoy *katharsis* of pity and fear despite not needing a moral education. In *Rhet.* Aristotle tells us that we fear dangerous things when they appear nearby (*Rhet.* II.4.1, 1382a37 *ff*), and dramatists manage to conjure fear by making it appear as if danger is close at hand (*Rhet.* II.5.1, 1383a). And since certain evils that appear ready to happen to others naturally excite pity, these are to be feared (*Rhet.* II.5.12, 1382b). It is through such things—the pity-inspiring fearful objects we can imagine happening to our loved ones—that the virtuous experience fear while attending a tragedy. While they know that they will never commit such *hamartia*, they can fear for loved ones and enjoy the *katharsis* at the end of the performance.

educated [...] In each case, the characters of the audience have been formed and ethical education would be either futile or superfluous."[28] But Lear's bifurcation is a false dichotomy. Surely not everyone in a tragic audience is either virtuous or vicious. Indeed, Aristotle is clear that both virtuous and vicious persons are rare. The vast majority of humans lie between the two extreme character types, and so the vast majority of humans have some moral knowledge, but also have room to improve. And while the plot of a tragic play alone may not suffice to educate the souls of young children or the vicious, attending live performances of such plays might be a good first step.

The moral of the story

We are approaching the position from where we may answer the two challenges listed earlier: the new Meno problem and the Spectator problem. The answers to these problems will not work for morally ignorant subjects. For that reason, we shall suggest an Aristotelian alteration of how tragedy can educate them; for the educative and pleasurable experience of the viewer depends on the moral condition of their soul.

But first let us revisit the question of what tragedy teaches morally knowing subjects. We stated above that, at the very least, tragedy teaches (since it is about) universals. However, we also noted that, for tragedy to do this, the subject must already grasp such universals. What more is there for morally knowing subjects to learn?

The virtuous are unlikely to learn from tragedy, though they can enjoy it. The continent, incontinent, and those between can easily identify sympathetic characters. For them, tragedy can be most instructive in at least two ways. First, tragedy teaches non-virtuous morally knowing subjects to continue to improve. Through identifying with the protagonist, such audience members are reminded that being a basically good person might not be good enough. Even continent persons could make the sort of error that destroys their happiness.[29] Only the virtuous are immune to misery

---

[28] Lear, "Katharsis," 320.

[29] Oedipus is a possible example, for he was *trying* to avoid the actions of the prophecy. However, we argue that, even if Oedipus were normally

(*NE* 1101a7-8). So, while it is tempting to halt moral progress once vice is eschewed, Aristotle warns against such complacency. In this regard, we have a solution for the Meno problem for non-virtuous morally knowing subjects. While they already know the good (in a nutshell), they must be reminded that striving for and maintaining goodness are lifetime pursuits.

We can also solve the spectator problem. While audience members are not physically acting and making decisions on what to do, they are mentally rehearsing and refamiliarizing themselves with their moral concepts. Recall that, for Aristotle, habits shape both actions and reactions (i.e., motivations and feelings) (*NE* 1103b15-19) and motivations and feelings are part of moral perception (*NE/EE* 1153a2-6; *EE* 1227a39-1227b1, 1235b26-29). But moral perception is perceptual knowledge, and it guides action (*DA* 433b12; *Met.* 1072a27-30). Therefore, while watching a tragedy is not *active per se*, it can be *pseudo-active*, since how one is affected can change one's sensitivity to moral matters.[30]

Since the average person's flaws stem from a discrepancy between their general moral knowledge and feelings on specific occasions when they act, emotional rehearsal could be instructive for them. For example, an akratic person might typically know that one ought not to drink to excess; however, when she is tempted to imbibe, she might temporarily forget this principle or fail to see how it applies to her on this occasion. As a result, she follows her desires to inebriation.

Such an agent is weak-willed when her own agency is in play; however, she might be perfectly capable of identifying right action for other people. Indeed, what allows an incontinent agent to act against her better judgment is the incontinent person's failure to access what she knows at the time of action (*NE/EE* 1146b32-35). We

---

a continent person, he certainly perpetrates a rare act of *incontinence* when he meets his biological father at the crossroads and kills him (and others) out of rage. Oedipus is a prime example for Vinje's argument.

[30] This is further evidenced at *NE* III.1 when Aristotle lists *pathē* among the behaviors that can be voluntary and for which we are praised and blamed (1109b30-33).

believe that, for this reason, Aristotle would encourage akratic persons to watch tragedy. Such persons are insufficiently "in touch" with their moral knowledge; it is not at their fingertips when it matters most. Perhaps through passive conjuring of their moral knowledge and mental rehearsal of apt feelings, akratic agents can strengthen the mental connection between their general moral knowledge and their immediate moral perception. As passive observers, their base desires need not be activated. While we noted earlier that men are the poorest judges of their own characters, it is possible that akratic agents are much better at identifying what *someone else* ought to do when tempted to behave contrary to what is good. While certainly not enough to become continent, we contend that even the akratic agent can benefit from tragedy insofar as mentally rehearsing apt emotional reactions might increase the incontinent person's chances of resisting temptations in the future.

This solution—emotional rehearsal and reconnection with knowledge—solves both problems illustrated earlier for non-virtuous knowing subjects. It solves the new Meno problem in that the accessibility of one's moral knowledge is increased even if the content is not.[31] It solves the spectator problem in that while emotional rehearsal is not truly active, it may prepare non-virtuous morally knowing subjects to act better than they may have otherwise.

What can ignorant subjects learn from tragedy?

But what of morally ignorant subjects? They do not have the moral concepts necessary for learning directly from a tragic plot. Might they learn from a different element of the tragedy? For example, individuals of all ages and characters can enjoy the pleasure of music. Aristotle tells us that music inspires enthusiasm in the listener, and enthusiasm is "an emotion of the ethical part of

---

[31] While Anton argues elsewhere ("Virtuous and Imperfect Moral Knowledge," 273, 277) that the content of a continent person's moral knowledge is richer than that of an incontinent person on account of routine active practice, she does not deny that intentional mental rehearsal of the sort that elicits moral judgments and feelings might contribute to one's moral knowledge as well (albeit likely less so than acting on such knowledge in real life).

the soul" (*Pol.* 1340a 10-14). Might music's tendency to inspire moral emotions provide the vicious person sufficient opportunity to learn what is morally good through the understanding of aesthetic value? After all, Aristotle writes, "rhythm [...] is the means in the dancer's imitations; for even he, by the rhythms of his attitudes, may represent men's characters as well as what they do and suffer" (*Poet.* 1447a25-28). If rhythm can communicate one's character, perhaps the morally ignorant subjects could identify the villain musically? Aristotle adds, "thought is shown in all they say when proving a particular point or, it may be, enunciating a general truth" (*Poet.*1450a5-7, *see also* 1450b10-11). Perhaps if a villainous character were introduced with ominous music, and if this particular character speaks a general (false) principle, morally ignorant subjects will know that they ought not to believe what they are hearing. And if they were able to draw this conclusion, they might imagine that the truth is the opposite of whatever the villain says.

While this *might* be the case, this specific combination (i.e., a villain making an incorrect moral declaration while nefarious music plays in the background) is not one that Aristotle explicitly prescribes. It also strikes us as too subtle for most morally ignorant subjects to grasp. Furthermore, if such a combination of events were necessary, we imagine Aristotle would have said as much, since he does make explicit many parts of a good tragedy.

On the other hand, Aristotle does state that "the tragic fear and pity may be aroused by the Spectacle," while still noting, "they may also be aroused by the very structure and incidents of the play—which is the better way and shows the better poet" (*Poet.* 1453b1-2). While the events in the plot are the preferred way to convey the moral of a tragedy to morally knowing subjects, Aristotle presents here a false dichotomy; a poet could, in theory, present the moral in both ways simultaneously.

Nevertheless, Aristotle is adamant that the spectacle is a cheap thrill: "the Spectacle, though an attraction, is the least artistic of all the parts, and has least to do with the art of poetry. The tragic effect is quite possible without a public performance and actors; and besides, the getting-up of the Spectacle is more a matter for the costumier than the poet" (*Poet.* 1450b19-20). Here it is important to recall Aristotle's intended audience. The morally knowing subjects need not witness a live performance to grasp a tragedy's meaning; they know enough to intuit it from simply reading the tragedy. But they are hardly the entirety of a tragedy's audience. For this reason, we suggest that morally ignorant subjects *can* learn from tragedy, but *only* when it is performed.

The tragic elements that are most accessible to morally ignorant subjects are performative. Only when tragedy is performed live will members of the audience be moved by music, rhythm, and the spectacle on stage. Therefore, morally ignorant subjects require this stimulation to be tuned in to the moral message in the first place. As they have no knowledge of the good, they cannot identify *imitation* in the plot of the play *as* imitation (see *Poet.* 1448b18-20 cited above).

Adjusting the spectacle

However, the music and rhythm are the same for both morally knowing and morally ignorant subjects. Perhaps the key to our puzzle is to admit that there are two different plays going on simultaneously in performed tragedy. There is the ostensible tragic performance on the stage, which morally knowing subjects access. But also, there is a broader spectacle that includes the former version: *the extended performance.* Morally ignorant subjects are not only engrossed in the play and its elements, but they will also take note of the reactions of the morally knowing members of the audience. In this regard, their fellow playgoers are as important an attraction as the actors.

To see how this is the case, let us also expand our notion of the tragic element of discovery so that something analogous is available to the morally ignorant subjects. In the play, the audience and the characters will learn something—usually something unpleasant— which explains why the tragic events unfold. Aristotle explains, "a discovery is, as the very word implies, a change from ignorance to knowledge, and thus to either love or hate, in the personages marked for good or evil fortune" (*Poet.* 1452a 30-31). Like the characters in the play, audience members "discover" things about characters and the consequences of their actions along the way.

While Aristotle speaks of discovery as something that happens to characters within the plot, morally knowing subjects can experience periodic "discoveries" alongside the characters on stage. Such discovery is a means by which the knowing viewer can insert themselves into the plotline of the tragedy, for the moment of discovery elicits a reflection of how the viewer's own life is similar.[32] Through such experiences, the spectator transforms from a passive viewer, who simply observes the plotline, to an active viewer, who deliberately allows the tragedy to intrude into their own moral understanding.

An analogous form of discovery could occur for morally ignorant audience members. After all, while "recognition is recognition *between* people," it only requires that one party is aware of it (*Poet.* 1452b3-4). We suggest that morally ignorant subjects experience something analogous to what Aristotle calls "Composite (*sunthetē*) Discovery"—through bad reasoning, the reasoner happens upon the truth anyway (*Poet.* 1455a 11-13). The morally ignorant viewer can "discover" moral truths vicariously through observing the reactions (i.e., signs of pity and fear) evident in the knowing subjects of the audience of a live performance. But such discovery is only noticeable to them when there is a discrepancy between their initial reaction and that of the knowing audience. Consider the following example. A vicious adult pities Medea when she is betrayed. However, when Medea exacts her revenge, this viewer is delighted! To her mind, justice has been served. However, she quickly notices that she alone is cheering. In fact, she hears gasps from the morally knowing audience members, who recognize Glauce and Creon as suffering punishments graver than they deserve, and they see Medea and Jason's children as completely innocent victims.

---

[32] While one might doubt that audience members can relate to one such as Oedipus, Aristotle explicitly uses Oedipus as such an example at 1453a8-12. We needn't also be royal or aristocratic to identify with the tragic hero. We must simply see ourselves as similarly good or as one who might act similarly if in the hero's shoes. For a discussion of the cultural notion of an *us* versus *them* mentality of social status, see G. Zanker, "Aristotle's Poetics and the Painters," *American Journal of Philology* 121.2 (2000): 225–35.

For the morally ignorant subject, they and the rest of the audience are part of what modern experts call a *dynamic audience.*[33] When viewing a tragedy, the audience itself is a part of the viewing experience for morally ignorant subjects. Because morally ignorant subjects will be in the presence of morally knowing subjects, the former can learn how to react to vicious deeds in the play from the latter. If such lessons are taken beyond the theatre and practiced in real life, morally ignorant subjects may ultimately learn how to behave. This phenomenon can be observed in modern day examples of spectators at a sporting event who are ignorant of the rules of the sport. For example, an individual who is unaware of the significance of certain plays in an American football game may learn when to cheer or groan accordingly by examining the ways that their fellow audience members react. Like the ignorant sports spectator, the morally ignorant subjects of a tragedy's audience will learn to stop cheering for the vicious character.

We consider this experience of the ignorant audience member merely analogous to discovery because it is incomplete and vicarious. The morally knowing subjects accurately grasp the discovery of the play; the morally ignorant subjects discover *that* they ought to react a certain way. While they remain ignorant of *why* the knowing subjects react as they do (since they lack the universal concepts), they do recognize their initial instinct as wrong (or, at the very least, unpopular). Morally ignorant subjects must first come to this realization before they can learn (and later recognize) the *imitative* aspect of good tragedy. In the meantime, they may imitate morally knowing subjects who are learning directly from the imitative aspects of the tragedy.

Conclusion

We have argued that tragedy provides a moral education first and foremost to the non-virtuous agents who already grasp basic

---

[33] Brown argues that this technique can be used to combat prejudice. See E. N. Brown, "Tragedy and The Vicious: Moral Education in Aristotle's *Poetics* and Future Applications to Contemporary Art," Honors College Capstone Experience/Thesis Projects. Paper 629, Western Kentucky University, 2016), especially section 7, pp. 23-30.

moral principles. Previous moral understanding is essential to recognizing the imitative aspects of moral elements in any tragic work of art. Typically, non-virtuous yet morally aware subjects do this best when they can identify with the protagonist, pity them when they suffer, and fear becoming like them. Continent viewers are reminded that they must continue to strive for virtue; they must not settle for being "good enough," for even continent people can err in ways that cause more harm than they imagined. Similarly, incontinent viewers are reminded of the importance of moral improvement, and they can increase their facility with their moral knowledge by associating it with the pity and fear induced by the tragic experience.

For those without such prior moral knowledge, the experience of tragic poetry is necessarily very different. They cannot identify the universal moral concepts underlying the imitative acts and events of the plot. If they were to merely read a good tragic play, they would certainly miss the point. Therefore, for tragedy to have its educative effect on morally ignorant subjects *it must be performed,* and those subjects must observe it in an audience comprised of mostly knowing subjects. Children may certainly benefit from the educational melodies and rhythm of live music. However, only through expanding the scope of the spectacle can morally ignorant subjects engage in the metacognition required to inform universal judgments (i.e., in the case of children) or to assess their initial judgments concerning the characters and actions in the plot (i.e., in the case of vicious people).

Through widening the scope of the spectacle to include the audience, morally ignorant subjects may experience revelations analogous to "discovery" within a standard tragic play. This "discovery" for the morally ignorant subject is not merely moving from ignorance of facts (e.g., *that* in killing the king, Oedipus committed patricide) but also values (Oedipus should not have killed anyone, and it is worse, in general, to commit patricide than the typical garden-variety homicide). While truly adopting such values takes time and practice in one's own life beyond the stage, it is possible that, through participation in a dynamic tragic audience, morally ignorant subjects can redirect their aesthetic attentions.

Much like the freed prisoner in Plato's famous allegory of the cave, morally ignorant subjects require a *turning of the soul* to be educated (*Rep.* 518c). In turning to the audience, their moral perspective broadens, and they see themselves within it. While not yet out of the cave, through experiencing tragedy among a live audience, such viewers may come to improve their orientation towards the good (if only in turning away from the bad momentarily). Ultimately, with time and other interventions, such viewers may even join the respectable ranks of the morally knowing subjects.

Georgios Mouratidis & Heather L. Reid[1]
From *Euexia* to *Eupraxia*:
Gymnastic Education and Moral Performance

In Chariton's *Callirhoe*, an ancient novel set in 5th century BCE Siracusa, the protagonist is introduced on his way out of the gymnasium. Chaereas is described as "radiant like a star [as] the flush of exercise bloomed on his beaming face like gold on silver."[2] His beauty is such that Callirhoe, the daughter of Hermocrates, falls for him immediately—as does the novel's audience. But what exactly should we "see" in the hero's gymnastic beauty? To be sure, the image of a fit body has special resonance in ancient Greek culture. It represented the divinity of gods, the nobility of heroes, and the excellence of athletes. As such, it symbolized a goal of Hellenic *paideia*—gymnastic education in particular—which staged contests and gave prizes for *euexia*—a concept conventionally construed as "good physical condition" or "bodily vigor."

The so-called *Gymnasiarchic Law*, a lengthy 2nd century BCE decree from Beroia that gives detailed information about its *gymnasion*, tells us that a prize for *euexia* went to "whoever seems [to the judges] to have developed the best body."[3] Scholars have

---

[1] Georgios Mouratidis is Assistant Director of the British School at Athens. A graduate of History and Archaeology of the Aristotle University of Thessaloniki, he earned his PhD in ancient history in 2020 from the University of St. Andrews, UK. Heather L. Reid is Professor Emerita at Morningside University in the USA and Scholar in Residence at Exedra Mediterranean Center in Siracusa, Sicily. She is a 2015 Fellow of the American Academy in Rome, 2018 Fellow of Harvard's Center for Hellenic Studies, and 2019 Fulbright Scholar at the Università degli Studi di Napoli Federico II.

[2] Chariton, *Callirhoe*, 1.1.5-6. τότε δὲ Χαιρέας ἀπὸ τῶν γυμνασίων ἐβάδιζεν οἴκαδε στίλβων ὥσπερ ἀστήρ· ἐπήνθει γὰρ αὐτοῦ τῷ λαμπρῷ τοῦ προσώπου τὸ ἐρύθημα τῆς παλαίστρας ὥσπερ ἀργύρῳχρυσός. Text and translation from the Loeb edited by G.P. Goold (Cambridge, MA: Harvard University Press, 1995).

[3] ὃς ἂν αὐτῶι δοκῆι ἄριστα τὸ σῶμα διακεῖσθαι. See L. Gounaropoulou, and B.H. Miltiades, *Epigraphes Katō Makedonias: Teuchos A'. Epigraphes*

interpreted *euexia* competitions as "male beauty contests" comparable to modern body-building competitions, judged on physical appearance.[4] A good *hexis* in philosophy, by contrast, is a moral condition achieved through training (*ethos*) that would be judged by a person's actions rather than their appearance.[5] So *euexia* as a goal of gymnastic *paideia* may be understood as a kind of fitness, but it cannot be merely physical. In what follows, we argue that gymnastic *euexia* must be fitness for a task, specifically the task of citizenship. As such it demands the training of body and mind alike—including the ability to be guided by the good and beautiful.

Euexia and the body

"Fitness," though modern, is a good translation for "*euexia*" because both are conditions achieved through training and defined by the activities that issue from them. As coaches love to remind us, fitness is readiness for a particular task. Even in the same sport, swimming for example, fitness for the 50-meter freestyle is qualitatively different from being fit for the 1,500 meters—and it demands a different preparation. Fitness, like *euexia*, is not confined to athletics, but since it is defined by action, it always involves the

---

Veroias (Athens: National Hellenic Research Foundation, 1998) 11-ll.50. Translation from Charles H. Stocking and Susan A. Stephens, *Ancient Greek Athletics: Primary Sources in Translation* (Oxford: Oxford University Press, 2021), 341.

[4] E.g., Nigel B. Crowther, "Male 'Beauty' Contests in Greece: The *Euandria* and *Euexia*" *L'Antiquité Classique,* 54 (1985): 285-91 and B.C. Perriello "Hermes and the *Euexia*: A Note on Nudity, Youth and Divinity in the Gymnasium," in *Dossier: Images mises en forme* (Paris: Éditions de l'École des hautes études en sciences sociales, 2009), 277-83.

[5] Aristotle's accounts of *hexis* are found in *Metaphysics* V.20, *Categories* VIII. *Aretē* (1106b36), *technē* (1140a7-8), and *phronēsis* (1140b4-5) are all *hexeis*: *aretē* for choosing, *technē* for producing, and *phronēsis* for acting. *Hexis* is distinct from activities (*energeiai*), emotions (*pathē*), dispositions (*diatheseis*), and capacities (*dynameis*). *Hexeis* arise in particular spheres of activity. Pleasures supervene on *energeia* (acts), but *energeiai* are specific to a particular *hexis*. For an analysis of *hexis* in Aristotle, see Pierre Rodrigo, "The Dynamic of *Hexis* in Aristotle's Philosophy," *Journal of the British Society for Phenomenology* 42.1 (2011): 6-17.

body. By the same token, it cannot refer merely to bodily condition since voluntary action involves both *psychē* (mind/soul) and *sōma* (body). The physical aspect of *euexia* is clearly the more visible, but just as we distinguish in modern English between "physical fitness" and fitness for tasks like parenthood or governance, ancient writers use modifiers to emphasize the bodily aspect of *euexia*. Xenophon, for example, specifies *"tou sōmatos euexias"* when his Socrates chastises a young man for being out of shape at *Memorabilia* 3.12.3.[6] Plato, at *Gorgias* 450a, *Protagoras* 354a, and *Laws* 7.789c also specifies that he is talking about somatic *euexia*. In another, later example, Polybius talks about the martial prowess of Macedonians by referring to their *euexia* in war affairs.[7]

Strangely, however, lexica and translators often render *euexia* as "bodily" or "physical" condition even when no such modifier appears in the Greek.[8] Thus, when Aristotle says in *Metaphysics*

---

[6] Xenophon, *Memorabilia* 3.12 [3] ἢ καταφρονεῖς τῶν ἐπιτιμίων τῆς κακεξίας τούτων, καὶ ῥᾳδίως ἂν οἴει φέρειν τὰ τοιαῦτα; καὶ μὴν οἶμαί γε πολλῷ ῥᾷω καὶ ἡδίω τούτων εἶναι ἃ δεῖ ὑπομένειν τὸν ἐπιμελόμενον τῆς τοῦ σώματος εὐεξίας. ἢ ὑγιεινότερόν τε καὶ εἰς τἄλλα χρησιμώτερον νομίζεις εἶναι τὴν κακεξίαν τῆς εὐεξίας, ἢ τῶν διὰ τὴν εὐεξίαν γιγνομένων καταφρονεῖς; Or do you despise these, the rewards of bad condition, and think that you can easily endure such things? And yet I suppose that what has to be borne by anyone who takes care to keep his body in good condition is far lighter and far pleasanter than these things. Or is it that you think bad condition healthier and generally more serviceable than good, or do you despise the effects of good condition?" Greek text from Xenophon. *Xenophontis opera omnia* (Oxford: Clarendon Press, 1921), translation from E.C. Marchant, *Xenophon in Seven Volumes* (Cambridge, MA: Harvard University Press; 1923). All Xenophon quotes are from these sources, unless otherwise noted.

[7] Polybius, *Histories*, III.6.12: Μακεδόνων εὐεξίαν ἐν τοῖς πολεμικοῖς.

[8] Brill defines *euexia* as (a) "good (physical) constitution, good health, health," and (b) "good state, vigor, excellent condition." LSJ's definition is similar, adding "good habit of body," a translation that picks up on the Latin *habitus,* which, like the Greek *hexis,* derives from the verb "to have." There is no consensus on the translation (or

6.1025b "ἔστι γάρ τι αἴτιον ὑγιείας καὶ εὐεξίας," it is translated "there is a cause of health and physical fitness."[9] And when he identifies *euexia* as the *telos* of *gymnastikē* in *Eudemian Ethics* 1.1218a35, Rackham unapologetically translates it as "bodily condition."[10] Aristotle is using gymnastics as an example here to illustrate the general point that each science aims at a particular good, but we think it dangerously misleading to suggest that the only good at which gymnastic education aims would be physical condition. It is especially troubling to supply the somatic modifier to *euexia* for Aristotle, since good *hexis* is for him an important moral concept, namely, the condition that agents must be in for their *praxis* (activity) to count as virtuous—literally "how they hold themselves" (*pōs hexōn*) when they act.[11] When Aristotle wants to talk specifically

---

definition) of this term. Examples include: "bodily vigor," "good physical conditioning," "good condition," "good health and strength," "comportment." In translating the Beroia Law, Stocking and Stephens, *Ancient Greek Athletics*, use "fitness."

[9] Greek text from Aristotle, *Aristotle's Metaphysics*, ed. W.D. Ross (Oxford: Clarendon Press, 1924). Translation from Hugh Tredennick, *Aristotle in 23 Volumes* (Cambridge, MA, Harvard University Press, 1989). W.D. Ross, translates the phrase "For there is a cause of health and of good condition..." in *The Complete Works of Aristotle*, ed. W.D. Ross (Princeton: Princeton University Press, 1984).

[10] *Eudemian Ethics* 1.1218a 35: "for instance the good of gymnastics is good bodily condition" οἶον γυμναστικῇ εὐεξία ἔτι καὶ τὸ ἐν τῷ λόγῳ γεγραμμένον. Greek text from Aristotle, *Aristotle's Eudemian Ethics*, ed. F. Susemihl (Leipzig: Teubner, 1884). H. Rackham's translation from *Aristotle in 23 Volumes* (Cambridge, MA, Harvard University Press, 1989). J. Solomon translates *euexia* identically in *The Complete Works of Aristotle*, ed. W.D. Ross (Princeton: Princeton University Press, 1984). All further translations of *Eudemian Ethics* are from this source.

[11] *Hexis* derives from the verb *echō*, to have or hold, similar to the Latin *habitus*. See Aristotle, *Nicomachean Ethics* 1105a.30: "...but if the acts that are in accordance with the excellences have themselves a certain character it does not follow that they are done justly or temperately. The agent also must be in a certain condition when he does them" τὰ δὲ κατὰ τὰς ἀρετὰς γινόμενα οὐκ ἐὰν αὐτά πως ἔχῃ, δικαίως ἢ

about the bodily aspect of a *hexis*, he is perfectly capable of making that clear. For example, at *Nicomachean Ethics* 1129a, he says that we can recognize *euexia* through "firmness of flesh" and *kakexia* through "flabbiness of flesh"—conditions which he links with proper diet and exercise (or lack thereof).[12]

When, however, Aristotle says in *Eudemian Ethics* 2.1220a that *euexia* is made up of the parts of *aretē* just as virtue of the soul is composed of separate virtues,

καὶ ὥσπερ ἡ εὐεξία σύγκειται ἐκ τῶν κατὰ μόριον ἀρετῶν, οὕτω καὶ ἡ τῆς ψυχῆς ἀρετὴ ᾗ τέλος

we find translations like Rackham's presumptuous:

> And just as a good constitution (*euexia*) consists of the separate excellences of the parts of the body, so also the goodness of the spirit, as being an End, is composed of the separate virtues.

σωφρόνως πράττεται, ἀλλὰ καὶ ἐὰν ὁ πράττων πῶς ἔχων πράττῃ. For an analysis, see Thornton Lockwood, "Habit, Habituation, and Character in Aristotle's *Nicomachean Ethics*," in *A History of Habit from Aristotle to Bordieu*, eds. T. Sparrow and A. Hutchinson, (Lanham, MD: Lexington Books, 2013), 19-36.

[12] Aristotle, *Nicomachean Ethics* 1129a: "Hence sometimes the nature of one of two opposite **dispositions** is inferred from the other, sometimes **dispositions** are known from the things in which they are found; for instance, if we know what **good bodily condition** is, we know from this what bad condition is as well, but we also know what good condition is from bodies in good condition, and know what bodies are in good condition from knowing what good condition is. Thus, supposing good condition is firmness of flesh, bad condition must be flabbiness of flesh, and a diet productive of good condition must be a diet producing firmness of flesh" (tr. Rackham). πολλάκις μὲν οὖν γνωρίζεται ἡ ἐναντία **ἕξις** ἀπὸ τῆς ἐναντίας, πολλάκις δὲ αἱ **ἕξεις** ἀπὸ τῶν ὑποκειμένων· ἐάν τε γὰρ ἡ **εὐεξία** ᾖ φανερά, καὶ ἡ **καχεξία** φανερὰ γίνεται, καὶ ἐκ τῶν εὐεκτικῶν ἡ **εὐεξία** καὶ ἐκ ταύτης τὰ εὐεκτικά. εἰ γὰρ ἐστιν ἡ **εὐεξία** πυκνότης σαρκός, ἀνάγκη καὶ τὴν **καχεξίαν** εἶναι μανότητα σαρκὸς καὶ τὸ εὐεκτικὸν τὸ ποιητικὸν πυκνότητος ἐν σαρκί (emphasis added).

Even though the second part of the quote talks specifically about the *psyche*, there is no reason to assume the first part is talking exclusively about the body, much less the parts of the body. "Firmness of flesh" may indeed be a sign that one has undertaken the training required to achieve *euexia*, but it cannot be identical with *euexia*. A perfectly toned and proportioned body may be unable to outrun a tortoise; likewise a champion athlete (and maybe especially a champion athlete) could be incapable of the kind of actions that philosophers like Aristotle, who taught in gymnasia, had in mind when they set *euexia* as the goal of gymnastic education.

In the gymnastic context, a body that exhibited *euexia* was a body that would be fit to serve the city effectively when needed, as illustrated by the example of Polemaios in the final section of this paper. It reflected the virtue of that person, which was demonstrated through virtuous actions within a community—and that is why, we believe, it is inextricably linked with citizenship. An indicative example is the decree from Sestos in honor of Menas, where we read about his second term as a *gymnasiarch*, at a time when his city was suffering raids from neighboring Thracian tribes as well as financial distress. To prepare the youth for their roles as citizens, Menas incentivized them by organizing contests, "urging the young men through such love of glory towards exercise and love of exertion, as a result of which the souls of the younger people, competing in bravery, are excellently directed in their characters towards virtue."[13] Bodily health and even vigor may be necessary conditions for achieving gymnastic *euexia*, but they certainly are not sufficient. In short, *euexia* may be a condition involving the body, but that is different from being a condition of the body alone.

---

[13] The Greek reads: προτρεπόμενος δὲ διὰ τῆς τοιαύτης φιλοδοξίας πρὸς ἄσκησιν καὶ φιλοπονίαν τοὺς νέους, ἐξ ὧν αἱ τῶν νεωτέρων ψυχαὶ πρὸς ἀνδρείαν ἀμιλλώμεναι καλῶς ἄγονται τοῖς ἤθεσιν πρὸς ἀρετήν. *Die Inschriften von Sestos und des thrakischen Chersones* 1 (133-120 BCE). Translation modified from Benjamin Gray, "Philosophy of education and the later Hellenistic polis," in *Epigraphical Approaches to the Post-classical Polis: Fourth Century BC to Second Century AD*, eds. P. Martzavou, and N. Papazarkadas (Oxford: Oxford University Press, 2012), 233-253, at 239.

Euexia and *paideia*

In understanding *euexia* as the telos of gymnastic *paideia*, we need first to distinguish gymnastic from athletic training, and second to appreciate the integration of mind and body in moral education. Gymnastic education in ancient Greece is frequently interpreted as the training of the *sōma* as distinct from that of the *psychē*. In Plato's *Republic*—a text with profound implications for ancient and modern education alike—*gymnastikē* is balanced with *mousikē* in the *paideia* of the guardians, the quintessential class of public servants from which philosopher rulers are selected. Translators render *gymnastikē* as "physical training" or even "athletic training," but just as *euexia* cannot be a purely physical condition, the training that produces it cannot involve the body alone.

Nor should the educational activities of gymnasia be confused with the preparation of athletes for the Panhellenic Games, which had different religious and political purposes. Gymnastic education is aimed not at athletic glory but rather the production of citizens— as exemplified by the inscription for Polemaios discussed below— and therefore it cultivates a different kind of *hexis*. Aristotle is clear on this point: "The athlete's *hexis* is not serviceable for the *euexia* required by a citizen," he says, explaining that athletes' exercises (*ponoi*) are too violent and specialized for "the pursuits (*praxeis*) of free men and women."[14] Gymnastic education is aimed at civic rather than athletic performance, then, but all forms of performance demand both mental and physical capacities, so the relevant education must engage mind and body alike, and even together.

Since Plato's educational program in the *Republic* included *mousikē*, construed as involving all the "arts of the muses," many take that part of *paideia* to condition the soul, while *gymnastikē* deals with

---

[14] Aristotle *Politics* 7.1335b: οὔτε γὰρ ἡ τῶν ἀθλητῶν χρήσιμος ἕξις πρὸς πολιτικὴν εὐεξίαν [...]. πεπονημένην μὲν οὖν ἔχειν δεῖ τὴν ἕξιν, πεπονημένην δὲ πόνοις μὴ [βιαίοις, μηδὲ πρὸς ἕνα μόνον, ὥσπερ ἡ τῶν ἀθλητῶν ἕξις, ἀλλὰ πρὸς τὰς τῶν ἐλευθερίων πράξεις. ὁμοίως δὲ δεῖ ταῦτα ὑπάρχειν ἀνδράσι καὶ γυναιξίν. Greek text from *Aristotle's Politica*, ed. W.D. Ross (Oxford: Clarendon Press, 1957); translation from H. Rackham, *Aristotle in 23 Volumes* (Cambridge, MA, Harvard University Press, 1944).

the body. But Plato's Socrates explicitly denies that dichotomy and states clearly that *gymnastikē* exists primarily for the sake of the soul.

> 'So then, Glaucon,' I said, 'it follows that those who established education in the arts and physical exercise didn't do this for the reasons that some think: to look to the needs of the body on the one hand, and the soul on the other, did they? [...] It can well be that they prescribe both especially for the good of the soul.'

> Ἆρ' οὖν, ἦν δ' ἐγώ, ὦ Γλαύκων, καὶ οἱ καθιστάντες μουσικῇ καὶ γυμναστικῇ παιδεύειν οὐχ οὗ ἕνεκά τινες οἴονται καθιστᾶσιν, ἵνα τῇ μὲν τὸ σῶμα θεραπεύοιντο, τῇ δὲ τὴν ψυχήν; [...] Κινδυνεύουσιν, ἦν δ' ἐγώ, ἀμφότερα τῆς ψυχῆς ἕνεκα τὸ μέγιστον καθιστάναι.[15]

Socrates also describes gymnastic activities in a way almost indistinguishable from athletic games.[16] So what exactly is the difference between athletic and gymnastic training, apart from the complementary practice of *mousikē*?

Another way to ask the same question is: how could athletic activities train the soul for citizenship? In *Memorabilia* 2.1.20, Xenophon points out that indolence and indulgence not only deprive the body of *euexia*, they deprive the soul of knowledge (*epistēmē*), whereas "strenuous effort leads up to good and noble deeds, as good men say."[17] He goes on to quote Epicharmus on the value of *ponos*

---

[15] Plato, *Republic*, 410bc. Unless otherwise stated, Greek text and translations or *Republic* are from Plato, *Republic, Volume I: Books 1-5*, edited and translated by Christopher Emlyn-Jones, William Preddy (Cambridge, MA: Harvard University Press, 2013).

[16] The *Republic* never defines *gymnastikē* except to say that it would follow existing patterns and to list as examples dancing, hunting, athletic contests, and horse races (412b). In *Gorgias* 464a ff., *gymnastikē* is described as a *technē* that establishes health through diet and exercise.

[17] Xenophon, *Memorabilia*, 2.1.20: ἔτι δὲ αἱ μὲν ῥᾳδιουργίαι ἐκ τοῦ παρα-χρῆμα ἡδοναὶ οὔτε σώμ, ατι εὐεξίαν ἱκαναί εἰσιν ἐνεργάζεσθαι, ὡς φασιν οἱ γυμνασταί, οὔτε ψυχῇ ἐπιστήμην ἀξιόλογον οὐδεμίαν ἐμποιοῦσιν, αἱ δὲ διὰ καρτερίας ἐπιμέλειαι τῶν καλῶν τε κἀγαθῶν ἔργων ἐξικνεῖσθαι ποιοῦσιν, ὡς φασιν οἱ ἀγαθοὶ ἄνδρες.

and Hesiod on the gods putting sweat before virtue. Plato cites the same quote in *Republic* and makes the same point, namely, that the efforts made in athletic activity educate the soul, specifically by promoting harmony among its three parts.[18] Rule-governed games, for example, prepare children to follow the laws,[19] and exposure to risk in contests prepares souls to face more serious risks later. Indeed, the gymnastic training and civic games proposed in the *Laws* for males and females alike incorporate dangers realistic enough to evoke real fear and thereby cultivate authentic courage.[20]

Plato's Socrates instructs Alcibiades that ruling oneself body and mind is a prerequisite to ruling the city. "Exercise yourself first (*gymnasai prōton*)," he says, "before entering politics."[21] In Plato's *Republic*, athletic contests are used to select future leaders—not, apparently, according to who wins, but according to who plays the game in a way that reveals their dedication to the city.[22] A pithy way

---

[18] Primarily by harmonizing the three parts of the soul, see Plato, *Republic* 410b: "What is more, he will toil at the gymnastics and physical exercise with a view to arousing the passionate side of his nature rather than cultivating mere strength, unlike other athletes who plan their diet and exercise with a view to developing muscle." Αὐτά μὴν τὰ γυμνάσια καὶ τοὺς πόνους πρὸς τὸ θυμοειδὲς τῆς φύσεως βλέπων κἀκεῖνο ἐγείρων πονήσει μᾶλλον ἢ πρὸς ἰσχύν, οὐχ ὥσπερ οἱ ἄλλοι ἀθληταὶ ῥώμης ἕνεκα σιτία καὶ πόνους μεταχειρίζονται. For analysis, see Heather Reid, "Sport as Moral Education in Plato's *Republic*," *Journal of the Philosophy of Sport* 34:2 (2007), 160-75.

[19] Plato *Republic* 4.424e.

[20] Plato, *Laws* 8.830e-831a.

[21] Plato, *Alcibiades I* 132b; this is the conclusion of an argument that begins at 129e with discussion of ruling the body. Text and translation from Plato, *Alcibiades I and II*, trans. W.R.M. Lamb (Cambridge, MA: Harvard University Press, 1927).

[22] Plato *Republic* 502e–503a: "We said, if you remember, that they must show themselves to be lovers of their city when tested by pleasure and pain and that they must hold on to their resolve through labors, fears, and all other adversities. Anyone incapable of doing so was to be rejected, while anyone who came through unchanged—like gold tested in a fire—was to be made ruler and receive prizes [*athla*] both while he

to put the distinction between athletic and gymnastic training is that, in the latter, what counts is not whether you win or lose but how you play the game. How people "hold themselves" when performing gymnastic tasks reveals their *hexis* of character. And parallel to the modern debate over whether sport builds character or reveals it, ancient philosophers identified a circular process by which virtuous activity cultivates virtue, which leads to virtuous activity.

For Aristotle, the *hexis* of *aretē* is achieved through "*ethos*" (a term typically translated as habituation, but better understood as training), which cultivates *ēthos*, moral character.[23] Emphasizing the importance of proper training (*ethismos*) at *Nicomachean Ethics* 1103b21-2e, he declares, "In a word, our moral dispositions (*hexeis*) are formed as a result of the corresponding activities (*energeiai*). Hence it is incumbent on us to control the character of our activities, since on the quality of these depends the quality of our dispositions (*hexeis*).[24] At *Eudemian Ethics* 2.1220a, Aristotle explains in a similar vein that the best disposition is produced from the best actions (*praxeis*), which result from the relevant excellences (*aretai*). "For example," he goes on, "it is the best exercises (*ponoi*) and food (*trophē*)

---

lived and after his death." ἐλέγομεν δ᾽, εἰ μνημονεύεις, δεῖν αὐτοὺς φιλοπόλιδάς τε φαίνεσθαι, βασανιζομένους ἐν ἡδοναῖς τε καὶ λύπαις, καὶ τὸ δόγμα τοῦτο μήτ᾽ ἐν πόνοις μήτ᾽ ἐν φόβοις μήτ᾽ ἐν ἄλλῃ μηδεμιᾷ μεταβολῇ φαίνεσθαι ἐκβάλλοντας, ἢ τὸν ἀδυνατοῦντα ἀποκριτέον, τὸν δὲ πανταχοῦ ἀκήρατον ἐκβαίνοντα ὥσπερ χρυσὸν ἐν πυρὶ βασανιζόμενον, στατέον ἄρχοντα καὶ γέρα δοτέον καὶ ζῶντι καὶ τελευτήσαντι καὶ ἆθλα. See also *Republic* 537b "...and moreover one of our tests of them, and not the least, will be their behavior in their physical exercises." καὶ ἅμα μία καὶ αὕτη τῶν βασάνων οὐκ ἐλαχίστη, τίς ἕκαστος ἐν τοῖς γυμνασίοις φανεῖται. Cf. *Laws* 829bc. On guardian selection, see *Republic* 7.537cd; for analysis see Reid, "Sport as Moral Education," 166-8.

[23] On the relation among *ethos*, *ēthos*, and *hexis* in Aristotle, as well as their relation to *kalon* and *metrion*, see Joe Sachs, "Three little words," transcription of a lecture from April, 1997, in *St. John's College Digital Archives*, online. Accessed July 9, 2020.

[24] Rackham translation; the Greek reads: καὶ ἑνὶ δὴ λόγῳ ἐκ τῶν ὁμοίων ἐνεργειῶν αἱ ἕξεις γίνονται. διὸ δεῖ τὰς ἐνεργείας ποιάς ἀποδιδόναι· κατὰ γὰρ τὰς τούτων διαφορὰς ἀκολουθοῦσιν αἱ ἕξεις.

that produce *euexia,* and *euexia* enables men to do the best work (*ponos*)." Rackham renders *euexia* here as "a good condition of body," but what follows shows the soul is also in play:

> Therefore *aretē* too is the sort of disposition that is created by the best movements in the spirit [*psychē*] and is also the source of the production [*prattein*] of the spirit's best actions [*erga*] and emotions....
>
> καὶ ἡ ἀρετὴ ἄρα ἡ τοιαύτη διάθεσίς ἐστίν, ἣ γίνεταί τε ὑπὸ τῶν ἀρίστων περὶ ψυχὴν κινήσεων καὶ ἀφ᾽ ἧς πράττεται τὰ ἄριστα τῆς ψυχῆς ἔργα καὶ πάθη...[25]

Plato likewise describes *aretē* as a *hexis* of the soul analogous to physical fitness; in *Republic*, Socrates calls it "the health [*hygeia*], and beauty [*kallos*], and good condition [*euexia*] of the soul," adding that it is achieved by "beautiful pursuits" (*kala epitēdeumata*).[26] Xenophon, furthermore, links such *epitēdeumata* explicitly with *eupraxia* (doing well), distinguishing it as the product of "study and practice," in contrast to states achieved through luck.[27] So, although the term *hexis* can apply to body and soul separately, virtuous actions and *eupraxia*

---

[25] Aristotle, *Eudemian Ethics* 2.1220a.

[26] Plato, *Republic* 444de (Shorey trans.). The Greek reads: ἀρετὴ μὲν ἄρα, ὡς ἔοικεν, ὑγίειά τέ τις ἂν εἴη καὶ κάλλος καὶ εὐεξία ψυχῆς, [...] ἆρ᾽ οὖν οὐ καὶ τὰ μὲν καλὰ ἐπιτηδεύματα εἰς ἀρετῆς κτῆσιν φέρει.

[27] Xenophon, *Memorabilia* 3.9.14: "When someone asked him what seemed to him the best pursuit for a man, he answered: "Doing well." Questioned further, whether he thought good luck a pursuit, he said: "On the contrary, I think luck and doing are opposite poles. To hit on something right by luck without search I call good luck, to do something well after study and practice I call doing well; and those who pursue this seem to me to do well." ἐρομένου δέ τινος αὐτὸν τί δοκοίη αὐτῷ κράτιστον ἀνδρὶ ἐπιτήδευμα εἶναι, ἀπεκρίνατο: εὐπραξία. ἐρομένου δὲ πάλιν εἰ καὶ τὴν εὐτυχίαν ἐπιτήδευμα νομίζοι εἶναι, πᾶν μὲν οὖν τοὐναντίον ἔγωγ᾽, ἔφ:η, τύχην καὶ πρᾶξιν ἡγοῦμαι: τὸ μὲν γὰρ μὴ ζητοῦντα ἐπιτυχεῖν τινι τῶν δεόντων εὐτυχίαν οἶμαι εἶναι, τὸ δὲ μαθόντα τε καὶ μελετήσαντά τι εὖ ποιεῖν εὐπραξίαν νομίζω, καὶ οἱ τοῦτο ἐπιτηδεύοντες δοκοῦσί μοι εὖ πράττειν.

in general are the product of both together. It is therefore important to recognize that the education of body and soul are not only analogous but also simultaneous in the activities of the *gymnasion*.

This, perhaps, is why the drafter of Beoria's *Gymnasiarchic Law* considered it important to use the word *diakeimai* to describe who deserved the prize for *euexia*[28] — a term that can be translated as "to be disposed or affected in a certain manner" or "to be in a certain state of mind, body, or circumstances."[29] Though scholars typically interpret it in this context to refer to the winner's physique, we would like to emphasize its affective aspects as evidenced in the way a man "carries himself," his "attitude," "presence," or "command."[30] Philo of Alexandria recounts some athletes' *euexia* being so impressive that they were awarded victory without having to compete.[31] In any case, being in a bodily condition worthy of reward in this context implies a long-term commitment to gymnastic training, rather than a one-time performance or mere appearance. We know that the ephebes' gymnastic commitment and progress was regularly tested in *apodeixis* (demonstration) contests, which included prizes for *euexia*, *eutaxia* and *philoponia*.[32] In the final Hermaia festival, this

---

[28] The verb *diakeimai* is used in a similar way in the *ephebarchic* law of Amphipolis, although in that case it refers to *eutaxia* and *philoponia* as well as *euexia*: Καλλιόπη Δ. Λαζαρίδου, 'Εφηβαρχικός Νόμος από την Αμφίπολη', *Αρχαιολογική Εφημερίς* 154 (2015), line 91.

[29] *Thesaurus Linguae Graecae, lemma* διάκειμαι.

[30] "Command appearance" is the translation of *euexia* found in Eran Lupu, *Greek Sacred Law* 2nd. ed. (Leiden: Brill, 2009), 258. P.H. Gauthier and M.B. Hatzopoulos, *La Loi Gymnasiarchique de Beroia* (Athens: Centre de Recherches de l'Antiquite, 1993), 102, translate τὸ σῶμα διακεῖσθαι as the French "attitude corporelle" (bodily attitude) and *euexia* as "prestance" (presence), explaining that it seems appropriate for evaluating the gait and condition of young men and adding that it denotes less beauty than balance, harmony, and vigor of the body.

[31] Philo of Alexandria, *The Worse Attacks the Better*, trans. F.H. Colson, G.H. Whitaker (Cambridge, MA: Harvard University Press, 1929), 29/197.

[32] These contests could take place monthly (see, e.g., Λαζαρίδου, Κ. Δ. 2015: 'Εφηβαρχικός Νόμος από την Αμφίπολη', *Αρχαιολογική Εφημερίς* 154, 1–48) or less frequently (e.g., every four months in Beroia, *EKM* 1 B.24). For more on the Hermaia, see Perriello "Hermes & the *Euexia*."

commitment was judged by the gymnasiarch and seven other "local" (ἐκ τοῦ τόπου) judges, most likely *gymnasion* attendees or officials who witnessed the contestants' character and commitment to their training over an extended period. The judgment was entirely subjective, as indicated by the verb *dokei*, which suggests that the *euexia* was probably not a performance event with a clear, undisputed victor, but like *philoponia*,[33] an extended evaluation of the contestant's character.

Despite its explicit mention of the body, we believe that the *Gymnasiarchic Law* helps to transcend the idea that *euexia* was a beauty contest, since the goal was not merely to have a well-proportioned and toned body, but to be ready mentally and physically to effectively serve the city. In practice, the link between *euexia* and *paideia* is first and foremost shown by the fact that such contests were not found in the program of athletic competitions, but only in the gymnastic festivals, which served as a kind of final exam for ephebes completing their civic training. In addition, surviving victory lists from these gymnastic festivals list the *euexia* victor separately from those of athletic events (i.e., boxing, pankration, or foot races) and military drills (i.e., catapult operation, archery, and javelin throw), showing that the *euexia* contest tested something different from those.[34] Finally, it is noteworthy that *euexia* does not appear in inscriptions that celebrate athletic victories, which suggests that it was not necessarily linked with athletic prowess. Conversely, the idea of training to serve the city is found in other (non-athletic) monuments honoring civic benefactors, as we demonstrate below. All of this evidence points to the fact that the *paideia* of the *gymnasium*, especially for ephebes, was aimed to develop a *hexis* of character useful for service to the city.

Euexia and citizenship

We are arguing that *euexia* is a condition, like *aretē*, produced from certain kinds of actions and productive of similar kinds of actions. The *euexia* that serves as the *telos* of gymnastic *paideia*,

---

[33] N.B. Crowther, "*Euexia, Eutaxia, Philoponia*: Three Contests of the Greek Gymnasium," *Zeitschrift für Papyrologie und Epigraphik* 85 (1991): 301-4.
[34] For example, *ITral* 107; *Inscriptiones Graecae* XII 6 1:183.

furthermore, is specific to citizenship. In Aristotelian terms, we may think of citizenship as a function (*ergon*) and gymnastic *euexia* as fitness for the performance of that function. But how exactly could gymnastic activities prepare someone for citizenship? The obvious answer is military training since ancient warfare demanded strength and endurance as well as skills in fighting and the use of weapons. It is a mistake, however, to construe athletic events such as wrestling, pankration, javelin, or discus-throwing as practical preparation for war; most likely these were a *mimēsis* of heroic actions from myths such as the Trojan War.[35] By the Classical period, troops fought in phalanx formations that emphasized social skills like coordination and cooperation, which were taught, in part through social activities like dance.[36] Plato's *Laws* gives an extensive account of gymnastic training (including dance) aimed at military service, it even restricts athletic competition to events useful for defense (832e). Running races, for example, are always done in armor (830d) and wrestling is replaced with armed combat for individuals and teams (833e). The question here is not whether gymnastic *paideia* involved exercises aimed at physical conditioning and military performance, it did.[37] The point is that gymnastic *paideia* just as importantly cultivated the social and moral capabilities of citizens.

Plato, in particular, looked to gymnastic education as a means for conquering appetitive desires; citizens can hardly obey their commander or the laws if they cannot first obey their own reason. In

---

[35] This idea originates with Gregory Nagy, *The Ancient Greek Hero in 24 Hours* (Cambridge, MA: Harvard University Press, 2013), 1§41, and is discussed and developed in Heather L. Reid, "Performing Virtue: Athletic *Mimēsis* in Platonic Education," in *Politics and Performance in Western Greece*, eds. H. Reid, D. Tanasi, and S. Kimbell (Sioux City: Parnassos Press, 2017), 260-272.

[36] See Stocking & Stephens, *Ancient Greek Athletics*, 4, Appendix II.

[37] Polybius, *Histories*, III.6.12 wrote about king Phillip II that he "perceived and reckoned on the cowardice and indolence of the Persians as compared with the military efficiency of himself and his Macedonians" κατανοήσας καὶ συλλογισάμενος τὴν Περσῶν ἀνανδρίαν καὶ ῥᾳθυμίαν καὶ τὴν αὑτοῦ καὶ Μακεδόνων εὐεξίαν ἐν τοῖς πολεμικοῖς Trans. W.R. Paton (Cambridge, MA: Harvard University Press, 2010).

Republic 8.559a, Socrates points out that the desire to eat is essential to *euexia*, but must be "disciplined and trained from an early age" to keep from harming one's capacity for *phronēsis* and *sōphrosynē*.[38] Not only must reason restrict appetites, it must overcome aversions to the pain and hard work (i.e., *ponos*) that is necessary to achieve a greater good. In *Protagoras* 354ab, Socrates cites gymnastics among things which are "good but painful," in part because they lead to *euexia*.[39] Xenophon adds that "toil and sweat" (*ponos kai idrota*) can train the body to serve the mind.[40] It is no accident that gymnastic exercises (like Heracles's labors) are often called *ponoi; ponos* is a term that can be translated as "pain" but always represents a voluntary effort to achieve some desired end.[41] As Aristotle says in *Metaphysics* 5, "there is a *ponos* of *euexia* and an *euexia* of *ponos*, but *euexia* is the 'end' and

---

[38] Plato *Republic* 8.559a.

[39] Plato *Protagoras* 354a-b: "Then again, suppose we should ask them the opposite: You, sirs, who tell us on the other hand that good things are painful—do you not give such instances as physical training, military service, and medical treatment conducted by cautery, incision, drugs, or starvation, and say that these are good, but painful? Would they not grant it? He agreed that they would. Then do you call them good because they produce extreme pangs and anguish for the moment, or because later on they result in health and good bodily condition, the deliverance of cities, dominion over others, and wealth? They would assent to this, I suppose." οὐκοῦν πάλιν ἂν αὐτοὺς τὸ ἐναντίον εἰ ἐροίμεθα: ὦ ἄνθρωποι οἱ λέγοντες αὖ ἀγαθὰ ἀνιαρὰ εἶναι, ἆρα οὐ τὰ τοιάδε λέγετε, οἷον τά τε γυμνάσια καὶ τὰς στρατείας καὶ τὰς ὑπὸ τῶν ἰατρῶν θεραπείας τὰς διὰ καύσεών τε καὶ τομῶν καὶ φαρμακειῶν καὶ λιμοκτονιῶν γιγνομένας, ὅτι ταῦτα ἀγαθὰ μέν ἐστιν, ἀνιαρὰ δέ; φαῖεν ἄν; συνεδόκει. πότερον οὖν κατὰ τόδε ἀγαθὰ αὐτὰ καλεῖτε, ὅτι ἐν τῷ παραχρῆμα ὀδύνας τὰς ἐσχάτας παρέχει καὶ ἀλγηδόνας, ἢ ὅτι εἰς τὸν ὕστερον χρόνον ὑγίειαί τε ἀπ᾽ αὐτῶν γίγνονται καὶ εὐεξίαι τῶν σωμάτων καὶ τῶν πόλεων σωτηρίαι καὶ ἄλλων ἀρχαὶ καὶ πλοῦτοι; φαῖεν ἄν, ὡς ἐγῷμαι. Greek text and translation from Plato. *Protagoras*, trans. W.R.M. Lamb (Cambridge, MA: Harvard University Press, 1924).

[40] Xenophon, *Memorabilia* 2.1.28.

[41] There is much more to say about *ponos* and we will in an upcoming paper.

ponos is the 'beginning.'"[42] Significantly, prizes for *philoponia* (love of hard work) were given alongside those for *euexia* in ancient gymnasia. We believe that both contests rewarded a particular mindset as much—or more—than a beautiful physique.

Beauty is nevertheless an important criterion for *euexia* because citizenship demands a sense of the beautiful and good. Plato, as we saw, described *aretē* as the *kallos* (beauty) of the soul—a form of the word applied specifically to beautiful bodies.[43] As in the concept of *kalokagathia* (beautiful goodness) espoused by Xenophon, Plato, and Aristotle alike, being beautiful is as much about aesthetic discernment and attraction to the good as it is about personal appearance.[44] Plato's philosopher-rulers, chosen in part on the moral *hexis* they exhibit in gymnastic competition, are tasked with discerning the beautiful and good for the entire Kallipolis.[45] Aristotle, meanwhile, applies aesthetic criteria like balance and proportion to his ethical theory—most clearly in his Doctrine of the Mean,[46] which is linked with *euexia* at *Nicomachean Ethics* 1119a, where the temperate person has moderate (*metriōs*) appetites and avoids pleasures detrimental to *euexia* and the beautiful (*to kalon*).[47]

---

[42] Aristotle, *Metaphysics* 5.1013b9-10, translation ours. The Greek reads: οἷον τὸ πονεῖν τῆς εὐεξίας καὶ αὕτη τοῦ πονεῖν: ἀλλ᾽ οὐ τὸν αὐτὸν τρόπον ἀλλὰ τὸ μὲν ὡς τέλος τὸ δ᾽ ὡς ἀρχὴ κινήσεως.

[43] Plato, *Republic*, 444d.

[44] For the full argument, see Heather L. Reid, "Athletic virtue and aesthetic values in Aristotle's ethics," *Journal of the Philosophy of Sport* 47.1 (2002), 63-74; id., "A Gentleman or a Philosopher? Xenophon vs. Aristotle on *Kalokagathia*," in *Philodorema: Essays in Greek and Roman Philosophy in Honor of Phillip Mitsis*, eds. David Konstan and David Sider (Siracusa: Parnassos Press, 2022), 212-34.

[45] For the full argument, see Reid "Sport as Moral Education," 160-175.

[46] Also explained at *Eudemian Ethics* 2.1222a.

[47] Aristotle, *Nicomachean Ethics* 1119a (Rackham trans.): "But such pleasures as conduce to health and fitness [The temperate man] will try to obtain in a moderate and right degree; as also other pleasures so far as they are not detrimental to health and fitness, and not ignoble, nor beyond his means." ὅσα δὲ πρὸς ὑγίειάν ἐστιν ἢ πρὸς εὐεξίαν ἡδέα ὄντα, τούτων ὀρέξεται μετρίως καὶ ὡς δεῖ, καὶ τῶν ἄλλων ἡδέων μὴ ἐμποδίων τούτοις ὄντων ἢ παρὰ τὸ καλὸν ἢ ὑπὲρ τὴν οὐσίαν.

Moderation is also the mark of the pentathlete's beauty extolled by Aristotle in the *Rhetoric*.[48] Let us remember that fitness is readiness for a task, or in Aristotelian terms, a *hexis* is linked to an *ergon*,[49] and it is by performing one's *ergon* that a person acts not only morally but beautifully.[50] Indeed, the natural capacity (*dynamis*) of cleverness becomes the virtuous *hexis* of *phronēsis* only once it is completed by a sense of the beautiful (*to kalon*).[51]

This idea about the link between *euexia* and civic service was not confined to the philosophical circle of Plato and Aristotle, however. Later Hellenistic decrees, heavily influenced by the pedagogical methodologies of these philosophers, regularly emphasized the

---

[48] Aristotle, *Rhetoric* 1361b11: "This is why the athletes in the pentathlon are most beautiful, because they are naturally adapted for bodily exertion and for swiftness of foot." διὸ οἱ πένταθλοι κάλλιστοι, ὅτι πρὸς βίαν καὶ πρὸς τάχος ἅμα πεφύκασιν. Aristotle, *Art of Rhetoric*, trans. J.H. Freese (Cambridge, MA: Harvard University Press, 2020).

[49] See Aristotle, *Eudemian Ethics* 2.1218b "Let these assumptions, then, be made, and let it be assumed as to *aretē* that it is the best disposition or state or faculty of each class of things that have some use or work (*ergon*)." ταῦτα δὴ οὕτως ὑποκείσθω καὶ περὶ ἀρετῆς, ὅτι ἐστὶν ἡ βελτίστη διάθεσις ἢ ἕξις ἢ δύναμις ἑκάστων, ὅσων ἐστί τις χρῆσις ἢ ἔργον. Rackham translation, modified.

[50] On the link between morality and beauty with respect to athletics in Aristotle, see Heather L. Reid, "Athletic virtue and aesthetic values in Aristotle's ethics," *Journal of the Philosophy of Sport* 47.1 (2020): 63-74.

[51] In Book VI of the *Nicomachean Ethics*, Aristotle contrasts the *hexis* of *phronēsis* with the *dynamis* of cleverness (*deinotēs*), to become *phronēsis*, the stump of cleverness must be completed by a sense of the beautiful (*kalon*) 1144a20-21: "There is a certain faculty called Cleverness, which is the capacity for doing the things aforesaid that conduce to the aim we propose, and so attaining that aim. If the aim is noble, this is a praiseworthy faculty: if base, it is mere knavery." ἔστι δὴ δύναμις ἣν καλοῦσι δεινότητα: αὕτη δ᾽ ἐστὶ τοιαύτη ὥστε τὰ πρὸς τὸν ὑποτεθέντα σκοπὸν συντείνοντα δύνασθαι ταῦτα πράττειν καὶ τυγχάνειν αὐτοῦ. ἂν μὲν οὖν ὁ σκοπὸς ᾖ καλός, ἐπαινετή ἐστιν, ἐὰν δὲ φαῦλος, πανουργία (Rackham trans.). See Lockwood, "Habit, " 26.

importance of training citizens through repeated action.[52] For example, a late 2ⁿᵈ century BCE decree from the city of Kolophon honors a citizen benefactor named Polemaios (or Ptolemaios) on the basis of his gymnastic *paideia*:

> since the age of the ephebes he frequented in the gymnasia and nourished his soul with the finest learning, trained his body in athletics through the habitual activities of the gymnasia and was crowned in sacred contests. [53]

> ...εν ἔτι τὴν ἀπὸ τῶν ἐφήβων ἔχων / ἡλικίαν προσεδρεύων τῶι γυμνα/σίωι καὶ τὴν μὲν ψυχὴν τοῖς καλλίσ/τοις συντρέφων μαθήμασιν, τὸ δὲ // σῶμα τοῖς ἀπὸ τῶν γυμνασιῶν ἐ/θισμοῖς ἐναθλήσας ἐστεφα/νώθη μὲν ἱεροὺς ἀγῶνας...

The decree drafter refers to the *hexis* that young Polemaios strived to develop as an ephebe, and it refers to his athletic victories. But it is his service as a citizen that earned him the monument; as the same document later confirms:

> ...considering good not only the renown imparted to his life and his fatherland by the achievements of his body, but also the renown from taking charge of common affairs with public speech and political action. [54]

> ...καλὸν δὲ κρί/νων οὐ μόνον τὸν ἀπὸ τοῦ σώ/ματος περιγινόμενον τῶι βίωι / καὶ τῆι πατρίδι κόσμον, ἀλλὰ καὶ // τὸν ἀπὸ τοῦ προΐστασθαι τῶν κοι/νῶν λόγωι καὶ πράξει πολιτι/κῆ.

Following Aristotelian doctrine, what made Polemaios an exemplary citizen and worthy of great honors was not only the *euexia* (good

---

[52] Gray, "Philosophy of Education" argues that later Hellenistic decrees have strong allusions to Aristotelian thinking, and include strong indications of support for the doctrine that the habituation of faculties of the soul beyond reason is a fundamental aspect of education, a necessary condition for the formation of virtuous character.

[53] *Supplementum Epigraphicum Graecum* XXXIX 1243, l.1-7 (130-110 BCE).

[54] *Supplementum Epigraphicum Graecum* XXXIX 1243, lines 16-22.

hexis) he developed as an ephebe, but also his *eupraxia* (good *praxis*) as a citizen—both of which are credited to his *paideia* in the *gymnasium*. When it was needed, we read that Polemaios risked his body, soul, and whole livelihood for the people.[55]

Conclusion

Speculating on the judgment of *euexia* contests in ancient gymnasia, Crowther concludes that it "was a kind of physique or body-building in which size was not a major criterion, but rather symmetry, bearing and especially a general fit and healthy appearance."[56] We have argued, in light of classical philosophy, that it was a kind beauty contest, but not the kind that can be judged by appearance. *Euexia* is more about putting one's abilities into the service of the ideal of the *kalon*, than exhibiting physical beauty. To be sure, *euexia* involves the body, in fact it can be seen as the mastery of the body. But because every *hexis* is defined by the *praxis* (action) that issues from it, *euexia* must involve the mind and body together. Rule-governed activities that require effort and control—not to mention social cooperation and moral judgment—constitute an appropriate education for it. *Gymnastikē*, therefore, aimed beyond physical fitness at the final goal of citizenship. The performance of that *ergon*, furthermore, requires an understanding of the good and beautiful, which, to the ancient mind, could manifest itself in the body. As Plato's Socrates says: "I, for my part, do not believe that a sound body by its excellence makes the soul good, but on the contrary that a good soul by its virtue renders the body the best that is possible."[57]

---

[55] *Supplementum Epigraphicum Graecum* XXXIX 1243, lines 19-24.

[56] Crowther, "Male 'Beauty' Contests," 291.

[57] Plato, *Republic* 403d: ἐμοὶ μὲν γὰρ οὐ φαίνεται, ὃ ἂν χρηστὸν ᾖ σῶμα, τοῦτο τῇ αὑτοῦ ἀρετῇ ψυχὴν ἀγαθὴν ποιεῖν, ἀλλὰ τοὐναντίον ψυχὴ ἀγαθὴ τῇ αὑτῆς ἀρετῇ σῶμα παρέχειν ὡς οἷόν τε βέλτιστον.

Made in the USA
Columbia, SC
17 June 2023

b8fac1bf-6516-45a2-b781-882badff4f5fR01